THE CONFESSIONS OF
ST. AUGUSTINE

The Confessions of St. Augustine

Books I - X

Translated by F. J. Sheed

Sheed & Ward

Sheed & Ward™ is a service of National Catholic Reporter Publishing Company, Inc.

ISBN: 1-55612-154-7

Published by: Sheed & Ward
           115 E. Armour Blvd. P.O. Box 414292
           Kansas City, MO 64141-4292

To order, call: (800) 333-7373

FOREWORD[1]

YOU CANNOT get the best out of the *Confessions* if you know nothing of Augustine save what he tells you there. Indeed, you would not even learn his name, for it is not mentioned anywhere in the book. But that is a trifle. What matters is that he has no conception of his own greatness or of his towering importance in the history of mankind. So that one might read it simply as the spiritual story of an able, pious man—it hardly matters who—living at some time in the past—it hardly matters when.

Reading it thus, one would miss too much of the significance. For the man who is here baring his mind and his soul to God and to us is one of the key figures of all history. "He was," says the Catholic historian Christopher Dawson, "to a far greater degree than any emperor or barbarian war lord, a maker of history and a builder of the bridge which was to lead from the old world to the new." The great liberal Protestant scholar Harnack writes as forcibly: "It would seem that the miserable existence of the Roman Empire in the West was prolonged until then, only to permit Augustine's influence to be exercised on universal history." In reading the *Confessions*, you are not reading the diary of a nobody. Every man living in the Western world would be a different man if Augustine had not been, or had been different. Naturally Augustine did not know this, but it is a pity if we do not.

Observe the moment. He was born in Africa, one of the mightiest provinces of the Church, in 354—forty years after Constantine had the dream or vision which swung the Roman Empire to Christianity. He died in 430, with the Vandals, who had wrested Africa from the Roman Empire, hammering at the gates of his episcopal city. It was the age of the dying of the Empire in the West and the passing of power to the Barbarians. The Empire had long been administered in two parts, with an Emperor in the East and an Emperor in the West: in 392 (the year after Augustine became a priest) Theodosius, the Eastern Emperor, became Emperor of the West as well. He died in 395, the last man to rule the whole Roman world. With his sons, the division was restored. The Eastern Empire,

[1] Reprinted from Vol. I of *The Great Books: A Christian Appraisal*, edited by Harold C. Gardiner, S.J., published by the Devin-Adair Company.

based upon Constantinople, was to last for another thousand years. The Western Empire fell to the Barbarians in a lifetime.

For Western civilization (which ultimately means ourselves among others!) the break was immense. It meant two things. In the secular order, the new rulers were men to whom the ancient classical tradition meant nothing. In the ecclesiastical order, the new situation meant the severance of the West from the East—the hierarchical unity lasted some centuries longer, but the old closeness was gone: and it was in the East that practically all the great theological thinking had been done. The Western world started on its new career under the double threat that civilization would be cut off from the Classics, that the Church would be cut off from its intellectual sources.

It did not happen so. It was Augustine who made the difference. "Single handed, he shifted the center of gravity," says Father Martindale. In himself he summed up and by his prestige gave to the new Europe all that was richest in the Classics: for the educators of the new Europe were to be the monks: and the monks took their curriculum from Augustine's treatise *De Doctrina Christiana* (not from the *Confessions,* where he dismisses the Classics pretty cavalierly). What he did for theology was even more remarkable. For in him—just at the moment of its most urgent need—the Western Church produced its first enormous intellect. Firmly, profoundly, *in Latin,* he stated all the great Christian truths: above all the doctrine of the Trinity, the supreme truth about God, and the doctrine of grace, the supreme truth about man's way to God. With the social order crashing about his ears, he went to the fundamentals of soul and society. His reaction to the sack of Rome by Alaric in 410 was to write *The City of God:*

Two loves had built two cities—love of self to the despising of God had built the earthly city; love of God to the despising of self, the heavenly city.

Or as he says in his Commentary on Psalm 64:

Two loves make up these two cities: love of God makes Jerusalem, love of the world makes Babylon. Let each question himself as to what he loves, and he shall find of which he is a citizen.

To write a book seemed a pitiful way to meet a catastrophe so vast, but the book laid the foundations of a Christian sociology; for Charlemagne, four hundred years later, it was a kind of Bible; more than any other single influence it shaped the Middle Ages. And just as Charlemagne was taught by *The City of God,* so two hundred years before him Gregory the Great in his mighty reform of the Church was nourished by the *Confessions*. By the twelfth century, first-rate thinkers were once more in action in the Church. But for the seven centuries between, the one light that shone steadily was Augustine's.

If you would know why this one man could throw his influence so far across the centuries, the *Confessions* will tell you. He was a genius, of course, and genius carries. But we can get closer to his secret.

To begin with, there is his personality. Reading the *Confessions*, you realize that you have never met a man even faintly like him. He joins the Church at the age of 33: twelve years later he writes the *Confessions*. By now he is a bishop, and he writes of himself with an unaffected candor that would be startling in a bartender.

Nor is he writing only of past sins, now happily conquered: there is the marvelous analysis of his present spiritual state in Book X— no one could read that section and not feel that Augustine is unique among the great. And uniqueness carries.

Then there is his power with words. You will meet with examples on every page of the *Confessions*; and remember that you are read-ing only what a wretched translator could make of them in English: the Latin is immeasurably more striking. No philosopher ever made such phrases, and great words carry.

For a third thing, there is his psychological insight, into himself and others. We could not have arrived at his psychological findings, but once he utters them we can check them from experience: they are dead right, and rightness carries.

But the heart of his secret is that his philosophy comes at us winged with passion: he was a passionate man, and the passion poured into his teaching not to muddy or confuse it but to give it impetus. He gives us his teaching and he gives us himself with it. In the experiences of life he learned certain truths: he does not skim the truth off the experience and give us that; he gives us the truth in the concrete experience in which he learned it. He gives us not the result only but the process. The problems he states are real prob-lems, they have given him years of anguish. The solutions then had to be real solutions. Colored water will cure an imaginary illness, but genuine disease needs a genuine remedy. When he tells you how he came to dominate (not eliminate, you notice, only dominate) sexual temptation, you know that he had really been tortured by it. And all men of turbulent passions recognize him for a brother.

What gives the *Confessions* their special quality is that Augustine was a passionate man with two passions not often found at such intensity in the one man: there was his bodily passion for women, which came to him with adolescence, and his intellectual passion for truth, which seems to have come a few years later with the reading of Cicero's *Hortensius*. A clamorous body and a clamorous mind both demanded satisfaction, and he could not silence either for the other. What the body wanted was simple enough. What the mind wanted was truth about God (especially how could He be everywhere unless He Himself had spatial dimensions); and it wanted the truth about God both because it was the primary truth and it was the condition of having any other truth at all.

And, as a problem that took in both the others, he saw that he must consider the origin of evil. He had come to know the sexual tyranny as evil: could God be the creator of evil? And if so, must He not be evil Himself? The Manichaeans and their heresy held him for nine years: it should have soothed the conflict in him, for it taught that evil had a separate creator over against God; and that the evil in himself was another will distinct from his own, and implying no guilt in him. But his intellect was not satisfied; he was totally incapable of the faintest intellectual dishonesty; he could not shirk a problem. Convenient for his own special case as their teachings were, he came to know them for false.

The book will tell you what he did about his three problems. He came to see that evil was not being but non-being, not something but the absence of something that should have been there: and as such it could not have a creator. Painfully he came to the truth about God: that He is pure spirit with no material element, and that He is in all things not by similarity of dimensions but by superiority of power. But with this came a new problem: how could God have become man, which meant uniting matter to Himself—for matter was surely a principle of degradation? And at last he knew the truth, that spirit has the primacy of matter, but that matter has its own sort of sacredness, too.

Don't dream that all this is an academic problem, suited to a fourth-century professor, but for us only a historical curiosity. It is the literal truth that this twin doctrine of matter's sacredness but spirit's primacy brought the Dark Ages through into the order of the great Middle Ages. It is the doctrine that our own age needs most urgently. It brought that world out of chaos and could bring our world out of chaos, too. Nothing else can. Further, it gave Augustine the mental framework within which he could see the truth about sexual appetite and, by God's grace, bring it under control. And in the matter of sex, our own age is as deadly sick as ever Augustine was.

F. J. S.

A NOTE ON THE MANICHEES

THE FOUNDER of Manichaeism, called Mani or (by the Greeks and Romans) Manes, was born in Babylonia about 215. At the age of 25 or 26 he first propounded his new religion in Persia; he was persecuted by the Zoroastrians, travelled widely, spreading his doctrines, and about the year 276 was crucified in Persia by Bahram I.

His religion, made up of borrowings from all the religions he met (including Christianity) with additional items and a general framework supplied by himself, is far too complicated to be set down shortly. There is much uncertainty as to almost every point of his teaching, and indeed it probably varied in different times and places. But these would seem to be its main points:

(1) In the beginning were two Principles, one Good, one Evil, God and Satan. Each of these has his kingdom, the Kingdom of Light and the Kingdom of Darkness. The two Kingdoms have one border in common, but in every other direction they are infinite.

(2) Each of these kingdoms is organised with incredible complexity. God, the Father of Light, has his kingdom proper with its Five Tabernacles (Intelligence, Reason, Thought, Reflection, Will) which are also called Aeons, and sometimes Angels. He also has his sub-kingdoms, Light-Air and Light-Earth, and each of these has five attributes. (The figure 5 is a key figure in Manes' doctrine because of some astrological significance he found in it.)

The Kingdom of Darkness has an organisation roughly parallel: the kingdom proper with its five Aeons (Wells of Poison, Columns of Smoke, Abysmal Depths, Fetid Marshes, Pillars of Fire) and sub-kingdoms each with five attributes.

(3) Satan invaded the Kingdom of Light. God himself did not fight Satan, but emanated Primal-Man (he is not to be confused with Adam) who in turn emanated Five Sons and these battled against Satan and his Five Elements. Satan won and devoured Primal-Man and his Five Elements; which thus remained as scattered Elements of Light in the Kingdom of Darkness.

(4) A male and female devil in the Kingdom of Darkness bring forth Adam and Eve; in Adam's body are a vast number of these

Seeds of Light, in Eve's a smaller number (this remains true of men
and women generally). Cain and Abel are sons of Satan and Eve,
Seth and the rest of the human race of Adam and Eve. Adam's fall
consisted in yielding to the seductions of sex: the generation of Seth
was his primary sin.

(5) The Spirits of Light took pity on men and sent Aeons to
help them. One of the Aeons thus sent to deliver man is Jesus—
not Jesus of Nazareth, who, according to Manes, was an impostor,
a devil, who interfered in the work of the real Jesus. It is difficult to
be quite clear about the Manichaean Jesus. He personifies the Light
imprisoned in matter. As such all that happens in matter happens
to him, so that he is always being born and suffering and dying. In
particular he is eaten in all food. But some part of that imprisoned
Light has already been released, and this is the same Jesus, but
luminous. It is in this capacity that he works to deliver man; in the
other he is in need of deliverance himself.

There is a continuing war for Men between Aeons of Light and
Demons. The Aeons try to deliver men by teaching them the truth
about nature and the powers of nature, and calling men from sensu-
ality. The Aeons work through Prophets of whom Manes is the last
and greatest, the "Paraclete."

(6) The whole of history is concerned with the effort to free
the Light elements imprisoned in the Kingdom of Darkness and
restore them to the Kingdom of Light. When all are thus restored,
a conflagration will destroy the world, the Kingdom of Light and
Darkness will be once more separated, and there will be no further
invasion.

(7) Men could co-operate either with the Aeons of Light or the
Demons. In general the use of matter was a co-operation with the
Demons: and the act of generation was the extreme point of this
co-operation. If at death a man was purified, his soul would go to
the Kingdom of Light; if not, there was a long process of purification. Some, of course, were beyond purification: they would be
damned: among these is Eve who went to eternal damnation for
seducing Adam. Here upon earth all believers were not in this
purified state. There were the small number of Elect and the great
body of Hearers. The Elect were bound to celibacy and were forbidden all flesh meat (for this is a special weapon of the powers of
Darkness); they ate vegetables, and some vegetables were especially
favored as containing a greater number of Light elements—of the
cosmic Jesus in fact; and when the Elect ate them, these Light
particles were set free. For the Hearers there were no such strict
rules. They were urged to virtue, but if they fell into sin they had

the consolation of knowing that these sins were something they were not responsible for but the acts of a foreign power working in them.

(8) Almost all rulers—Christian and pagan—persecuted Manichaeism as an enemy of morality. But it proved hard to destroy, and in the form of Albigensianism was an immense threat to mediaeval civilisation.

CONTENTS

Book One: THE FIRST FIFTEEN YEARS

I–V	Prayer to God and Meditation upon God	3
VI–VII	Augustine's Infancy	5
VIII	Learning to Speak	9
IX–XIX	Schooldays	10
XX	Reasons for Gratitude to God	19

Book Two: THE SIXTEENTH YEAR

I–III	Adolescence	23
IV–X	Robbing a Pear-tree	26

Book Three: FROM SIXTEEN TO EIGHTEEN

I–III	First Days at Carthage	35
IV–V	Cicero and Scripture	38
VI–X	Joins the Manichees	39
XI–XII	His Mother's Anxiety	45

Book Four: FROM EIGHTEEN TO TWENTY–SEVEN

I–III	Searching for Deliverance	51
IV–IX	Loss of a Friend	54
X–XII	The Transience of Created Things	58
XIII–XV	He Writes a Book	61
XVI	Reads Aristotle on the Categories	64

Book Five: AGED TWENTY–EIGHT

I–II	Prayer	69
III–VII	Faustus Comes to Carthage	70
VIII–XII	Augustine Goes to Rome	76
XIII–XIV	At Milan	81

Book Six: AGED TWENTY–NINE

I–II	Monica Comes to Milan	87
III–V	His Mind Still Searches	89
VI	Disappointments in Worldly Affairs	92
VII–X	Alypius and Nebridius	94
XI–XVI	The Problem of Continence	99

Book Seven: AGED THIRTY

I–II   Realisation That God Is Incorruptible   107
III–V   The Problem of the Origin of Evil   109
VI   Finally Rejects Astrology   112
VII–XVII Beginning of Emancipation from Too Corporeal
          Thinking   114
XVIII–XXI The Need for Christ   122

Book Eight: AGED THIRTY–ONE

I–IV   The Conversion of Victorinus   129
V–XII   Augustine's Conversion   134

Book Nine: AGED THIRTY–TWO

I–VII   Reception into the Church   151
VIII–XIII The Death of Monica   160

Book Ten: CONCLUDES AUGUSTINE'S CONFESSION

I–V   Why He Makes This Confession   173
VI–VII   What Is God?   176
VIII–XXV Analysis of Memory   178
XXVI–XXIX Prayer   192
XXX–XLI   Augustine's Present State   193
XLII–XLIII The True Mediator   207

TRANSLATOR'S NOTE

The use of *Thou* or *You* in speaking to God presented a real problem. St. Augustine, of course, knew nothing of *Thou* as a term reserved for religious use. He, like any other writer of Latin, used *Tu* when he was talking to one (whether it were God or his mother or his mistress or an opponent in controversy), *Vos* when he was talking to more than one. It would seem therefore that our usage of *Thou*, with the special religious atmosphere that now goes with it, introduces a note into the translation that was not in the original.

On the other hand, Christians of the English tongue are so accustomed to using *Thou* in their prayers, that *You* would sound odd.

St. Augustine is addressing God all the time: he relates the story of his life to God, discusses philosophical problems with God, and from time to time breaks into what we should more naturally regard as prayer to God. If *Thou* is used throughout, the effect is quite intolerably archaic and untrue to the extreme modernness of St. Augustine's Latin. I have therefore made a compromise: in passages of straight prayer, I have used *Thou*; but when he addresses God in narrative or discussion, I have used *You*.

The border-line between prayer and discussion (or narrative) is not always quite clear. And, even apart from that, it has not been possible to apply the rule with entire consistency. Where St. Augustine uses Scripture passages in which our English version uses *Thou*, I have kept *Thou*; and in his own comments arising out of or linking such Scripture passages, it seemed best to keep to *Thou*.

Texts of Scripture, even where Augustine modifies them a little, are printed in italics; but not scattered phrases from Scripture.

I have occasionally inserted a phrase for greater clarity. Such phrases will be found in square brackets.

BOOK ONE

THE FIRST FIFTEEN YEARS

I–V   *Prayer to God and Meditation upon God*
      I   Prayer, and questions about prayer
     II   Since God is in man, why do we pray that God should come to us?
    III   How is God everywhere?
    IV   Praise of God
     V   Prayer for forgiveness and for light

VI–VII   *Augustine's Infancy*
    VI   The providence of God; did infancy follow some earlier age?
    VII   Where is the innocence of infancy?

VIII   *Learning to Speak*

IX–XIX   *Schooldays*
    IX   Going to school; the idleness of boys and of men
    X   Love of play
    XI   Early illness and postponement of baptism
    XII   Dislike of learning
    XIII   Useful and less useful studies
    XIV   Learning Latin and learning Greek
    XV   Prayer that he may rightly use what he has learned
    XVI   The moral danger of classical studies
    XVII   Contest in declamation
    XVIII   The rules of grammar and the laws of God
    XIX   His faults of character

XX   *Reasons for Gratitude to God*

GREAT ART THOU, O *Lord, and greatly to be praised; great is Thy power, and of Thy wisdom there is no number.* And man desires to praise Thee. He is but a tiny part of all that Thou hast created. He bears about him his mortality, the evidence of his sinfulness, and the evidence that *Thou dost resist the proud*: yet this tiny part of all that Thou hast created desires to praise Thee.

Thou dost so excite him that to praise Thee is his joy. For Thou hast made us for Thyself and our hearts are restless till they rest in Thee. Grant me, O Lord, to know which is the soul's first movement toward Thee—to implore Thy aid or to utter its praise of Thee; and whether it must know Thee before it can implore. For it would seem clear that no one can call upon Thee without knowing Thee, for if he did he might invoke another than Thee, knowing Thee not. Yet may it be that a man must implore Thee before he can know Thee? But, *how shall they call on Him in Whom they have not believed? or how shall they believe without a preacher?* And, *they shall praise the Lord that seek Him*; for those that seek shall find; and finding Him they will praise Him. Let me seek Thee, Lord, by praying Thy aid, and let me utter my prayer believing in Thee: for Thou hast been preached to us. My faith, Lord, cries to Thee, the faith that Thou hast given me, that Thou hast inbreathed in me, through the humanity of Thy Son and by the ministry of Thy Preacher.

But how can I call unto my God, my God and Lord? For in calling unto Him, I am calling Him to me: and what room is there in me for my God, the God who made heaven and earth? Is there anything in me, O God, that can contain You? All heaven and earth cannot contain You for You made them, and me in them. Yet, since nothing that is could exist without You, You must in some way be in all that is: [therefore also in me, since I am]. And if You are already in me, since otherwise I should not be, why do I cry to You to enter into me? Even if I were in Hell You would be there *for if*

I go down into hell, Thou art there also. Thus, O God, I should be nothing, utterly nothing, unless You were in me—or rather unless I were in You, *of Whom and by Whom and in Whom are all things.* So it is, Lord; so it is. Where do I call You to come to, since I am in You? Or where else are You that You can come to me? Where shall I go, beyond the bounds of heaven and earth, that God may come to me, since He has said: *Heaven and earth do I fill.*

III

But if You fill heaven and earth, do they contain You? Or do You fill them, and yet have much over since they cannot contain You? Is there some other place into which that overplus of You pours that heaven and earth cannot hold? Surely You have no need of any place to contain You since You contain all things, and fill them indeed precisely by containing them. The vessels thus filled with You do not render You any support: for though they perished utterly, You would not be spilt out. And in pouring Yourself out upon us, You do not come down to us but rather elevate us to You: You are not scattered over us, but we are gathered into one by You. You fill all things: but with Your whole being? It is true that all things cannot wholly contain You: but does this mean that they contain part of You? and do they all contain the same part at the same time? or do different parts of creation contain different parts of You—greater parts or smaller according to their own magnitude? But are there in You parts greater and smaller? Or are You not in every place at once in the totality of Your being, while yet nothing contains You wholly?

IV

What then is my God, what but the Lord God? *For Who is Lord but the Lord, or Who is God but our God?* O Thou, the greatest and the best, mightiest, almighty, most merciful and most just, utterly hidden and utterly present, most beautiful and most strong, abiding yet mysterious, suffering no change and changing all things: never new, never old, making all things new, *bringing age upon the proud and they know it not;* ever in action, ever at rest, gathering all things to Thee and needing none; sustaining and fulfilling and protecting, creating and nourishing and making perfect; ever seeking though lacking nothing. Thou lovest without subjection to passion, Thou art jealous but not with fear; Thou canst know repentance but not sorrow, be angry yet unperturbed by anger. Thou canst change the

works Thou hast made but Thy mind stands changeless. Thou dost
find and receive back what Thou didst never lose; art never in need
but dost rejoice in Thy gains, art not greedy but dost exact interest
manifold. Men pay Thee more than is of obligation to win return
from Thee, yet who has anything that is not already Thine? Thou
owest nothing yet dost pay as if in debt to Thy creature, forgivest
what is owed to Thee yet dost not lose thereby. And with all this,
what have I said, my God and my Life and my sacred Delight?
What can any one say when he speaks of Thee? Yet woe to them
that speak not of Thee at all, since those who say most are but dumb.

V

Who shall grant me to rest in Thee? By whose gift shalt Thou
enter into my heart and fill it so compellingly that I turn no
more to my sins but embrace Thee, my only good? What art Thou
to me? Have mercy, that I may tell. What rather am I to Thee, that
Thou shouldst demand my love and if I do not love Thee be angry
and threaten such great woes? Surely not to love Thee is already
a great woe. For Thy mercies' sake, O Lord my God, tell me what
Thou art to me. *Say unto my soul, I am Thy salvation.* So speak that
I may hear, Lord, my heart is listening; open it that it may hear Thee
say to my soul *I am Thy salvation.* Hearing that word, let me come
in haste to lay hold upon Thee. Hide not Thy face from me. Let
me see Thy face even if I die, lest I die with longing to see it.

The house of my soul is too small to receive Thee: let it be
enlarged by Thee. It is all in ruins: do Thou repair it. There are
things in it that must offend Thy gaze, I confess and know. But
who shall cleanse it? or to what other besides Thee shall I cry out:
*From my secret sins cleanse me, O Lord, and from those of others
spare Thy servant? I believe, and therefore do I speak.* Lord Thou
knowest, *Have I not confessed against myself my transgressions
against Thee, and Thou, my God, hast forgiven the iniquities of my
heart? I contend not in judgment with Thee,* who art the truth; and
I have no will to deceive myself, *lest my iniquity lie unto itself.* Therefore I contend not in judgment with Thee, for *if Thou, O Lord, wilt
mark iniquities, Lord, who shall endure it?*

VI

Yet, though I am but dust and ashes, suffer me to utter my plea
to Thy mercy; suffer me to speak since it is to God's mercy that I
speak and not to man's scorn. From Thee too I might have scorn, but

Thou wilt return and have compassion on me. What have I to say to Thee, God, save that I know not where I came from, when I came into this life-in-death—or should I call it death-in-life? I do not know. I only know that the gifts Your mercy had provided sustained me from the first moment: not that I remember it but so I have heard from the parents of my flesh, the father from whom, and the mother in whom, You fashioned me in time.

Thus for my sustenance and my delight I had woman's milk: yet it was not my mother or my nurses who stored their breasts for me: it was Yourself, using them to give me the food of my infancy, according to Your ordinance and the riches set by You at every level of creation. It was by Your gift that I desired what You gave and no more, by Your gift that those who suckled me willed to give me what You had given them: for it was by the love implanted in them by You that they gave so willingly that milk which by Your gift flowed in the breasts. It was a good for them that I received good from them, though I received it not *from* them but only through them: since all good things are from You, O God, and *from God is all my health*. But this I have learnt since: You have made it abundantly clear by all that I have seen You give, within me and about me. For at that time I knew how to suck, to lie quiet when I was content, to cry when I was in pain: and that was all I knew.

Later I added smiling to the things I could do, first in sleep, then awake. This again I have on the word of others, for naturally I do not remember; in any event, I believe it, for I have seen other infants do the same. And gradually I began to notice where I was, and the will grew in me to make my wants known to those who might satisfy them; but I could not, for my wants were within me and those others were outside: nor had they any faculty enabling them to enter into my mind. So I would fling my arms and legs about and utter sounds, making the few gestures in my power—these being as apt to express my wishes as I could make them: but they were not very apt. And when I did not get what I wanted, either because my wishes were not clear or the things not good for me, I was in a rage —with my parents as though I had a right to their submission, with free human beings as though they had been bound to serve me; and I took my revenge in screams. That infants are like this, I have learnt from watching other infants; and that I was like it myself I have learnt more clearly from these other infants, who did not know me, than from my nurses who did.

That infancy of mine died long since, yet I still live. But there is something I would enquire of You, Lord, because Your life is for ever and in You nothing dies: for before the beginning of time.

before anything that can even be called "before," You are—and You are the God and Lord of all that You have created: and before Your face stand the causes of all things transient and the changeless principles of all things that change, and the eternal reasons of all the things of unreason and of time. Therefore, O God, tell me I beg, in pity to a creature who needs pity, whether my infancy followed upon some earlier age of my life that had passed away before it. Was the time I spent in my mother's womb such another age? I have heard something of [my mother's condition at] that time, and I have seen women big with child. And before that again, O God of my joy? Was I anywhere? Was I anyone? There is none to tell me— neither my parents, nor any man's experience, nor any memory of my own. Perhaps You laugh at me for seeking to know of such things since it is Your will that I adore You and praise You for what I do know. And I do truly, Lord of heaven and earth, adore You and praise You for my first being and the infancy of which I have now no memory: for You have left man to learn these things about him- self from others, to accept much that touches him so closely on the word of his womenfolk.

Clearly then I had being and I had life: and toward the end of my infancy I tried hard to find ways of making my feelings known to others. Whence could such a living being come but from You, Lord? Could any man be his own maker? Or is there any other channel through which being and life should flow into us, save that we are made by You, Lord, to whom "being" and "being alive" are not two separate things, since infinite Being is identical with infinite Life? For You are infinite and in You is no change, nor does today pass away in You. Yet in another sense in You it does pass away, for in You are all such things—they could not even have any being that could pass away unless You upheld them in being. And because Your years do not pass, Your years are today; and no matter how many our days and our fathers' days have been, they have all passed in Your undying day and from it have received such being and meas- ures as they had: and all the days to come shall similarly pass in Your undying day and shall receive from it their being and measures. But You are still the same. All our tomorrows to the end of time You shall make to be in this Your day; and all our yesterdays from the beginning of time You have made to be in this Your day. What is it to me, if anyone does not understand this? Let him rejoice as he asks: *What is this?* Let him rejoice, and let him prefer to find You even if he does not find this, rather than to find it and not You with it.

VII

O God hear me! Woe unto men for their sins! When man cries thus, You have mercy upon him, for You made man but not the sin in him. Who shall remind me of the sins of my infancy: *for in Thy sight there is none pure from sin, not even the infant whose life is but a day upon the earth.* But who is to inform me? Perhaps this or that tiny child in whom I can see what I no longer remember of myself [If he is to teach me] what then were my sins at that age? That I wailed too fiercely for the breast? For if today I were to make as gluttonously and as clamorously, not of course for my mother's breasts, but for the food I now eat, I should be ridiculed and quite properly condemned. This means that what I did then was in fact reprehensible, although, since I could not understand words of blame, neither custom nor commonsense allowed me to be blamed. As we grow older we root out such ways and cast them from us: [which means that we hold them to be bad]—for no man engaged in removing evil would knowingly cast out what is good. Surely it was not good, even for that time of life, to scream for things that would have been thoroughly bad for me; to fly into hot rage because older persons—and free, not slaves—were not obedient to me; to strike out as hard as I could, with sheer will to hurt, at my parents and other sensible folk for not yielding to demands which could only have been granted at my peril. Thus the innocence of children is in the helplessness of their bodies rather than any quality in their minds. I have myself seen a small baby jealous; it was too young to speak, but it was livid with anger as it watched another infant at the breast.

There is nothing unusual in this. Mothers and nurses will tell you that they have their own way of curing these fits of jealousy. But at any rate it is an odd kind of innocence when a baby cannot bear that another—in great need, since upon that one food his very life depends—should share the milk that flows in such abundance. These childish tempers are borne with lightly, not because they are not faults, or only small faults; but because they will pass with the years. This is clearly so: for though we bear with them now, the same things would not be tolerated in an older person.

You, O Lord my God, gave me in my infancy life and a body; and You supplied the body with senses, fitted it with limbs, gave it shape and proportion, and for its general well-being and security implanted in it all the instincts of a living being. And You, Lord, doer of all these things, command me to praise You in them, *to confess unto Thee and sing to Thy name, O most high*; because You are

God, omnipotent and good, even if You had done these things alone: for none other can do them save You, the One, who are the exemplar of all things, the All-Beautiful, who form and set in order all things by Your law.

Thus, Lord, I do not remember living this age of my infancy; I must take the word of others about it and can only conjecture how I spent it—even if with a fair amount of certainty—from watching others now in the same stage. I am loth, indeed, to count it as part of the life I live in this world. For it is buried in the darkness of the forgotten as completely as the period earlier still that I spent in my mother's womb. But if *I was conceived in iniquity, and in sin my mother nourished me in the womb,* then where, my God, where, O Lord, where or when was I, Your servant, innocent? But I pass now from that time. For what concern have I now with a time of which I can recall no trace?

VIII

From infancy I came to boyhood, or rather it came to me, taking the place of infancy. Yet infancy did not go: for where was it to go to? Simply it was no longer there. For now I was not an infant, without speech, but a boy, speaking. This I remember; and I have since discovered by observation how I learned to speak. I did not learn by elders teaching me words in any systematic way, as I was soon after taught to read and write. But of my own motion, using the mind which You, my God, gave me, I strove with cries and various sounds and much moving of my limbs to utter the feelings of my heart—all this in order to get my own way. Now I did not always manage to express the right meanings to the right people. So I began to reflect. [I observed that] my elders would make some particular sound, and as they made it would point at or move towards some particular thing: and from this I came to realize that the thing was called by the sound they made when they wished to draw my attention to it. That they intended this was clear from the motions of their body, by a kind of natural language common to all races which consists in facial expressions, glances of the eye, gestures, and the tones by which the voice expresses the mind's state—for example whether things are to be sought, kept, thrown away, or avoided. So, as I heard the same words again and again properly used in different phrases, I came gradually to grasp what things they signified; and forcing my mouth to the same sounds, I began to use them to express my own wishes. Thus I learnt to convey what I meant to those about me; and so took another long step along the stormy way of human

life in society, while I was still subject to the authority of my parents
and at the beck and call of my elders.

IX

O God, my God, what emptiness and mockeries did I now experience: for it was impressed upon me as right and proper in a boy to
obey those who taught me, that I might get on in the world and excel
in the handling of words to gain honor among men and deceitful
riches. I, poor wretch, could not see the use of the things I was sent
to school to learn; but if I proved idle in learning, I was soundly
beaten. For this procedure seemed wise to our ancestors: and many,
passing the same way in days past, had built a sorrowful road by
which we too must go, with multiplication of grief and toil upon
the sons of Adam.

Yet, Lord, I observed men praying to You: and I learnt to do
likewise, thinking of You (to the best of my understanding) as
some great being who, though unseen, could hear and help me. As
a boy I fell into the way of calling upon You, my Help and my
Refuge; and in those prayers I broke the strings of my tongue—praying to You, small as I was but with no small energy, that I might not
be beaten at school. And when You did not hear me (*not as giving
me over to folly*), my elders and even my parents, who certainly
wished me no harm, treated my stripes as a huge joke, which they
were very far from being to me. Surely, Lord, there is no one so
steeled in mind or cleaving to You so close—or even so insensitive, for
that might have the same effect—as to make light of the racks and
hooks and other torture instruments (from which in all lands men
pray so fervently to be saved) while truly loving those who are in
such bitter fear of them. Yet my parents seemed to be amused at the
torments inflicted upon me as a boy by my masters, though I was no
less afraid of my punishments or zealous in my prayers to You for
deliverance. But in spite of my terrors I still did wrong, by writing or
reading or studying less than my set tasks. It was not, Lord, that I
lacked mind or memory, for You had given me as much of these as
my age required; but the one thing I revelled in was play; and for this
I was punished by men who after all were doing exactly the same
things themselves. But the idling of men is called business; the idling
of boys, though exactly like, is punished by those same men: and
no one pities either boys or men. Perhaps an unbiased observer would
hold that I was rightly punished as a boy for playing with a ball:
because this hindered my progress in studies—studies which would
give me the opportunity as a man to play at things more degraded.

Thanks so
much Marg.

Marilyn

And what difference was there between me and the master who flogged me? For if on some trifling point he had the worst of the argument with some fellow-master, he was more torn with angry vanity than I when I was beaten in a game of ball.

X

Yet in acting against the commands of my parents and school-masters, I did wrong, O Lord my God, Creator and Ruler of all things, but of sin not Creator but Ruler only: for I might later have made good use of those lessons that they wanted me to learn, whatever may have been their motive in wanting it. I disobeyed, not because I had chosen better, but through sheer love of play: I loved the vanity of victory, and I loved too to have my ears tickled with the fictions of the theatre which set them to itching ever more burningly: and in my eyes a similar curiosity burned increasingly for the games and shows of my elders. Yet those who put on such shows are held in high esteem. And most people would be delighted to have their sons grow up to give similar shows in their turn—and meanwhile fully concur in the beatings those same sons get if these shows hinder study: for study is the way to the prosperity necessary for giving them! Look down in mercy, Lord, upon such things; and set us free who now beseech Thee: and not only us, but those also who have never besought Thee—that they may turn to Thee and be made free.

XI

Even as a boy, of course, I had heard of an eternal life promised because the Lord our God had come down in His humility upon our pride. And I was signed with the sign of His Cross and seasoned with His salt as I came new from the womb of my mother, who had great trust in You. When I was still a child, I fell gravely ill with some abdominal trouble and was close to death. You saw, Lord—for You were even then guarding me—with what earnest faith I besought the piety of my own mother, and of the Church which is the mother of us all, that I might receive the baptism of Your Christ, my Lord and my God. The mother of my flesh was in heavy anxiety, since with a heart chaste in Your faith she was ever in deep travail for my eternal salvation, and would have proceeded without delay to have me consecrated and washed clean by the Sacrament of salvation, while I confessed You, Lord Jesus, unto the remission of sins: but I made a sudden recovery. This caused my baptismal cleansing to be postponed: for it was argued that if I lived I should inevitably fall again into the filth of sin: and after baptism the guilt of sin's defilement would be in itself graver and put the soul in graver peril. I then believed, as did my mother and all our household, except my father: yet he did not prevail over the hold my mother's piety had upon me, to lead me not to believe in Christ because he did not as yet. She used all her endeavor, O God, that I should hold You for my father rather than him: and in this with Your aid she overcame her husband, in her greater virtue serving him because in serving him she served Your command likewise.

I ask You, my God—for I would know, if it is Your will to tell me— to what end was my baptism deferred? was it for my good that I was left to sin with a loose rein, or was the rein not truly loosed? Why do we constantly hear such phrases as: "Let him alone, let him keep on with what he is doing, he is not yet baptized"? In the matter of the body's health we do not say: "Let him be wounded worse, he is not yet cured." It would have been far better had I been made whole at once and had so used my own efforts and the aid of my friends that the health brought to my soul should be safe in Your keeping, by whose gift it was given me. Far better, I say. But it was obvious that many mighty waves of temptation threatened to break upon me as I grew out of boyhood. So my mother knew: and she thought it better to let them break upon the clay before it was moulded to Christ's image rather than let the clay be moulded and then assailed.

XII

But to continue with my boyhood, which was in less peril of sin than my adolescence. I disliked learning and hated to be forced to it. But I *was* forced to it, so that good was done to me though it was not my doing. Short of being driven to it, I certainly would not have learned. But no one does well against his will, even if the thing he does is a good thing to do. Nor did those who forced me do well: it was by You, O God, that well was done. Those others had no deeper vision of the use to which I might put all they forced me to learn, but to sate the insatiable desire of man for wealth that is but penury and glory that is but shame. But You, Lord, *by Whom the very hairs of our head are numbered,* used for my good the error of those who urged me to study; but my own error, in that I had no will to learn, you used for my punishment—a punishment richly deserved by one so small a boy and so great a sinner. Thus, You brought good for me out of those who did ill, and justly punished me for the ill I did

myself. So You have ordained and so it is: that every disorder of the
soul is its own punishment.

XIII

To this day I do not quite see why I so hated the Greek tongue
that I was made to learn as a small boy. For I really liked Latin—not
the rudiments that we got from our first teachers but the literature
that we came to be taught later. For the rudiments—reading and
writing and figuring—I found as hard and hateful as Greek. Yet
this too could come only from sin and the vanity of life, because *I
was flesh, and a wind that goes away and returns not.* For those first
lessons were the surer. I acquired the power I still have to read what
I find written and to write what I want to express; whereas in the
studies that came later I was forced to memorise the wanderings of
Aeneas—whoever *he* was—while forgetting my own wanderings; and
to weep for the death of Dido who killed herself for love, while
bearing dry-eyed my own pitiful state, in that among these studies
I was becoming dead to You, O God, my life.

Nothing could be more pitiful than a pitiable creature who does
not see to pity himself, and weeps for the death that Dido suffered
through love of Aeneas and not for the death he suffers himself
through not loving You, O God, Light of my heart, Bread of my soul,
Power wedded to my mind and the depths of my thought. I did not
love You and I went away from You in fornication: and all around
me in my fornication echoed applauding cries: "Well done! Well
done!" *For the friendship of this world is fornication against Thee*:
and the world cries "Well done" so loudly that one is ashamed of
unmanliness not to do it. And for this I did not grieve; but I grieved
for Dido, slain as she sought by the sword an end to her woe, while
I too followed after the lowest of Your creatures, forsaking You,
earth going unto earth. And if I were kept from reading, I grieved at
not reading the tales that caused me such grief. This sort of folly
is held nobler and richer than the studies by which we learn to
read and write!

But now let my God cry aloud in my soul, and let Your truth
assure me that it is not so: the earlier study is the better. I would
more willingly forget the wanderings of Aeneas and all such
things than how to write and read. Over the entrance of these
grammar schools hangs a curtain: but this should be seen not as
lending honor to the mysteries, but as a cloak to the errors taught
within. Let not those masters—who have now lost their terrors for me
—cry out against me, because I confess to You, my God, the desire

of my soul, and find soul's rest in blaming my evil ways that I may love Your holy ways. Let not the buyers or sellers of book-learning cry out against me. If I ask them whether it is true, as the poet says, that Aeneas ever went to Carthage, the more ignorant will have to answer that they do not know, the more scholarly that he certainly did not. But if I ask with what letters the name Aeneas is spelt, all whose schooling has gone so far will answer correctly, according to the convention men have agreed upon for the use of letters. Or again, were I to ask which loss would be more damaging to human life—the loss from men's memory of reading and writing or the loss of these poetic imaginings—there can be no question what anyone would answer who had not lost his own memory. Therefore as a boy I did wrong in liking the empty studies more than the useful—or rather in loving the empty and hating the useful. For one and one make two, two and two make four, I found a loathsome refrain; but such empty unrealities as the Wooden Horse with its armed men, and Troy on fire, and Creusa's Ghost, were sheer delight.

XIV

But why did I hate Greek literature, which is filled with similar tales? Homer is as skilled in the invention of such things, and has the same charm and the same unreality: yet as a boy I could not abide him. I suppose that Virgil affects Greek boys when they are compelled to learn him as Homer affected me. For the drudgery of learning a foreign language sprinkled bitterness over all the sweetness of the Greek tales. I did not know a word of the language: and I was driven with threats and savage punishments to learn. There had been a time of infancy when I knew no Latin either. Yet I learnt it without threat or punishment merely by keeping my eyes and ears open, amidst the flatterings of nurses and the jesting and pleased laughter of elders leading me on. I learned it without the painful pressure of compulsion, by the sole pressure of my own desire to express what was in my mind, which would have been impossible unless I had learnt words: and I learnt them not through people teaching me but simply through people speaking: to whom I was striving to utter my own feelings. All this goes to prove that free curiosity is of more value in learning than harsh discipline. But by Your ordinance, O God, discipline must control the free play of curiosity—for Your ordinance ranges from the master's cane to the torments suffered by the martyrs, and works that mingling of bitter with sweet which brings us back to You from the poison of pleasure that first drew us away from You.

XV

Hear my prayer, O Lord; let not my soul fail under Thy discipline, nor let me fail in uttering to Thee Thy mercies: by them Thou hast drawn me out of all my most evil ways, that I should find more delight in Thee than in all the temptations I once ran after, and should love Thee more intensely, and lay hold upon Thy hand with all my heart's strength, and be delivered from every temptation unto the end.

O Lord, my King and my God: may whatever of value I learnt as a boy be used for Thy service, and what I now do in speaking and writing and reading and figuring. When I was learning vain things, Thou didst discipline me: and the sin of the delight I had in those vain things, Thou hast forgiven me. Among those studies, I learnt many a useful word, but these might have been learnt equally well in studies not vain: and that surely is the safe way for the young to tread.

XVI

But [in this matter of classical studies] how woeful are you, O torrent of established custom. Who can resist you or when will you run dry? How long will you continue to roll the sons of Eve into that vast and terrible sea in which even those who mount the cross scarcely escape drowning? In you I read of Jove, both as the God of thunder and as an adulterer. How could he be both? But so the story goes: and so sham thunder is made to legitimize and play pander to real adultery: yet these robed and gowned masters are furious when Cicero, a man trained in their own school, protests: "Homer invented these stories, ascribing things human to the Gods: would that he had brought down things divine to us." It would have been even truer to say that Homer invented them, attributing divinity to the vilest of men, with the result that crimes are held not to be crimes, and those who do commit them are regarded as acting not like abandoned men but like Gods from Olympus.

And still, O torrent from hell, the sons of men pay fees to be hurled into you in order that they may learn such things. And there is great interest when this sort of teaching is carried on publicly in the forum under the very eye of laws allotting salaries to the masters over and above the fees paid by the pupils. And all the while the torrent lashes its rocks and roars: "By these studies words are learned and the eloquence acquired which is so necessary for persuasion and exposition." Apparently the argument is that we should not have come to know words like "golden," "shower," "lap," "deceive," "the temple of Heaven," and others of the sort, unless Terence had brought a vicious youth upon the stage, setting up Jove as a model for his own fornication, and all the while gazing upon a picture on the wall of Jove deceiving Danae by descending into her lap as a golden shower. Note how the youth incites himself to lust as though commanded from Heaven:

And what a God! [Jove] who shakes the temples of heaven with the
    roar of his thunder!
And I, a mere mortal, should I not do what he does? I have done it,
    and with joy.

The words are not learned one whit more easily because of all this vileness: but the vileness is committed all the more boldly because of the words. I make no accusation against the words, which in themselves are choice and precious vessels, but against the wine of error that is in them, and is poured out to us by teachers already drunken with it. And we, unless we drank, were flogged and had no right of appeal to any sober judge. And I, my God, in Whose sight I can now recall these things without peril, learnt them willingly, and sinfully delighted in them, and so was regarded as a youth of much promise.

XVII

Give me leave, O my God, to speak of my mind, Your gift, and of the follies in which I wasted it. It chanced that a task was set me, a task which I did not like but had to do. There was the promise of glory if I won, the fear of ignominy, and a flogging as well, if I lost. It was to declaim the words uttered by Juno in her rage and grief when she could not keep the Trojan prince from coming to Italy. I had learnt that Juno had never said these words, but we were compelled to err in the footsteps of the poet who had invented them: and it was our duty to paraphrase in prose what he had said in verse. In this exercise that boy won most applause in whom the passions of grief and rage were expressed most powerfully and in the language most adequate to the majesty of the personage represented.

What could all this mean to me, O My true Life, My God? Why was there more applause for the performance I gave than for so many classmates of my own age? Was not the whole business so much smoke and wind? Surely some other matter could have been found to exercise mind and tongue. Thy praises, Lord, might have upheld the fresh young shoot of my heart, so that it might not have been whirled away by empty trifles, defiled, a prey to the spirits of the air. For there is more than one way of sacrificing to the fallen angels.

XVIII

Yet it was no wonder that I fell away into vanity and went so far from Thee, My God, seeing that men were held up as models for my imitation who were covered with shame if, in relating some act of theirs in no way evil, they fell into some barbarism or grammatical solecism: yet were praised, and delighted to be praised, when they told of their lusts, provided they did so in correct words correctly arranged. All these things Thou seest, O Lord, and art silent: for Thou art patient and plenteous in mercy and truth. But wilt Thou always stay silent? Even now Thou dost draw out of this pit of horror the soul that seeks Thee and thirsts for Thy joys, *the heart that says to Thee I have sought Thy face: Thy face, Lord, will I still seek:* for to be darkened in heart is to be far from Thy face. It is not on our feet or by movement in space that we go from Thee or return to Thee: Thy prodigal son did not charter horses or chariots or ships, or fly with wings or journey on his two feet to that far country where he wasted in luxurious living what Thou as a loving father hadst given him on his departure—loving when Thou didst give, more loving still to Thy son when he returned, all poor and stripped. To be lustful, that is darkened, in heart, is to be far from Thy face.

Behold, O Lord My God, and, seeing, see patiently, with what anxious care the sons of men observe the rules of letters and syllables taught by the speakers of our tongue before us, while they neglect the eternal rules of everlasting salvation taught by You. The learner or teacher of the established rules of pronunciation is held more contemptible if he drops an 'h' and speaks of a 'uman being*—thus breaking a law of language—than if he hates a human being—thus breaking a law of God. It is strange that we should not realise that no enemy could be more dangerous to us than the hatred with which we hate him, and that by our efforts against him we do less damage to our enemy than is wrought in our own heart. Obviously the knowledge of letters is not more deeply engraved in us than the law of conscience against doing to another what one would not bear if

---

* Thus neatly does Dr. Pusey represent the man who for "hominem" says "ominem."

done to oneself. How hidden art Thou, O God the only great, dwelling in silence in the high places, and by Thy untiring law sending blindness as the punishment for unlawful lusts. A man seeking the fame of eloquence—before a judge who is also a man, with a multitude of men standing about—inveighs against his adversary with inhuman hatred. Such a man will be most vigilantly on guard lest by a slip of the tongue he drop an 'h' and murder the word "human": yet worries not at all that by the fury of his mind he may murder a real human.

XIX

These were the ways of the world upon whose threshold I stood as a boy, and such was the arena for which I was training—more concerned to avoid committing a grammatical error than to be void of envy in case I did commit one and another did not. This I say and confess to Thee, O My God: and in this I was praised by those whom my one idea of success was to please. I did not see the whirl of vileness into which I had been cast away from Thy eyes: for what was more unclean than I, seeing that I did not win the approval even of my own kind: I told endless lies to my tutors, my masters and my parents: all for the love of games, the craving for stage shows, and a restlessness to do what I saw done in these shows.

I stole from my parents' cellar and table, sometimes because I was gluttonous myself, sometimes to have something to give other boys in exchange for implements of play which they were prepared to sell although they loved them as much as I. Even in games, when I was clearly outplayed I tried to win by cheating, from the vain desire for first place. At the same time I was indignant and argued furiously when I caught anyone doing the very things that I had done to others. When I was caught myself, I would fly into a rage rather than give way.

Is this boyhood innocence? It is not, Lord. I cry Thy mercy, O My God. Yet as we leave behind tutors and masters and nuts and balls and birds and come to deal with prefects and kings and the getting of gold and estates and slaves, these are the qualities which pass on with us, one stage of life taking the place of another as the greater punishments of the law take the place of the schoolmaster's cane. Therefore, O God our King, when you said "of such is the Kingdom of Heaven," it could only have been humility as symbolised by the low stature of childhood that you were commending.

XX

Yet, Lord, I should have owed thanks to You, My God and the most excellent Creator and Ruler of the Universe, even if it had been Your will that I should not live beyond boyhood. For even then I was; I lived: I felt: even so early I had an instinct for the care of my own being, a trace in me of that most profound Unity whence my being was derived; in my interior sense I kept guard over the integrity of my outward sense perception, and in my small thoughts upon small matters I had come to delight in the truth. I hated to be wrong, had a vigorous memory, was well trained in speech, delighted in friendship, shunned pain, meanness and ignorance. In so small a creature was not all this admirable and reason for praise? Yet all these were the gifts of my God, for I did not give them to myself. All these were good and all these were I. Therefore He Who made me is good and He is my Good: and in Him I shall exult for all the good qualities that even as a boy I had. But in this lay my sin: that I sought pleasure, nobility, and truth not in God but in the beings He had created, myself and others. Thus I fell into sorrow and confusion and error. Thanks be to Thee, my Joy and my Glory and my Hope and my God: thanks be to Thee for Thy gifts: but do Thou preserve them in me. Thus Thou wilt preserve me, and the things Thou hast given me will increase and be made perfect, and I shall be with Thee: because even that I exist is Thy gift.

BOOK TWO

THE SIXTEENTH YEAR

I–III   *Adolescence*
      I   The sinfulness of his adolescence
     II   Lust takes hold: it might have been checked either by marriage or by knowledge of the true doctrine of virginity
   III   The year at home between Madaura and Carthage; father's and mother's reactions to his sexual development

IV–X   *Robbing a Pear-tree*
    IV   Why did he do it, given that he did not want the pears?
     V   No one sins for no cause at all
    VI   Why then did he steal the pears? All sin is a perverse imitation of God: what excellence of God did this sin imitate?
   VII   Prayer of thanksgiving to God for repentance
  VIII   Was it for the sake of companionship that he stole?
    IX   The danger that lies in companionship
     X   "I became to myself a barren land"

I

I PROPOSE NOW to set down my past wickedness and the carnal corruptions of my soul, not for love of them but that I may love Thee, O my God. I do it for love of Thy love, passing again in the bitterness of remembrance over my most evil ways that Thou mayest thereby grow ever lovelier to me, O Loveliness that dost not deceive, Loveliness happy and abiding: and I collect my self out of that broken state in which my very being was torn asunder because I was turned away from Thee, the One, and wasted myself upon the many.

Arrived now at adolescence I burned for all the satisfactions of hell, and I sank to the animal in a succession of dark lusts: *my beauty consumed away,* and I stank in Thine eyes, yet was pleasing in my own and anxious to please the eyes of men.

II

My one delight was to love and to be loved. But in this I did not keep the measure of mind to mind, which is the luminous line of friendship; but from the muddy concupiscence of the flesh and the hot imagination of puberty mists steamed up to becloud and darken my heart so that I could not distinguish the white light of love from the fog of lust. Both love and lust boiled within me, and swept my youthful immaturity over the precipice of evil desires to leave me half drowned in a whirlpool of abominable sins. Your wrath had grown mighty against me and I knew it not. I had grown deaf from the clanking of the chain of my mortality, the punishment for the pride of my soul: and I departed further from You, and You left me to myself: and I was tossed about and wasted and poured out and boiling over in my fornications: and You were silent, O my late-won Joy. You were silent, and I, arrogant and depressed, weary and restless, wandered further and further from You into more and more sins which could bear no fruit save sorrows.

If only there had been some one then to bring relief to the wretchedness of my state, and turn to account the fleeting beauties of these new temptations and bring within bounds their attractions for me: so that the tides of my youth might have driven in upon the shore of marriage: for then they might have been brought to calm with the having of children as Your law prescribes, O Lord, for in this way You form the offspring of this our death, able with gentle hand to blunt the thorns that You would not have in Your paradise. For Your omnipotence is not far from us, even when we are far from You. Or, on the other hand, I might well have listened more heedfully to the voice from the clouds: *"Nevertheless such [as marry] shall have tribulation of the flesh; but I spare you"*; and *"It is good for a man not to touch a woman"*; and *"He that is without a wife is solicitous for the things that belong to the Lord, how he may please God: but he that is with a wife is solicitous for the things of the world, how he may please his wife."* I should have listened more closely to these words and made myself a eunuch for the kingdom of heaven; and so in all tranquillity awaited Your embraces. Instead I foamed in my wickedness, following the rushing of my own tide, leaving You and going beyond all Your laws. Nor did I escape Your scourges. No mortal can. You were always by me, mercifully hard upon me, and besprinkling all my illicit pleasures with certain elements of bitterness, to draw me on to seek for pleasures in which no bitterness should be. And where was I to find such pleasures save in You O Lord, You who use sorrow to teach, and wound us to heal, and kill us lest we die to You. Where then was I, and how far from the delights of Your house, in that sixteenth year of my life in this world, when the madness of lust—needing no licence from human shamelessness, receiving no licence from Your laws—took complete control of me, and I surrendered wholly to it? My family took no care to save me from this moral destruction by marriage: their only concern was that I should learn to make as fine and persuasive speeches as possible.

III

In that year my studies were interrupted. I had come back from Madaura, a neighboring city to which I had been sent to study grammar and rhetoric, and the money was being got together for the longer journey to Carthage, where I was to go because my father was set upon it—not that he was rich, for he was only a poor citizen of Tagaste. But to whom am I telling this? Not to Thee, O my God, but in Thy presence I am telling it to my own kind, to the race of men, or rather to that small part of the human race that may come upon these writings. And to what purpose do I tell it? Simply that I and any other who may read may realise out of what depths we must cry to Thee. For nothing is more surely heard by Thee than a heart that confesses Thee and a life in Thy faith.

Everyone of course praised my father because, although his means did not allow it, he had somehow provided the wherewithal for his son to travel so far for the sake of his studies. Many a very much richer citizen did no such thing for his children. Yet this same father never bothered about how I was growing towards You or how chaste or unchaste I might be, so long as I grew in eloquence, however much I might lack of Your cultivation O God, who are the one true and good Lord of your field, my heart.

But during that sixteenth year between Madaura and Carthage, owing to the narrowness of the family fortunes I did not go to school, but lived idly at home with my parents. The briars of unclean lusts grew so that they towered over my head, and there was no hand to root them out. On the contrary my father saw me one day in the public baths, now obviously growing towards manhood and showing the turbulent signs of adolescence. The effect upon him was that he already began to look forward to grandchildren, and went home in happy excitement to tell my mother. He rejoiced, indeed, through that intoxication in which the world forgets You its Creator and loves what You have created instead of You, the intoxication of the invisible wine of a will perverted and turned towards baseness. But in my mother's breast You had already laid the foundation of Your temple and begun Your holy habitation: whereas my father was still only a catechumen, and a new catechumen at that. So that she was stricken with a holy fear. And though I was not as yet baptised, she was in terror of my walking in the crooked ways of those who walk with their backs towards You and not their faces.

I have dared to say that You were silent, my God, when I went afar from You. But was it truly so? Whose but Yours were the words You dinned into my ears through the voice of my mother, Your faithful servant? Not that at that time any of it sank into my heart to make me do it. I still remember her anxiety and how earnestly she urged upon me not to sin with women, above all not with any man's wife. All this sounded to me womanish and I should have blushed to obey. Yet it was from You, though I did not know it and thought that You were silent and she speaking: whereas You were speaking to me through her, and in ignoring her I was ignoring You: I, her son, the son of Your handmaid, Your servant. But I realised none of this and went headlong on my course, so blinded that I was ashamed among the other youths that my viciousness was less than theirs; I heard them boasting of their exploits, and the viler the exploits the louder the boasting; and I set about the same exploits not only for the pleasure of the act but for the pleasure of the boasting.

Nothing is utterly condemnable save vice: yet I grew in vice through desire of praise; and when I lacked opportunity to equal others in vice, I invented things I had not done, lest I might be held cowardly for being innocent, or contemptible for being chaste. With the basest companions I walked the streets of Babylon [the city of this World as opposed to the city of God] and wallowed in its filth as if it had been a bed of spices and precious ointments. To make me cleave closer to that city's very center, the invisible Enemy trod me down and seduced me, for I was easy to seduce. My mother had by now fled out of the center of Babylon, but she still lingered in its outskirts. She had urged me to chastity but she did not follow up what my father had told her of me: and though she saw my sexual passions as most evil now and full of peril for the future, she did not consider that if they could not be pared down to the quick, they had better be brought under control within the bounds of married love. She did not want me married because she feared that a wife might be a hindrance to my prospects—not those hopes of the world to come which my mother had in You, O God, but my prospects as a student. Both my parents were unduly set upon the success of my studies, my father because he had practically no thought of You and only vain ambition for me, my mother because she thought that the usual course of studies would be not only no hindrance to my coming to You but an actual help. Recalling the past as well as I can, that is how I read my parents' characters. Anyhow, I was left to do pretty well as I liked, and go after pleasure not only beyond the limit of reasonable discipline but to sheer dissoluteness in many kinds of evil. And in all this, O God, a mist hung between my eyes and the brightness of Your truth: *and mine iniquity had come forth as it were from fatness.*

IV

Your law, O Lord, punishes theft; and this law is so written in the hearts of men that not even the breaking of it blots it out: for no thief bears calmly being stolen from—not even if he is rich and the other steals through want. Yet I chose to steal, and not because want drove me to it—unless a want of justice and contempt for it and an excess of iniquity. For I stole things which I already had in plenty and of better quality. Nor had I any desire to enjoy the things I stole, but only the stealing of them and the sin. There was a pear tree near our vineyard, heavy with fruit, but fruit that was not particularly tempting either to look at or to taste. A group of young blackguards, and I among them, went out to knock down the pears and carry them off late one night, for it was our bad habit to carry

on our games in the streets till very late. We carried off an immense
load of pears, not to eat—for we barely tasted them before throwing
them to the hogs. Our only pleasure in doing it was that it was
forbidden. Such was my heart, O God, such was my heart: yet in
the depth of the abyss You had pity on it. Let that heart now tell
You what it sought when I was thus evil for no object, having no
cause for wrongdoing save my wrongness. The malice of the act was
base and I loved it—that is to say I loved my own undoing, I loved
the evil in me—not the thing for which I did the evil, simply the
evil: my soul was depraved, and hurled itself down from security
in You into utter destruction, seeking no profit from wickedness but
only to be wicked.

V

There is an appeal to the eye in beautiful things, in gold and
silver and all such; the sense of touch has its own powerful pleasures;
and the other senses find qualities in things suited to them. Worldly
success has its glory, and the power to command and to overcome:
and from this springs the thirst for revenge. But in our quest of all
these things, we must not depart from You, Lord, or deviate from
Your Law. This life we live here below has its own attractiveness,
grounded in the measure of beauty it has and its harmony with the
beauty of all lesser things. The bond of human friendship is admirable,
holding many souls as one. Yet in the enjoyment of all such things
we commit sin if through immoderate inclination to them—for though
they are good, they are of the lowest order of good—things higher and
better are forgotten, even You, O Lord our God, and Your Truth
and Your Law. These lower things have their delights but not such
as my God has, for He made them all: *and in Him doth the righteous
delight, and He is the joy of the upright of heart.*

Now when we ask why this or that particular evil act was done, it
is normal to assume that it could not have been done save through
the desire of gaining or the fear of losing some one of these lower
goods. For they have their own charm and their own beauty, though
compared with the higher values of heaven they are poor and mean
enough. Such a man has committed a murder. Why? He wanted the
other man's wife or his property; or he had chosen robbery as a means
of livelihood; or he feared to lose this or that through his victim's
act; or he had been wronged and was aflame for vengeance. Would
any man commit a murder for no cause, for the sheer delight of
murdering? The thing would be incredible. There is of course the
case of the man [Catiline] who was said to be so stupidly and savagely

cruel that he practised cruelty and evil even when he had nothing to gain by them. But even there a cause was stated—he did it, he said, lest through idleness his hand or his resolution should grow slack. And why did he want to prevent that? So that one day by the multiplication of his crimes the city should be his, and he would have gained honors and authority and riches, and would no longer be in fear of the law or in the difficulties that want of money and the awareness of his crimes had brought him. So that not even Catiline loved his crimes as crimes: he loved some other thing which was his reason for committing them.

VI

What was it then that in my wretched folly I loved in You, O theft of mine, deed wrought in that dark night when I was sixteen? For you were not lovely: you were a theft. Or are you anything at all, that I should talk with you? The pears that we stole were beautiful for they were created by Thee, Thou most Beautiful of all, Creator of all, Thou good God, my Sovereign and true Good. The pears were beautiful but it was not pears that my empty soul desired. For I had any number of better pears of my own, and plucked those only that I might steal. For once I had gathered them I threw them away, tasting only my own sin and savouring that with delight; for if I took so much as a bite of any one of those pears, it was the sin that sweetened it. And now, Lord my God, I ask what was it that attracted me in that theft, for there was no beauty in it to attract. I do not mean merely that it lacked the beauty that there is in justice and prudence, or in the mind of man or his senses and vegetative life: or even so much as the beauty and glory of the stars in the heavens, or of earth and sea with their oncoming of new life to replace the generations that pass. It had not even that false show or shadow of beauty by which sin tempts us.

[For there *is* a certain show of beauty in sin.] Thus pride wears the mask of loftiness of spirit, although You alone, O God, are high over all. Ambition seeks honor and glory, although You alone are to be honored before all and glorious forever. By cruelty the great seek to be feared, yet who is to be feared but God alone: from His power what can be wrested away, or when or where or how or by whom? The caresses by which the lustful seduce are a seeking for love: but nothing is more caressing than Your charity, nor is anything more healthfully loved than Your supremely lovely, supremely luminous Truth. Curiosity may be regarded as a desire for knowledge, whereas You supremely know all things. Ignorance and sheer stupidity hide

under the names of simplicity and innocence: yet no being has simplicity like to Yours: and none is more innocent than You, for it is
their own deeds that harm the wicked. Sloth pretends that it wants
quietude: but what sure rest is there save the Lord? Luxuriousness
would be called abundance and completeness; but You are the
fullness and inexhaustible abundance of incorruptible delight. Waste-
fulness is a parody of generosity: but You are the infinitely generous
giver of all good. Avarice wants to possess overmuch: but You
possess all. Enviousness claims that it strives to excel: but what can
excel before You? Anger clamors for just vengeance: but whose
vengeance is so just as Yours? Fear is the recoil from a new and sudden
threat to something one holds dear, and a cautious regard for one's
own safety: but nothing new or sudden can happen to You, nothing
can threaten Your hold upon things loved, and where is safety secure
save in You? Grief pines at the loss of things in which desire delighted:
for it wills to be like to You from whom nothing can be taken away.

Thus the soul is guilty of fornication when she turns from You and
seeks from any other source what she will nowhere find pure and
without taint unless she returns to You. Thus even those who go from
You and stand up against You are still perversely imitating You. But
by the mere fact of their imitation, they declare that You are the
creator of all that is, and that there is nowhere for them to go where
You are not.

So once again what did I enjoy in that theft of mine? Of what
excellence of my Lord was I making perverse and vicious imitation?
Perhaps it was the thrill of acting against Your law—at least in
appearance, since I had no power to do so in fact, the delight a
prisoner might have in making some small gesture of liberty—getting
a deceptive sense of omnipotence from doing something forbidden
without immediate punishment. I was that slave, who fled from his
Lord and pursued his Lord's shadow. O rottenness, O monstrousness
of life and abyss of death! Could you find pleasure only in what was
forbidden, and only because it was forbidden?

VII

What shall I render unto the Lord, that I can recall these things
and yet not be afraid! *I shall love Thee, Lord, and shall give thanks
to Thee and confess Thy name,* because Thou hast forgiven me such
great sins and evil deeds. I know that it is only by Thy grace and
mercy that Thou hast melted away the ice of my sins. And the evil I
have not done, that also I know is by Thy grace: for what might I not
have done, seeing that I loved evil solely because it was evil? I confess

that Thou hast forgiven all alike—the sins I committed of my own motion, the sins I would have committed but for Thy grace.

Would any man, considering his own weakness, dare to attribute his chastity or his innocence to his own powers and so love Thee less—as if he did not need the same mercy as those who return to Thee after sin. If any man has heard Thy voice and followed it and done none of the things he finds me here recording and confessing, still he must not scorn me: for I am healed by the same doctor who preserved him from falling into sickness, or at least into such grievous sickness. But let him love Thee even more: seeing me rescued out of such sickness of sin, and himself saved from falling into such sickness of sin, by the one same Saviour.

VIII

What fruit therefore had I (in my vileness) *in those things of which I am now ashamed?* Especially in that piece of thieving, in which I loved nothing except the thievery—though that in itself was no *thing* and I only the more wretched for it. Now—as I think back on the state of my mind then—I am altogether certain that I would not have done it alone. Perhaps then what I really loved was the companionship of those with whom I did it. If so, can I still say that I loved nothing over and above the thievery? Surely I can; that companionship was nothing over and above, because it was nothing. What is the truth of it? Who shall show me, unless He that illumines my heart and brings light into its dark places? What is the thing that I am trying to get at in all this discussion? If I had liked the pears that I stole and wanted to enjoy eating them, I might have committed the offence alone, if that had been sufficient, to get me the pleasure I wanted; I should not have needed to inflame the itch of my desires by rubbing against accomplices. But since the pleasure I got was not in the pears, it must have been in the crime itself, and put there by the companionship of others sinning with me.

IX

What was my feeling in all this? Depraved, undoubtedly, and woe is me that I had it. But what exactly was it? *Who can understand sins?* We laughed together as if our hearts were tickled to be playing a trick upon the owners, who had no notion of what we were doing and would very strongly have objected. But what delight did I find in that, which I should not equally have found if I had done it alone? Because we are not much given to laughing when we are alone? Not much given, perhaps, but laughter does sometimes overcome a man when no one else is about, if something especially ridiculous is seen or heard or floats into the mind. Yet I would not have done this by myself: quite definitely I would not have done it by myself.

Here, then, O God, is the memory still vivid in my mind. I would not have committed that theft alone: my pleasure in it was not what I stole but that I stole: yet I would not have enjoyed doing it, I would not have done it, alone. O friendship unfriendly, unanalysable attraction for the mind, greediness to do damage for the mere sport and jest of it, desire for another's loss with no gain to oneself or vengeance to be satisfied! Someone cries "Come on, let's do it"—and we would be ashamed to be ashamed!

X

Who can unravel that complex twisted knottedness? It is unclean, I hate to think of it or look at it. I long for Thee, O Justice and Innocence; Joy and Beauty of the clear of sight, I long for Thee with unquenchable longing. There is sure repose in Thee and life untroubled. He that enters into Thee, enters into the joy of his Lord and shall not fear and shall be well in Him who is the Best. I went away from Thee, my God, in my youth I strayed too far from Thy sustaining power, and I became to myself a barren land.

BOOK THREE

FROM SIXTEEN TO EIGHTEEN

I–III   *First Days at Carthage*
      I   Comes to Carthage: in love with love: "a cauldron of illicit loves"
     II   Passion for stage plays: pity superficial and real
    III   "An act worthy of the fruits of death"; a student of Rhetoric; the *eversores*

IV–V   *Cicero and Scripture*
    IV   The profound effect of Cicero's *Hortensius*
     V   Scripture seemed less majestic than Cicero

VI–X   *Joins the Manichees*
    VI   The fantasies the Manichees offered when he hungered for real food; especially their corporeal notion of God
   VII   Manichean objections to Catholic truth: the nature of God; the actions of the Old Testament patriarchs
  VIII   An analysis of sins—(i) sins which corrupt our own nature (*flagitia*) and (ii) sins which damage others (*facinora*)
    IX   Further analysis; God's command is absolute
     X   Manichean absurdity about the fig-tree

XI–XII   *His Mother's Anxiety*
    XI   Monica reassured in a vision
   XII   "The son of these tears"

I

I CAME TO CARTHAGE, where a cauldron of illicit loves leapt and boiled about me. I was not yet in love, but I was in love with love, and from the very depth of my need hated myself for not more keenly feeling the need. I sought some object to love, since I was thus in love with loving; and I hated security and a life with no snares for my feet. For within I was hungry, all for the want of that spiritual food which is Thyself, my God; yet [though I was hungry for want of it] I did not hunger for it: I had no desire whatever for incorruptible food, not because I had it in abundance but the emptier I was, the more I hated the thought of it. Because of all this my soul was sick, and broke out in sores, whose itch I agonized to scratch with the rub of carnal things—carnal, yet if there were no soul in them, they would not be objects of love. My longing then was to love and to be loved, but most when I obtained the enjoyment of the body of the person who loved me.

Thus I polluted the stream of friendship with the filth of unclean desire and sullied its limpidity with the hell of lust. And vile and unclean as I was, so great was my vanity that I was bent upon passing for clean and courtly. And I did fall in love, simply from wanting to. O my God, my Mercy, with how much bitterness didst Thou in Thy goodness sprinkle the delights of that time! I was loved, and our love came to the bond of consummation: I wore my chains with bliss but with torment too, for I was scourged with the red hot rods of jealousy, with suspicions and fears and tempers and quarrels.

II

I developed a passion for stage plays, with the mirror they held up to my own miseries and the fuel they poured on my flame. How is it that a man wants to be made sad by the sight of tragic sufferings that he could not bear in his own person? Yet the spectator does want to feel sorrow, and it is actually his feeling of sorrow that he enjoys. Surely this is the most wretched lunacy? For the more a man feels such sufferings in himself, the more he is moved by the sight of them on the stage. Now when a man suffers himself, it is called misery;

35

when he suffers in the suffering of another, it is called pity. But
how can the unreal sufferings of the stage possibly move pity? The
spectator is not moved to aid the sufferer but merely to be sorry for
him; and the more the author of these fictions makes the audience
grieve, the better they like him. If the tragic sorrows of the characters—whether historical or entirely fictitious—be so poorly represented that the spectator is not moved to tears, he leaves the theatre
unsatisfied and full of complaints; if he *is* moved to tears, he stays to
the end, fascinated and revelling in it. So that tears and sorrow, it
would seem, are things to be sought. Yet surely every man prefers to
be joyful. May it be that whereas no one wants to be miserable,
there is real pleasure in pitying others—and we love their sorrows
because without them we should have nothing to pity?

All this takes its rise in that stream of friendship [of which we have
been speaking]. But where does that stream go to? What is the direction of its flow? Why must it run into—and lose itself in—that torrent
of pitch which boils out in great waves of vile lust? For by some
inclination in itself friendship is twisted and torn away from its
heavenly cleanness.

Is compassion, feeling for others, therefore to be shunned? By no
means. The sorrows of others must move our love. But beware of
uncleanness, O my soul, under the protection of my God, the God
of our fathers who is to be praised and exalted above all forever;
beware of uncleanness. I can still feel for others. But in those days
when I went to the theatres I was glad with lovers when they
sinfully enjoyed each other—although the whole thing was merely
fictitious and part of a stage play—and when they lost each other I
was sad for them; but either way I enjoyed the play. But today I have
more pity for the sinner getting enjoyment from his sin than when
he suffers torment from the loss of pleasure which is ultimately
destructive, and the loss of happiness which is only misery. This
clearly is the truer compassion, but the sorrow I feel for him gives
me no pleasure. Although he that grieves with the grief-stricken is
to be commended for his work of charity, yet the man who is frater-
nally compassionate would prefer to find nothing in others to need his
compassion. Only in the impossible event of good-will being malevo-
lent, could a man who is truly and sincerely filled with pity desire
that there should be miserable people for him to pity. There is a
kind of compassionate sorrow that is good, but there is no kind that
we should rejoice to feel. And thus do you act, Lord God, for You
love souls with a greater and deeper purity than we can, and are
more incorruptibly compassionate because no sorrow can reach to
wound You. *And who is sufficient for these things?*

But to return to that time. In my wretchedness I loved to be made sad and sought for things to be sad about: and in the misery of others—though fictitious and only on the stage—the more my tears were set to flowing, the more pleasure did I get from the drama and the more powerfully did it hold me. There I was, a wretched sheep strayed from Your fold and impatient of the Shepherd: what wonder that I became infected with a foul disease? That is why I loved those sorrows—not that I wanted them to bite too deep (for I had no wish to suffer the sorrows I loved to look upon), but simply to scratch the surface of my heart as I saw them on the stage: yet, as if they had been fingernails, their scratching was followed by swelling and inflammation and sores with pus flowing. Such was my life; but was that a life, my God?

III

Yet from afar off Your faithful mercy hovered over me. I wasted myself in baseness, pursuing a sacrilegious curiosity which led me once I had deserted You to the uttermost treason and the deceiving service of devils, to whom I made offering of my vile deeds. And in all this You chastised me with Your scourges. For I dared so far one day within the walls of Your church and during the very celebration of Your mysteries to desire and carry out an act worthy of the fruits of death. For this You lashed me with the heaviest punishments, yet the punishments were as nothing to the guilt of my act, O my God, my exceeding great Mercy, my Refuge from the fierce dangers among which I wandered in my arrogance, going ever further from You, loving my way and not Your ways, in love with my runaway liberty.

Those of my occupations at that time which were held as reputable were directed towards the study of the law, in which I meant to excel—and the less honest I was, the more famous I should be. The very limit of human blindness is to glory in being blind. By this time I was a leader in the School of Rhetoric and I enjoyed this high station and was arrogant and swollen with importance: though You know, O Lord, that I was far quieter in my behaviour and had no share in the riotousness of the *eversores*—the Overturners—for this blackguardly diabolical name they wore as the very badge of sophistication. Yet I was much in their company and much ashamed of the sense of shame that kept me from being like them. I was with them and I did for the most part enjoy their companionship, though I abominated the acts that were their specialty—as when they made a butt of some hapless newcomer, assailing him with really cruel mockery for no reason whatever, save the malicious pleasure they got from it. There was something very like the action of devils in their behaviour. They were rightly called Overturners, since they had themselves been first overturned and perverted, tricked by those same devils who were secretly mocking them in the very acts by which they amused themselves in mocking and making fools of others.

IV

With these men as companions of my immaturity, I was studying the books of eloquence; for in eloquence it was my ambition to shine, all from a damnable vaingloriousness and for the satisfaction of human vanity. Following the normal order of study I had come to a book of one Cicero, whose tongue practically everyone admires, though not his heart. That particular book is called *Hortensius* and contains an exhortation to philosophy. Quite definitely it changed the direction of my mind, altered my prayers to You, O Lord, and gave me a new purpose and ambition. Suddenly all the vanity I had hoped in I saw as worthless, and with an incredible intensity of desire I longed after immortal wisdom. I had begun that journey upwards by which I was to return to You. My father was now dead two years; I was eighteen and was receiving money from my mother for the continuance of my study of eloquence. But I used that book not for the sharpening of my tongue; what won me in it was what it said, not the excellence of its phrasing.

How did I then burn, my God, how did I burn to wing upwards from earthly delights to You. But I had no notion what You were to do with me. For with You is wisdom. Now love of wisdom is what is meant by the Greek word philosophy, and it was to philosophy that that book set me so ardently. There are those who seduce men's minds by philosophy, colouring and covering their errors with its great and fine and honourable name: almost all who in Cicero's own time and earlier had been of that sort are listed in his book and shown for what they are. Indeed it illustrates the wholesome advice given by the Spirit through Your good and loving servant: *Beware lest any man cheat you by philosophy, and vain deceits; according to the tradition of men, according to the elements of the world, and not according to Christ: for in Him dwelleth all the fulness of the Godhead corporeally.* At that time, You know, O Light of my heart, those writings of the Apostle were not yet known to me. But the one thing that delighted me in Cicero's exhortation was that I should love, and seek, and win, and hold, and embrace, not this or that philosophical school but

Wisdom itself, whatever it might be. The book excited and inflamed me; in my ardour the only thing I found lacking was that the name of Christ was not there. For with my mother's milk my infant heart had drunk in, and still held deep down in it, that name according to Your mercy, O Lord, the name of Your Son, my Saviour; and whatever lacked that name, no matter how learned and excellently written and true, could not win me wholly.

V

So I resolved to make some study of the Sacred Scriptures and find what kind of books they were. But what I came upon was something not grasped by the proud, not revealed either to children, something utterly humble in the hearing but sublime in the doing, and shrouded deep in mystery. And I was not of the nature to enter into it or bend my neck to follow it. When I first read those Scriptures, I did not feel in the least what I have just said; they seemed to me unworthy to be compared with the majesty of Cicero. My conceit was repelled by their simplicity, and I had not the mind to penetrate into their depths. They were indeed of a nature to grow in Your little ones. But I could not bear to be a little one; I was only swollen with pride, but to myself I seemed a very big man.

VI

I fell in with a sect of men [the Manicheans] talking high-sounding nonsense, carnal and wordy men. The snares of the devil were in their mouths, to trap souls with an arrangement of the syllables of the names of God the Father and of the Lord Jesus Christ and of the Paraclete, the Holy Ghost, our Comforter. These names were always on their lips, but only as sounds and tongue noises; for their heart was empty of the true meaning. They cried out "Truth, truth;" they were forever uttering the word to me, but the thing was nowhere in them; indeed they spoke falsehood not only of You, who are truly Truth, but also of the elements of this world, Your creatures. Concerning these I ought to have passed beyond even the philosophers who spoke truly, for love of You, O my supreme and good Father, Beauty of all things beautiful. O Truth, Truth, how inwardly did the very marrow of my soul pant for You when time and again I heard them sound Your name. But it was all words—words spoken, words written in many huge tomes. In these dishes—while I hungered for You— they served me up the sun and the moon, beautiful works of Yours, but works of Yours all the same and not Yourself: not even Your mightiest works. For Your spiritual creation is greater than these material things, brilliantly as they shine in the sky.

Yet not even for the noblest of Your works did I hunger and thirst but for Yourself, the Truth, *with whom there is no change nor shadow of alteration.* And still in those poor dishes they set before me splendid fantasies: it would indeed have been better to love the sun, which is at least true to the eyes, than those falsities which deceive the mind through the eyes. All the same, I swallowed them because I thought that they were Yourself: yet I did not swallow them with much appetite, because You did not taste in my mouth as You are—for after all You were not those empty falsehoods—and I was not nourished by them, but utterly dried up. Food in dreams is exactly like real food, yet what we eat in our dreams does not nourish: for we are dreaming. But those fantasies of theirs were not in any way like You, as You have since spoken to me; for they were material images, false shows of bodies. The true bodies that we see with our bodily vision, whether in the sky or on the earth, are truer than they: we see them as beasts and birds do, and they are more certain than our images of them. And again these images have more reality than the grandiose infinite bodies we deduced from them, which have no being at all. On such emptiness did I then feed and was not fed.

But You, God of my Love, for whom I long that I may find strength, are not those bodies which we see, though it is in the heavens that we see them; nor are You those bodies which we do not see in the heavens, because You have created them too, nor do You hold them among Your mightiest works. How far then is the reality of You from those empty imaginings of mine, imaginings of bodies which had no being whatever. The images of those bodies which do have being are more certain than they, and the bodies themselves more certain than the images. Yet even these You are not. You are not even the soul, which is the life of bodies—and therefore obviously better and more certain than the bodies it vivifies: but You are the Life of souls, the Life of lives, Livingness itself, and You shall not change, O Life of my soul.

Where then were You and how far from me? I had indeed straggled far from You, not even being allowed to eat the husks of the swine whom I was feeding with husks. How much better were the sheer fables of the poets and literary men than all the traps [that Manes set for souls]. Verses, and poems, and Medea flying, were less harmful than the Five Elements, variously transformed in strife with the five Dens of Darkness, which have no being whatsoever and are death to the soul that believes them. It is possible to get real food for the mind out of verses and poems; and though I sang of Medea flying, I did not think it was true; and when I heard it sung I did not believe it. But these fantasies of the Manichees I did believe. Alas, by what stages was I brought down to the deepest depths of the pit, giving myself needless labour and turmoil of spirit for want of the truth: in that I sought You my God—to You I confess it, for You had pity on me even when I had not yet confessed—in that I sought You not according to the understanding of the mind by which You have set us above the beasts, but according to the sense of the flesh. Yet all the time You were more inward than the most inward place of my heart and loftier than the highest. But I had come upon the woman of Solomon's parable, the shameless woman, knowing nothing, who sits on a seat at the door of her house and says: *Eat ye the bread of secrecies willingly, and drink ye stolen waters which are sweet.* She seduced me because she found me dwelling externally in the eye of my flesh, and ruminating within myself upon such food as, through the body's eye, the mind had swallowed.

VII

But I did not know that other reality which truly is; and through my own sharpness I let myself be taken in by fools, who deceived me with such questions as: Whence comes evil? And is God bounded by a bodily shape and has he hair and nails? And are those [patriarchs] to be esteemed righteous who had many wives at the same time and slew men and offered sacrifices of living animals? By all this my ignorance was much troubled, and it seemed to me that I was coming to the truth when I was in fact going away from it. I did not know that evil has no being of its own but is only an absence of good, so that it simply is not. How indeed should I see this, when the sight of my eyes saw no deeper than bodies and the sight of my soul no deeper than images of bodies? I did not even know that God is a spirit, having no parts extended in length and breadth, to whose being bulk does not belong: for bulk is less in its part than in its whole: and if it be infinite, it is less in the part circumscribed by a certain space than in its infinity: and so could not be wholly itself in every place, as a spirit is, as God is. And I was further ignorant what is the principle in us by which we are; and what Scripture meant by saying that we are made to the image of God.

Nor did I know that true and inward righteousness which judges not according to custom but according to the most righteous law of Almighty God. By that law the ways of conduct of different places and times are shaped as is best for those places and times, though the law itself is always and everywhere the same, not different in different places or changing with the ages. By this righteousness, Abraham and Isaac and Jacob and Moses and David and all those others praised by God were righteous, although they are judged not so by ignorant men who apply the tests of their human minds, and measure all the conduct of the human race by the measure of their own custom. They are like a man handling armour and not knowing what piece is meant for what part of the body and so putting a greave on his head and a helmet on his feet and complaining that they do not fit; or as if on a given day on which it was illegal to do business in the afternoon, a man should grumble because he was not allowed to go on selling in the afternoon, though he had been in the morning; or as if in a given house he should see something handled by one servant but not allowed to the one who has to pour the wine; or that something were done behind the stable which is forbidden in the dining room: as if, in short, he should be angry because in the one dwelling house and the one family the same things are not allowed to every member of the household and in all parts of the house. Such are those who are scandalized when they hear that something was permitted to righteous men in one age, and not permitted in another; and that God gave one man this command, another that, as the difference of the age required, yet both alike served the same righteousness: just as in one man and in one day and in one house different things are held fitting for different members, and a particular act is lawful now but not lawful an hour hence, and something is allowed or indeed commanded in one corner which is forbidden and punished in another. Does this mean that justice is unstable and changeable? No, but the times over which justice presides are not alike, for they are times. Men, because their life upon earth is short, are unable of their own observation to compare the conditions of past ages and foreign nations which they have not experienced with those which they have experienced. In the matter of one body or day or house, they can readily see what is fitting for this or that member, this or that moment, this or that part of the house or rank in the household; they accept such differences [because they fall within their experience]: yet remain scandalised at the differences shown in Scripture.

But all this I did not then know or realise; it was beating in on me the whole time and I had not eyes to see. Thus when I composed verses, I was not free to put any foot where I pleased, but in different places according to the metre I was using; and in one line I could not use the same foot in every position: none the less the art I was practising, the art of poetry, did not have a different law for different places, but the same law throughout. Yet I failed to see that the justice obeyed by these good and holy men was all the more excellent and admirable because while it contained all its precepts in one and never varied: yet it did not order and decree all things alike but to each age what was proper to each. Thus in my blindness I blamed those holy patriarchs who not only used things present as God commanded and inspired them, but also foretold the future as God revealed it to them.

VIII

In no time or place could it be wrong for a man to love God with his whole heart and his whole soul and his whole mind, and his neighbor as himself. Therefore those sins which are against nature, like those of the men of Sodom, are in all times and places to be detested and punished. Even if all nations committed such sins, they should all alike be held guilty by God's law which did not make men so that they should use each other thus. The friendship which should be between God and us is violated when that nature—whose author He is—is polluted by so perverted a lust. Actions which are against the customs of human societies are to be avoided according to the variety of such customs; so that that which is agreed upon by the custom, or decreed by the law, of state or people, is not to be violated at the mere pleasure whether of citizen or alien. For every part is defective that is not in harmony with the whole.

But when God orders something against the custom or covenant of a state, though it never had been done it must be done; and if it was [once done but] allowed to lapse, it must be restored; and if it was not a law before, it must be made a law now. In a state it is lawful for the reigning monarch to command something which none had ever commanded before him and he himself had never commanded before; and obedience in this event is not against the fellowship of that state: indeed disobedience would be against the fellowship, for it is the general agreement of all societies of men to obey their kings. How much more then may God so act, the ruler of all Creation, whose commands are to be obeyed without hesitation. For as among the powers of human society the greater power has a right to the obedience of the lesser, so God to the obedience of all.

In sins where there is a real will to harm another, it may be either by calumny or injury; and, whichever of these two it is, the sin is committed either for the sake of revenge (as when one enemy attacks another); or to gain something that another has (as when a bandit sets upon a traveller); or to escape some danger (as when one man is afraid of another); or through envy (as when a man in poverty attacks one more prosperous, or one who has prospered attacks another

whom he fears as likely to equal him or hates for having already
equalled him); or for mere pleasure in another's suffering (like
the spectators at gladiatorial shows, or people who are always mocking and deriding their neighbors). These are the main heads of sin,
which swarm forth from the lust for holding the first place, or the lust
of the eye, or the lust of the senses, or from any one or two of them,
or from all together. By these we live evilly against the three and the
seven, the ten-stringed harp, the Ten Commandments given by You,
O God Most High and Most Gracious.

But how are sins of the first sort against You, who can suffer no
corruption; or how are sins of the second sort against You, who can
suffer no harm? You punish the sins men commit against themselves,
because though their sin is against You, they are wronging their own
souls and their iniquity gives itself the lie. Either they corrupt and
pervert their own nature, which You have created and set in order
—by making wrong use of the things You have permitted, or by burning towards a use of things not permitted which is against nature; or
their guilt lies in raging against You in thought and word and kicking
against the prick; or else, in complete contempt of the existing order
of society, they go their own insolent way with private agreements or
private feuds according to their personal likes or dislikes.

And all this happens, O Fountain of Life, the only and the true
Creator and Ruler of the universe, whenever You are forsaken, and
out of the pride of the individual a part is loved as though it were the
whole. Therefore by lowly love of You must we return to You: and
You cleanse us from evil habit, and You are merciful to the sins of
those who confess to You, and You hear the groans of those chained
in sin and You loose us from the fetters we have made for ourselves
—all this You do unless we raise against You the arrogance of a sham
liberty, and through the greedy desire to have more (at the risk of
losing all) love our own private good more than You, who are the
common good of all.

IX

But amongst these vices and crimes and countless iniquities are
the sins into which men fall although they are in general on the
right way. By those who judge rightly, these sins are blamed according to the rule of perfection, but the persons themselves may still be
praised for the hope of a better harvest, as the blade gives hope of
the growing corn. And there are some actions again that are very
much like sins and yet are not sins, since they neither offend You,
our Lord God, nor the bond of society: thus when certain things are

set aside to meet the requirements of life or some given circumstance, and it is not clear whether this is done through a mere liking to hoard; or certain actions are punished by a person in authority for the sake of correcting the wrongdoer, and it is not clear whether he may not have done it through a mere desire to cause pain. Thus many actions that to men seem blameworthy, are approved in Your sight; and many that are praised by men are condemned by You, O God—all because often the appearance of the act may be quite different from the mind of the doer or because there is some unrealized element in the situation. But when on a sudden You order something unusual and improbable, even if You had formerly forbidden it, it must obviously be done—though You may conceal the cause of Your command for the time and though it may be against the ordinance of this or that society of men: a society of men is just, only if it obeys You. But happy are they who know that it was You who commanded. For by those that serve You all things are done either to supply what is needful for the present moment or to foreshadow things to come.

X

But I knew nothing of all this and so I derided those Your holy servants and prophets. And I gained nothing by mocking them, except that I should myself be mocked by You. Gradually and inevitably I was drawn to accept every kind of nonsense—as that a fig weeps when it is plucked and its mother tree sheds tears of sap. But provided the fig had been plucked by another man's sin and not his own, some Manichean saint might eat it, digest it in his stomach and groaning and sighing in prayer breathe out from it angels: nay more, he might breathe out certain particles of the Godhead; and these particles of the true and supreme God would have remained in bondage in the fruit unless set free by the teeth and belly of some holy Elect one. And I believed, poor wretch, that more mercy was to be shown to the fruits of the earth than to men, for whose use they were created. For if any man, being hungry—and not being a Manichean—should ask for some, I should have held it worthy of the punishment of death to give him even a mouthful.

XI

And You *sent Your hand from above,* and raised my soul out of that depth of darkness, because my mother, Your faithful one, wept to You for me more bitterly than mothers weep for the bodily deaths of their children. For by the faith and the spirit which she had from You, she saw me as dead; and You heard her, Lord. You heard her

and did not despise her tears when they flowed down and watered
the earth against which she pressed her face wherever she prayed. You
heard her. What else could have been the cause of that dream by
which You so comforted her that she consented to live with me and
to eat at the same table in the house: which previously she had
refused to do, because she shunned and detested the blasphemies
of my error. In her dream she saw herself standing on a wooden rule
and a youth all radiant coming to her cheerful and smiling upon
her, whereas she was grieving and heavy with her grief. He asked
her—not to learn from her but, as is the way of visions, to teach her—
the causes of her sorrow and the tears she daily shed. She replied that
she was mourning for the loss of my soul. He commanded her to be
at peace and told her to observe carefully and she would see that
where she was, there was I also. She looked, and saw me standing
alongside her on the same rule. How should she have had this dream
unless Your ears had heard her heart, O Good Omnipotent, You who
have such care for each one of us as if You had care for him alone,
and such care for all as if we were all but one person?

And the same must have been the reason for this too: that when she
had told me her vision and I tried to interpret it to mean that she
must not despair of one day being as I was, she answered without an
instant's hesitation: "No. For it was not said to me where he is, you
are, but where you are, he is." I confess to You, O Lord, that if I
remember aright—and I have often spoken of it since—I was more
deeply moved by that answer which You gave through my mother—
in that she was not disturbed by the false plausibility of my interpreta-
tion and so quickly saw what was to be seen (which I certainly had
not seen until she said it)—than by the dream itself: by which the joy
that was to come to that holy woman so long after was foretold so
long before for the relief of her present anguish. Nine years were to
follow in which I lay tossing in the mud of that deep pit and the
darkness of its falsity, though I often tried to rise and only fell the
more heavily. All that time this chaste, god-fearing and sober widow—
for such You love—was all the more cheered up with hope. Yet she
did not relax her weeping and mourning. She did not cease to pray
at every hour and bewail me to You, and her prayers found entry into
Your sight. But for all that You allowed me still to toss helplessly in
that darkness.

XII

One other answer I remember You gave her in that time. Many
such things I pass over, because I am hastening on to the matters

which I am more urgently pressed to confess to You, and many I have simply forgotten. But You gave her another assurance by the mouth of Your priest, a certain bishop reared up in the Church and well grounded in Your Scriptures. My mother asked him in his kindness to have some discussion with me, to refute my errors, to unteach me what was evil and teach me what was good, for he often did this when he found such people as it might profit. He refused, rightly as I have realized since. He told her that I was as yet not ripe for teaching because I was all puffed up with the newness of my heresy and had already upset a number of insufficiently skilled people with certain questions—as she had, in fact, told him. "But," said he, "let him alone. Only pray to the Lord for him: he will himself discover by reading what his error is and how great his impiety."

The bishop went on to tell her that his mother had been seduced by the Manichees so that as a small child he had been given over to them; and he had not only read practically all their books but had also copied them out; and had found out for himself, with no need for anyone to argue or convince him, that he must leave the sect. And he had left it. When he had told her this, my mother would not be satisfied but urged him with repeated entreaties and floods of tears to see me and discuss with me. He, losing patience, said: "Go your way; as sure as you live, it is impossible that the son of these tears should perish." In the conversations we had afterwards, she often said that she had accepted this answer as if it had sounded from heaven.

BOOK FOUR

FROM EIGHTEEN TO TWENTY–SEVEN

I-III   *Searching for Deliverance*
     I   Worldly pursuits and Manichean practice
     II Teaches rhetoric in Tagaste: takes a mistress (with whom he is to live for fifteen years): contempt for magical practices
     III Attracted by astrology

IV–IX *Loss of a Friend*
     IV Sickness, baptism and death of a friend; "my heart was black with grief"
     V   Meditation on grief
     VI The paradox of grief
     VII Grief drove him from Tagaste; he returned to Carthage
     VIII New friends: the nature of friendship
     IX Only a friend loved in God cannot be lost

X–XII *The Transience of Created Things*
     X   The necessity of transience
     XI God does not pass
     XII How material things are to be loved: Christ has conquered death

XIII–XV *He Writes a Book*
     XIII *De pulchro et apto*
     XIV Why he dedicated it to Hiereus
     XV He is still unable to conceive an incorporeal substance, is troubled as to the relation of the soul to God and as to the source of evil

XVI *Reads Aristotle on the Categories*
     He understood the book but misapplied its teaching to God

I

THROUGHOUT that nine-year period, from my nineteenth year to my twenty-eighth, I was astray myself and led others astray, was deceived and deceived others in various forms of self-assertion, publicly by the teaching of what are called the liberal arts, privately under the false name of religion; in the one proud, in the other superstitious, in both vain. On the one side of my life I pursued the emptiness of popular glory and the applause of spectators, with competition for prize poems and strife for garlands of straw and the vanity of stage shows and untempered lusts; on the other side I was striving to be made clean of all this same filth, by bearing food to those who were called elect and holy, that in the factory of their own stomachs they should turn it into angels and deities by whom I was to be set free. And I followed out this line of conduct; and so did my friends who were deceived by me and with me. Let the proud of heart deride me now and all who have never been brought low and broken by Thee unto salvation, O my God: it is only for Thy glory that I confess to Thee all my ingloriousness. Grant me, I beseech Thee, to retraverse now in memory the past ways of my error and to *offer Thee a sacrifice of rejoicing*. For without Thee, what am I but a guide to my own destruction? Or at my best what am I but an infant suckled on Thy milk and feeding upon Thee, O Food incorruptible? What indeed is any man, seeing that he is but a man? Let the strong in their own power mock on, I in my weakness and neediness will confess unto Thee.

II

In those years I taught the art of Rhetoric. Overcome myself by the desire of money, I offered for sale skill in speech to overcome others by. But You know, O Lord, I preferred to have honest scholars as honesty is nowadays reckoned: and without guile I taught them guilefulness, that they might use it not against the life of an innocent man, but for the life of a guilty man. And You, O God, saw me far from You stumbling in that slippery way, showing amidst much smoke some small spark of honour: for in my schoolmastership I honestly did my best for men who loved vanity and sought after lying: and in truth I was one with them. In those years I took one woman, not joined to me in lawful marriage, but one whom wandering lust and no particular judgement had brought my way. Yet I had but that one woman, and I was faithful to her. And with her I learnt by my own experience what a gulf there is between the restraint of the marriage-covenant entered into for the sake of children and the mere bargain of a lustful love, where if children come they come unwanted —though when they are born, they compel our love.

I remember once, when I had made up my mind to enter a contest for a poem to be recited on the stage, some magician, I have forgotten his name, demanded how much I would be willing to give him to be certain of victory. I loathed and abominated the filthy rites they practiced, and I told him that if the wreath were of gold, and immortal at that, I would not allow a fly to be slain that I might win it. For it seems that he was to slay certain living creatures in his rites, and by such compliments to persuade the devils to favor me. Yet, O God of my heart, it was not from any purity towards You that I rejected this evil thing. I did not know how to love You, since in its thinking upon You my mind did not rise above a sort of material resplendence. A soul that pants after such idle imaginations simply commits fornication against You, and trusts in shadows, and feeds the winds. I would not have him offer sacrifice on my behalf to devils, and all the while I was myself offering them sacrifice by the superstition I was in. For surely to feed them—that is by our error to become their sport and their derision—is to feed the winds.

III

For the impostors who were called mathematicians [astrologers] I did not scruple to consult, because they offered no sacrifice, and directed no prayers to any spirit to aid their divination. Yet true Christian piety necessarily rejects and condemns their art. For *it is good to confess unto Thee, Lord* and say, *Be merciful to me, heal my soul, for I have sinned against Thee;* and not to misuse Thy mercy as a license to sin but to remember the words of our Lord: *Behold, Thou art made whole: sin no more, lest some worse thing happen to thee.* All this saving truth the astrologers strive to destroy, when they teach that the inevitable cause of sin is in the heavens, that it is the doing of Venus or Saturn or Mars: in other words that man, flesh and blood and proud corruption, is guiltless, and that the guilt lies with the Creator and Ruler of heaven and the stars of heaven. And He is none other than our God, very Loveliness and Well-spring of Justice, *who shall render to every man according to his works:* and *a broken and a contrite heart wilt Thou not despise.*

The proconsul at that time was a man of much wisdom, skilled in medicine and famed for his skill. He set upon my distempered head the wreath I won in the contest: but not as a healer of my distemper. For that disease You alone cure who *resist the proud and give grace to the humble.* Yet You did not fail to aid me through that old man and to use him for the healing of my soul. I came to know him better and pay the closest attention to his words, for without particular pretence, his talk was at once grave and gay from the sheer vitality of his thought. When I told him that I was much given to the books of the horoscope-casters, with much fatherly kindness he advised me to throw them away and not waste upon such nonsense time and trouble that could be put to better use. He told me that in his earlier years he had had some idea of studying that same art and indeed of making it his profession; obviously, since he had understood Hippocrates, he was quite able to understand this other kind of learning as well. But he had given it up and concentrated upon the study of medicine simply because he had found it false, and as an honest man had no desire to make his living by cheating people. "But you," he said, "have the profession of rhetoric to support yourself by, and are pursuing this astrological nonsense voluntarily and not through financial necessity. Therefore you ought all the more to trust me in the matter, for when I sought to attain sufficient skill in it, it was because I meant to make it my sole means of livelihood."

I asked him how he explained the fact that many things were foretold truly by it. He answered, very reasonably, that it was due to the force of chance, which is always to be allowed for in the order of things. Thus if one happened to consult the pages of some poet, who was singing (and thinking) of quite other matters, the eye often fell on a verse quite extraordinarily relevant to the matter in one's own mind; and, he said, it was not more extraordinary if from the mind of man—by some higher but quite blind instinct, not by art but merely by chance—things should sometimes emerge that should seem to have a bearing upon the affairs and actions of the inquirer.

Surely it was You who from him or through him procured this for me and gave my memory the hint of the answer that I was later to arrive at for myself. But at the time neither he nor my close friend Nebridius—a young man of great worth and high moral character, who laughed at the whole business of divination—could persuade me to give up these studies: the authority of the writers of the books still had the greater power with me and I had not yet found the certain proof I sought that would settle beyond doubt that the truths they foretold came by chance or luck, and not by the art of the star-gazers.

IV

During the period in which I first began to teach in the town of my birth, I had found a very dear friend, who was pursuing similar studies. He was about my own age, and was now coming, as I was, to the very flowering-time of young manhood. He had indeed grown up with me as a child and we had gone to school together and played together. Neither in those earlier days nor indeed in the later time of which I now speak was he a friend in the truest meaning of friendship: for there is no true friendship unless You weld it between souls that cleave together through that charity which is shed in our hearts by the Holy Ghost who is given to us. Yet it had become a friendship very dear to us, made the warmer by the ardor of studies pursued together. I had turned him from the true faith—in which being little more than a boy he was not deeply grounded—towards those super-stitious and soul-destroying errors that my mother bewailed in me. With me he went astray in error, and my soul could not be without him. But You are ever close upon the heels of those who flee from You, for You are at once God of Vengeance and Fount of Mercy, and You turn us to Yourself by ways most wonderful. You took this man from the life of earth when he had completed scarcely a year in a friendship that had grown sweeter to me than all the sweetness of the life I knew.

What man could recount all Your praises for the things he has experienced in his own single person? What was it, O my God, that You accomplished then and how unsearchable is the abyss of Your judgements! For he was in a high fever and when he had for a long time lain unconscious in a deathly sweat so that his life was despaired of, he was baptized. Naturally he knew nothing of it, and I paid little heed, since I took for granted that his mind would retain what he had learned from me and not what was done upon his body while he was unconscious. But it turned out very differently. The fever left him and he recovered. As soon as I could speak to him—which was as soon as he could speak to me, for I had not left him and indeed we de-pended too much upon each other—I began to mock, assuming that he would join me in mocking, the baptism which he had received when he had neither sense nor feeling. For by now he had been told of it. But he looked at me as if I had been his deadly enemy, and in a burst of independence that startled me warned me that if I wished to continue his friend I must cease that kind of talk. I was stupefied and deeply perturbed. I postponed telling him of my feelings until he should be well again, and thus in such condition of health and strength that I could discuss what was in my mind. But he was snatched from the reach of my folly, that he might be safe with You for my future consolation. Within a few days he relapsed into his fever and died. And I was not there.

My heart was black with grief. Whatever I looked upon had the air of death. My native place was a prison-house and my home a strange unhappiness. The things we had done together became sheer torment without him. My eyes were restless looking for him, but he was not there. I hated all places because he was not in them. They could not say "He will come soon," as they would in his life when he was absent. I became a great enigma to myself and I was forever asking my soul why it was sad and why it disquieted me so sorely. And my soul knew not what to answer me. If I said "Trust in God" my soul did not obey—naturally, because the man whom she had loved and lost was nobler and more real than the imagined deity in whom I was bidding her trust. I had no delight but in tears, for tears had taken the place my friend had held in the love of my heart.

V

But now, Lord, all that has passed and time has dulled the ache of the wound. May I learn from You who are Truth, may I make the ear of my heart attentive to the word of Your mouth, that You may tell me why tears are so sweet to the sorrowful. Have You, for all that You are everywhere, cast our misery from You? You abide in Yourself, we are tossed from trial to trial: yet if we might not utter our sorrow to Your ears, nothing should remain for our hope. How does it come then that from the bitterness of life we can pluck fruit so sweet as is in mourning and weeping and sighing and the utterance of our woe? Are all these things such relief to our misery because of our hope that You hear them? Obviously this is so of our prayers, because they are uttered with the sole aim of reaching You. But is it so also of the sorrow and grief for a thing lost, in which I was then overwhelmed? I had no hope of bringing him back to life, nor for all my tears did I ask for this: simply I grieved and wept. For I was in misery and had lost my joy. Or is weeping really a bitter thing, pleasing to us only from a distaste for the things we once enjoyed and only while the distaste remains keen?

VI

But why do I speak of these things? I should not be asking questions but making my confession to You. I was wretched, and every

soul is wretched that is bound in affection of mortal things: it is
tormented to lose them, and in their loss becomes aware of the
wretchedness which in reality it had even before it lost them. Such
was I at that time. And I wept most bitterly and in that bitterness
found my only repose. I was wretched, yet I held my wretched life
dearer than the friend for whose loss I was wretched. For although
I would have liked to change the unhappiness of my life, yet I was
more unwilling to lose my life itself than I had been to lose my friend;
and I doubt if I would have been willing to lose it even to be with
him—as the tradition is, whether true or false, of Orestes and Pylades,
who wanted to die for each other and both together, because for
either life without the other was worse than death. But in me there
was an odd kind of feeling, the exact opposite of theirs, for I was at
once utterly weary of life and in great fear of death. It may be that
the more I loved him the more I hated and feared, as the cruellest
enemy, that death which had taken him from me; and I was
filled with the thought that it might snatch away any man as suddenly
as it had snatched him. That this was then my mind, I still remember. Behold my heart, O my God, look deep within it; see how I
remember, O my Hope, You who cleanse me from all the uncleanness
of such affections *directing my eyes towards You and plucking my
feet out of the snare.* I wondered that other mortals should live when
he was dead whom I had loved as if he would never die; and I
marvelled still more that he should be dead and I his other self living
still. Rightly has a friend been called "the half of my soul." For I
thought of my soul and his soul as one soul in two bodies; and my life
was a horror to me because I would not live halved. And it may be
that I feared to die lest thereby he should die wholly whom I had
loved so deeply.

VII

O madness that knows not how to love men as men! O foolish man
to bear the lot of man so rebelliously! I had both the madness and the
folly. I raged and sighed and wept and was in torment, unable to
rest, unable to think. I bore my soul all broken and bleeding and
loathing to be borne by me; and I could find nowhere to set it
down to rest. Not in shady groves, nor in mirth and music, nor
in perfumed gardens, nor in formal banquets, nor in the delights of
bedroom and bed, not in books nor in poetry could it find peace. I
hated all things, hated the very light itself; and all that was not he
was painful and wearisome, save only my tears: for in them alone
did I find a little peace. When my soul gave over weeping, it was

still crushed under the great burden of a misery which only by You, Lord, could be lightened and lifted. This I knew; but I had neither the will nor the strength—and what made it more impossible was that when I thought of You it was not as of something firm and solid. For my God was not yet You but the error and vain fantasy I held. When I tried to rest my burden upon that, it fell as through emptiness and was once more heavy upon me; and I remained to myself a place of unhappiness, in which I could not abide, yet from which I could not depart. For where was my heart to flee for refuge from my heart? Whither was I to fly from myself? To what place should I not follow myself? Yet leave my native place I did. For my eyes would look for him less where they had not been accustomed to see him. I left the town of Tagaste and came to Carthage.

VIII

Time takes no holiday. It does not roll idly by, but through our senses works its own wonders in the mind. Time came and went from one day to the next; in its coming and its passing it brought me other hopes and other memories, and little by little patched me up again with the kind of delights which had once been mine, and which in my grief I had abandoned. The place of that great grief was slowly taken, not perhaps by new griefs, but by the seeds from which new griefs should spring. For that first grief had pierced so easily and so deep only because I had spilt out my soul upon the sand, in loving a mortal man as if he were never to die. At any rate the comfort I found in other friends—and the pleasure I had with them in things of earth—did much to repair and remake me. And it was all one huge fable, one long lie; and by its adulterous caressing, my soul, which lay itching in my ears, was utterly corrupted. For my folly did not die whenever one of my friends died.

All kinds of things rejoiced my soul in their company—to talk and laugh and do each other kindnesses; read pleasant books together, pass from lightest jesting to talk of the deepest things and back again; differ without rancour, as a man might differ with himself, and when most rarely dissension arose find our normal agreement all the sweeter for it; teach each other or learn from each other; be impatient for the return of the absent, and welcome them with joy on their home-coming; these and such like things, proceeding from our hearts as we gave affection and received it back, and shown by face, by voice, by the eyes, and a thousand other pleasing ways, kindled a flame which fused our very souls and of many made us one.

IX

This is what men value in friends, and value so much that their conscience judges them guilty if they do not meet friendship with friendship, expecting nothing from their friend save such evidences of his affection. This is the root of our grief when a friend dies, and the blackness of our sorrow, and the steeping of the heart in tears for the joy that has turned to bitterness, and the feeling as though we were dead because he is dead. Blessed is the man that loves Thee, O God, and his friend in Thee, and his enemy for Thee. For he alone loses no one that is dear to him, if all are dear in God, who is never lost. And who is that God but our God, the God who made heaven and earth, who fills them because it is by filling them with Himself that he has made them? No man loses Thee, unless he goes from Thee; and in going from Thee, where does he go or where does he flee save from Thee to Thee—from God well-pleased to God angered? For where shall he not find Thy law fulfilled in his punishment? Thy law is truth and truth is Thou.

X

Convert us, O God of hosts, and show us Thy face, and we shall be saved. Wherever the soul of man turns, unless towards God, it cleaves to sorrow, even though the things outside God and outside itself to which it cleaves may be things of beauty. For these lovely things would be nothing at all unless they were from Him. They rise and set: in their rising they begin to be, and they grow towards perfection, and once come to perfection they grow old, and they die: not all grow old but all die. Therefore when they rise and tend toward being, the more haste they make toward fullness of being, the more haste they make towards ceasing to be. That is their law. You have given them to be parts of a whole: they are not all existent at once, but in their departures and successions constitute the whole of which they are parts. Our own speech, which we utter by making sounds signifying meanings, follows the same principles. For there never could be a whole sentence unless one word ceased to be when its syllables had sounded and another took its place. In all such things let my soul praise You, O God, Creator of all things, but let it not cleave too close in love to them through the senses of the body. For they go their way and are no more; and they rend the soul with desires that can destroy it, for it longs to be one with the things it loves and to repose in them. But in them is no place of repose, because they do not abide. They pass, and who can follow them with any bodily sense? Or who can grasp them firm even while they are still here?

Our fleshly sense is slow because it is fleshly sense: and that is the limit of its being. It can do what it was made to do; but it has no power to hold things transient as they run their course from their due beginning to their due end. For in Your word, by which they are created, they hear their law: "From this point: not beyond that."

XI

Be not foolish, my soul, nor let the ear of your heart be deafened with the clamor of your folly. Listen. The Word Himself calls to you to return, and with Him is the place of peace that shall not be broken, where your love will not be forsaken unless it first forsake. Things pass that other things may come in their place and this material universe be established in all its parts. "But do I depart anywhere?" says the Word of God. Fix your dwelling in Him, commit to God whatsoever you have: for it is from God. O my soul, wearied at last with emptiness, commit to Truth's keeping whatever Truth has given you, and you shall not lose any; and what is decayed in you shall be made clean, and what is sick shall be made well, and what is transient shall be reshaped and made new and established in you in firmness; and they shall not set you down where they themselves go, but shall stand and abide and you with them, before God who stands and abides forever.

Why, O perverse soul of mine, will you go on following your flesh? Rather turn, and let it follow you. Whatever things you perceive by fleshly sense you perceive only in part, not knowing the whole of which those things are but parts and yet they delight you so much. For if fleshly sense had been capable of grasping the whole—and had not for your punishment received part only of the whole as its just limit—you would wish that whatever exists in the present might pass on, that the whole might be perceived by you for your delight. What we speak, you hear by a bodily sense: and certainly you do not wish the same syllable to go on sounding but to pass away that other syllables may come and you may hear the whole speech. It is always so with all things that go to make up one whole: all that goes to make up the whole does not exist at one moment. If all could be perceived in one act of perception, it would obviously give more delight than any of the individual parts. But far better than all is He who made all; and He is our God. He does not pass away and there is none to take His place.

XII

If material things please you then praise God for them, but turn back your love upon Him who made them: lest in the things that please you, you displease Him. If souls please you, then love them in God because they are mutable in themselves but in Him firmly established: without Him they would pass and perish. Love them, I say, in Him, and draw as many souls with you to Him as you can, saying to them: "Him let us love: He made this world and is not far from it." For He did not simply make it and leave it: but as it is from Him so it is in Him. See where He is, wherever there is a savour of truth: He is in the most secret place of the heart, yet the heart has strayed from Him. O sinners, return to your own heart and abide in Him that made you. Stand with Him and you shall stand, rest in Him and you shall be at peace. Where are you going, to what bleak places? Where are you going? The good that you love is from Him: and insofar as it is likewise *for* Him it is good and lovely; but it will rightly be turned into bitterness, if it is unrightly loved and He deserted by whom it is. What goal are you making for, wandering around and about by ways so hard and laborious? Rest is not where you seek it. Seek what you seek, but it is not where you seek it. You seek happiness of life in the land of death, and it is not there. For how shall there be happiness of life where there is no life?

But our Life came down to this our earth and took away our death, slew death with the abundance of His own life: and He thundered, calling to us to return to Him into that secret place from which He came forth to us—coming first into the Virgin's womb, where humanity was wedded to Him, our mortal flesh, though not always to be mortal; and thence *like a bridegroom coming out of his bride chamber, rejoicing as a giant to run his course.* For He did not delay but rushed on, calling to us by what He said and what He did, calling to us by His death, life, descent, and ascension to return to Him. And He withdrew from our eyes, that we might return to our own heart and find Him. For He went away and behold He is still here. He would not be with us long, yet He did not leave us. He went back to that place which He had never left, for the world was made by Him. And He was in this world, and He came into this world to save sinners. Unto Him my soul confesses and He hears it, for it has sinned against Him. O ye sons of men, how long will ye be so slow of heart? Even now when Life has come down to you, will you not ascend and live? But to what high place shall you climb, since you are in a high place and have *set your mouth against the heavens?* First descend that you may ascend, ascend to God. For in mounting up *against* God you fell. Tell the souls of men to weep in this valley of tears, and so bear them up with you to God, because it is by His Spirit that you are speaking this to them, if in your speaking you are on fire with the fire of charity.

XIII

But these things I did not at that time know, and I was in love with those lower beauties. I was sinking into the very depths and I said to my friends: "Do we love anything save what is beautiful? What then is beautiful? and what is beauty? What is it that allures us and delights us in the things we love? Unless there were grace and beauty in them they could not possibly draw us to them." Looking deeper I saw that in things themselves we must distinguish between the beauty which belongs to the whole in itself, and the becomingness which results from right relation to some other thing, as a part of the body to the whole body, or a shoe to the foot, and such like. This thought surged up into my mind from the very depths of my heart and I composed certain books *De Pulchro et Apto*—on the Beautiful and the Fitting—two books or three, I fancy; You know, O God, for I do not remember. I no longer have them. Somehow or other they have been lost.

XIV

What was it, O Lord my God, that moved me to dedicate these books to Hiereus, an Orator of Rome? I had never seen him, but I was won to him for the fame of his learning, which was indeed very notable, and I had heard things he had said which seemed to me admirable. But he pleased me mainly because he pleased others; they praised him highly, amazed that a Syrian, brought up on Greek, should afterwards prove so wonderful a speaker in the Latin tongue, amazed too at his great learning in the field of philosophy. Thus a man is praised and we love him though we have in fact never seen him. Does such a love pass from the lips of the one who praises into the heart of the one who hears the praise? Not at all. Simply one lover is inflamed by another. That is why we are won to a man we hear praised only if we believe that the praise comes from a sincere heart, that is when the praise is uttered by one who truly loves.

Thus I then loved men upon the judgement of men, but not upon

Your judgement, my God, in whom no man is deceived. But yet it is to be noted that the feeling I had for such men was not like the feeling I had for some great charioteer, say, or fighter with beasts, whose popularity was so great with the crowd. I admired *them* far differently and for more serious reasons, admired them indeed as I would myself wish to have been admired. I certainly had no desire to be praised and liked as actors are, though I myself both liked them and praised them. For myself I would have chosen to remain utterly unknown rather than so known, and to be hated rather than so loved. How are the balances of these varied and diverse loves so distributed within one soul? How is it that I admire a quality in another and yet seem to hate it too, since I should detest and despise it in myself. After all, he and I are both men. It is not as a man might admire a good horse and yet have no desire to be a horse, even if he could manage it. The matter of myself and the actor is different, for he and I share the same nature. How then do I admire a man for being what I should hate to be, although I too am a man? Man is a great deep, Lord. You number his very hairs and they are not lost in Your sight: but the hairs of his head are easier to number than his affections and the movements of his heart.

But that orator whom I so admired was the kind of man that I should have wished myself to be; and I erred through swollen pride, and I was blown about by every wind, and You steered my course for me too hiddenly. And I know now and with sure confidence confess to You that I loved the man more for the love of those who praised him than for the qualities for which he was praised: if those same people had not praised but abused him, and had described the very same qualities in him abusively and with scorn, I should not have been kindled towards him nor brought to admire him. Yet obviously the qualities would have been the same and the man himself not different: only the attitude of the speakers would have been different. Thus the soul is prostrate and helpless, when it does not adhere to the stability of truth. According as the winds of speech blow from the lungs of those who think they know, so is the soul twisted and turned, and twisted and turned again, and the light shines not for it and it cannot see the truth. Yet the truth is right before it. I thought I should be very much the gainer if my style and my ideas might come to the knowledge of so famous a man. If he thought well of them, I should be still more on fire for him; but if he thought ill, my vain heart, all void of Your stability, would have been wounded deep. All the same I enjoyed setting my meditation to work upon the theme of the Beautiful and the Fitting which I dedicated to him; and with no one else to admire it, I admired it myself.

XV

But I had not yet seen that this great matter [of the Beautiful and the Fitting] turns upon Your workmanship, O Almighty by whom alone things marvellous are done; and my mind considered only corporeal forms. I defined and distinguished the Beautiful as that which is so of itself, the Fitting as that which is excellent in its relation of fitness to some other thing; and it was by corporeal examples that I supported my argument. I did consider the nature of the soul, but again the false view I had of spiritual things would not let me get at the truth—although by its sheer force the truth was staring me in the face. I turned my throbbing mind away from the incorporeal to line and colour and bulk, and because I did not see these things in my mind, I concluded that I could not see my mind. Further, loving the peace I saw in virtue and hating the discord in vice, I noted the unity of the one and the dividedness of the other; and it seemed to me that in the unity lay the rational mind and the nature of truth and the supreme Good: but in the dividedness I thought I saw some substance of irrational life, and the nature of a supreme Evil. This Evil I saw not only as substance but even as life: and yet, poor wretch, I held that it was not from You, my God, from Whom all things are. I called the first a Monad seeing it as a mind without sex, and the other I called a Dyad—the anger I saw in deeds of violence, the lust I saw in deeds of impurity: but I was talking blindly. For I did not as yet know, I had not been taught, that evil was not any substance, nor was this soul of ours the supreme and immutable good.

Just as we have sins against others if our emotion, in which lies the impetus to act, is vicious and thrusts forward arrogantly and without measure, and damage to self if that affection of the soul whence carnal desires rise is ungoverned: similarly errors and false opinions contaminate life if the rational soul itself is corrupted. So was my soul at that time, for I did not realise that it had to be illumined by another light, if it was to be a partaker of truth, because it is not itself the essence of truth. For *Thou lightest my lamp, O Lord; O my God, enlighten my darkness:* and *of Thy fullness we all have received.* For *Thou art the true Light which enlighteneth every man that cometh into this world:* because *in Thee there is neither change nor shadow of alteration.*

But I was at once striving towards You and thrust back from You, so that I knew the taste of death: for You resist the proud. What could be worse pride than the incredible folly in which I asserted that I was by nature what You are? Since I was not myself immutable

—as was clear enough from the fact of my desire to become wise and change from worse to better—I chose rather to think You mutable than to think I was not as You are. Thus I was thrust back: You resisted my windy pride. So that I went on imagining corporeal forms: and being flesh I accused the flesh, and being a wayfaring spirit I did not return to You but in my drifting was borne on towards imaginings which have no reality either in You or in me or in the body, and were not created for me by Your truth but were invented by my own folly playing upon matter. And I spoke much to the little ones of Your flock—my own fellow citizens from whom I was in exile, though I did not know it,—and like the argumentative fool that I was I put to them the question: "Why does the soul err if God created it?" But I would not have any one ask me: "Why then does God err?" And I preferred to maintain that Your immutable substance had been constrained to suffer error, rather than admit that my own mutable substance had gone astray through its own fault and fallen into error for its punishment.

I was around twenty-six or twenty-seven when I wrote these books, revolving within my mind the corporeal imaginings whose clamour filled the ears of my heart, while I was straining them, O Loveliness of Truth, to catch Your inner melody, meditating upon the Beautiful and the Fitting, and yearning that I might stand and hearken to You and rejoice with joy for the voice of the Bridegroom. But for this I had not the strength. I was drawn out of myself by the voices of my error and went falling ever lower through the sheer weight of my own pride. You did not *make me to hear joy and gladness,* nor *did the bones exult which were not yet humbled.*

XVI

And what did it profit me that when I was barely twenty years old there came into my hands, and I read and understood, alone and unaided, the book of Aristotle's Ten Categories—a book I had longed for as for some great and divine work because the master who taught me Rhetoric at Carthage, and others held learned, mouthed its name with such evident pride? I compared notes with others, who admitted that they had scarcely managed to understand the book even with the most learned masters not merely lecturing upon it but making many diagrams in the dust: and they could not tell me anything of it that I had not discovered in reading it for myself. For it seemed to me clear enough what the book had to say of substances, like man, and of the accidents that are in substances, like the figure of a man, what sort of man he is, and of his stature,

how many feet high, and of his family relationships, whose brother
he is, or where he is placed, or when he was born, or whether he is
standing or sitting or has his shoes on or is armed, or whether he is
doing something or having something done to him—and all the other
countless things that are to be put either in these nine categories of
which I have given examples, or in the chief category of substance.

Not only did all this not profit me, it actually did me harm, in that I
tried to understand You, my God, marvellous in Your simplicity and
immutability, while imagining that whatsoever had being was to be
found within these ten categories—as if You were a substance in which
inhered Your own greatness of beauty, as they might inhere in a
body. In fact Your greatness and Your beauty are Yourself: whereas
a body is not large and beautiful merely by being a body, because it
would still be a body even if it were less large and less beautiful. The
idea I had of You was falsehood and not truth, a fiction of my own
littleness, not the solid ground of Your beatitude. For it was Your
command, and so it came to pass in me, that *the earth should bring
forth thorns and thistles* for me and that *in the sweat of my brow I
should eat my bread.*

And what did it profit me that I read and understood for myself
all the books of what are called the Liberal Arts that I was able to get
hold of, since I remained the vile slave of evil desires? I enjoyed the
books, while not knowing Him from whom came whatever was true
or certain in them. For I had my back to the light and my face to the
things upon which the light falls: so that my eyes, by which I looked
upon the things in the light, were not themselves illumined. Whatever was written either of the art of rhetoric or of logic, of the dimensions of figures or music or arithmetic I understood with no great difficulty and no need of an instructor: this You know, Lord my God,
because swiftness of understanding and keenness of perceiving are
Your gift. But none of this did I offer in sacrifice to You. Therefore
it was not for my profit but rather for my harm, that I laboured so to
have so great a part of my substance in my own power, and preserved
my strength but not for You, going from You into a far country to
waste my substance upon loves that were only harlots. For what did
it profit me to have good ability since I did not use it well? I did not
discover that these matters were very difficult even for the studious
and intelligent to grasp, until I tried to teach them to others—and that
pupil was regarded as the most excellent who could follow my exposition least laggingly.

But what did all this profit me while I held that You, Lord God of
truth, were a luminous immeasurable body and I a kind of particle
broken from that body? It was an extreme of perverseness, but so I

then was: and I do not now blush to confess to You the mercies You have shown me, O my God, and to call upon You, any more than I then blushed to profess my blasphemies before men and to bark at You. Of what use to me then was my intelligence, swift to run clear through those sciences, of what use were all those knotty books I unravelled without the aid of any human teacher, when in the doctrine of love of You I erred so far and so foully and so sacrilegiously? Or what great harm to Your little ones was their far slower intelligence: since they strayed not far from You and so could fledge their wings in safety in the nest of Your church, and nourish the wings of charity with the food of solid faith?

O Lord our God let us hope in the protecting shadow of Thy wings. Guard us and bear us up. Bear us up Thou wilt, as tiny infants and on to our gray hairs: for when Thou art our strength, it is strength indeed, but when our strength is our own it is only weakness. With Thee our good ever lives, and when we are averted from Thee we are perverted. Let us now return to Thee, O Lord, that we may not be overturned, for with Thee lives without any defect our good which is Thyself. We have no fear that there should be no place of return, merely because by our own act we fell from it: our absence does not cause our home to fall, which is Thy Eternity.

BOOK FIVE

AGED TWENTY–EIGHT

I–II   *Prayer*
      I   The whole creation speaks God's praise
     II   Man cannot escape from God's presence

III–VII   *Faustus Comes to Carthage*
     III   Augustine could not reconcile the astronomical doctrines of Manes with the proved science of the astronomers
     IV   Astronomy does not matter to the soul's life
     V   But Manes so taught it that his reputation rested on it
     VI   The Manicheans had told him that Faustus would satisfy him: Faustus fails
     VII   He loses confidence in the Manichees but does not leave them

VIII–XII   *Augustine Goes to Rome*
     VIII   Decision to go to Rome, mainly to escape the *eversores;* had to deceive Monica to get away
     IX   In Rome fell ill and nearly died
     X   Associated with the Manichees, yet without great faith in them; attracted by the scepticism of the Academics; still unable to think of God save as a bodily magnitude and troubled by problem of origin of evil; in error as to Christ
     XI   Certain Scriptural difficulties
     XII   Teaching Rhetoric at Rome had its drawbacks

XIII–XIV   *At Milan*
     XIII   Applied for and got professorship at Milan; met St. Ambrose
     XIV   Helped by Ambrose's figurative explanations of Scripture; becomes a Catechumen

I

ECEIVE the sacrifice of my Confessions offered by my tongue, which Thou didst form and hast moved to confess unto Thy name. *Heal Thou all my bones* and *they shall say: Lord, who is like to Thee?* A man who makes confession to Thee does not thereby give Thee any information as to what is happening within him. The closed heart does not close out Thy eye, nor the heart's hardness resist Thy hand. For Thou dost open it at Thy pleasure whether for mercy or for justice, and *there is nothing that can hide itself from Thy heat.* But let my soul praise Thee that it may love Thee, and let it tell Thee Thy mercies that it may praise Thee. Without ceasing Thy whole creation speaks Thy praise—the spirit of every man by the words that his mouth directs to Thee, animals and lifeless matter by the mouth of those who look upon them: that so our soul rises out of its mortal weariness unto Thee, helped upward by the things Thou hast made and passing beyond them unto Thee who hast wonderfully made them: and there refreshment is and strength unfailing.

II

Let the wicked in their restlessness go from Thee and flee away. Yet Thou dost see them, cleaving through their darkness. And all the universe is beautiful about them, but they are vile. What harm have they done Thee? Or have they brought dishonour upon Thy government, which from the heavens unto the latest things of earth is just and perfect? Where indeed did they flee to when they fled from Thy face? Or where dost Thou not find them? The truth is that they fled, that they might not see Thee who sawest them. And so with eyes blinded they stumbled against Thee—for Thou dost not desert any of the things that Thou hast made—they stumbled against Thee in their injustice and justly suffered, since they had withdrawn from Thy mercy and stumbled against Thy justice and fallen headlong upon Thy wrath. Plainly they do not know that Thou art everywhere whom no place compasses in, and that Thou alone art ever present even to those that go furthest from Thee. Let them therefore turn back and seek Thee because Thou hast not deserted Thy creatures as they have deserted their Creator. Let them turn back, and behold Thou art there in their hearts, in the hearts of those that confess to Thee and cast themselves upon Thee and weep on Thy breast as they return from ways of anguish. Gently Thou dost wipe away their tears and they weep the more and are consoled in their weeping: because Thou, Lord, and not any man that is only flesh and blood, Thou, Lord who hast made them, dost remake them and give them comfort. But where was I when I sought after Thee? Thou wert there before me, but I had gone away from myself and I could not even find myself, much less Thee.

III

I now set before the face of my God the twenty-ninth year of my age. There had just come to Carthage one Faustus, a bishop of the Manichees. He was a great snare of the devil and many were caught in the snare through the charm of his speech. In fact I found this admirable myself, but I was coming to distinguish between it and the truth for which I was then so hungry. I was concerned not with the dish, but with such knowledge as this Faustus, of whom they thought so highly, might set before me to feed upon. Report had already told me great things of him, as a man learned in all profitable learning and especially learned in the liberal sciences.

Now I had read many works of the philosophers and retained a great deal in my memory, and I compared certain of these things with the long-winded fables of the Manichees. What the philosophers taught seemed to me the more probable, though their power was limited to making judgment of this world and they could not pierce through to its Lord. For *the Lord is high and looks on the low: and the proud He knows afar off.* Nor do You draw near, Lord, to any save the contrite of heart; the proud cannot find You, not even if they have skill beyond the natural to number the stars and the grains of sand, and measure out the places of the constellations and plot the courses of the planets. For with the mind and understanding that Thou hast given them they investigate such things: and indeed they have discovered much, and foretold many years in advance eclipses of the sun and the moon, the day, the hour and what part should be in eclipse, and their calculations proved right. It happened as they had foretold; and they put in writing the rules they had arrived at, and these may be read to-day: and by these rules can be foretold the year and the month of the year and the day of the month and the hour of the day and the part of its light that sun or moon is to suffer eclipse: and it will happen as foretold. And men who do not know this art marvel and are amazed, and those that know it boast and are made much of, in their evil pride turning from You and losing Your light: an eclipse of the sun they see so long before it happens, yet they fail to see their own eclipse actually present. They do not religiously enquire what is the source of that gift of understanding by which they enquire these lesser things: and if they find that it is You that have made them, they do not give themselves to You that You should preserve what You have made: nor do they slay in sacrifice to You what they have made themselves to be: for they do not slaughter their self-conceits like birds, nor the curiosities—by which they voyage through the secret ways of the abyss—like the fish of the sea, nor their carnal lusts like the beasts of the field: that You, O God, You the consuming fire, should burn up those dead cares and renew the men themselves to immortal life.

They do not know that way which is Your Word, by which You have made not only the things that they number but also themselves who do the numbering, and the bodily sense by which they see what they number, and the mind from which their numbering comes: *and of Thy wisdom there is no number.* But the Only-Begotten was Himself *made unto us Wisdom and Justice and Sanctification,* and was numbered amongst us and *paid tribute to Caesar.* They do not know the way by which they should descend from themselves to Him, and by Him ascend to Him. They do not know this way, and they fancy themselves raised on high and shining with the stars, whereas they fall upon the earth and *their foolish heart is darkened.*

Much that they say of the created universe is true, but they do not religiously seek the Truth, the architect of the created universe; so that they either do not find Him, or if they find Him and know Him to be God, they do not honour him as God or give Him thanks, but become vain in their imaginings and profess themselves to be wise, attributing to themselves what is Yours and at the same time in a kind of perverse blindness attributing their own qualities to You —so that they load with their falsehoods You who are the Truth, and *changing the glory of the incorruptible God into the likeness of the image of a corruptible man, and of birds, and of four-footed beasts, and of creeping things, and changing the truth of God into a lie, they worship and serve the creature rather than the creator.*

All the same I remembered many truths that they had spoken of the created world itself, and I saw their theories justified by numbers and the order of time and the visible evidence of the stars. I compared all this with what Manes had said, for he wrote at great length upon such matters and quite wildly: but I did not find in him any explanation of the solstices or the equinoxes or the eclipses of sun and moon; nor any of such things as I had learnt in the books of worldly philosophy. I was commanded to believe [what Manes wrote], yet it did not harmonize with the principles I had arrived at by mathematics and indeed by my own eyes, but was far otherwise.

IV

Yet, Lord God of truth, is any man pleasing to You for knowing such things? Surely a man is unhappy even if he knows all these things but does not know You; and that man is happy who knows You even though he knows nothing of them. And the man who knows both You and them is not the happier for them but only on account of You: if knowing You he glorifies You as You are and gives thanks and does not become vain in his thoughts. For just as he is better who knows he possesses a tree and gives thanks to You for the use it is to him, although he does not know how many cubits high it is or the width of its spread, than another man who can measure it and number its branches but neither possesses it nor knows and loves Him who created it; so it would be absurd to doubt that a true Christian— who in some sense possesses all this world of riches and who having nothing yet possesses all things, by cleaving unto You whom all things serve—is better though he does not even know the circles of the Great Bear than one who can measure the heavens and number the stars and balance the elements, if in all this he neglects You who have *ordered all things in measure and number and weight.*

V

Who then asked this Manes to write of such things, when piety can be acquired without knowledge of them? For You have said unto man: *Behold the fear of the Lord, that is wisdom.* Manes might very well have been totally without wisdom even though he knew these things perfectly: but in that he had the impudence to presume to teach them when he did not know them, he obviously could not know fear of the Lord. For it is vanity to profess these worldly matters even when one knows them, but piety to confess unto You. Thus he had gone astray and had spoken much of these things: to the sole end that he might be convicted of ignorance by those who had learned them aright, and so his competence upon other more abstruse matters could be readily judged. He did not want to be thought little of, but tried to persuade men that the Holy Ghost, the Comforter and Enricher of Your faithful, was resident in himself personally, with plenary authority. Therefore when he was caught

out in error about the sky and the stars and the movements of
sun and moon, though these things do not pertain to religious doctrine,
yet his sacrilegious audacity was apparent in that he said things not
only unknown to him but plainly false: and in the swollen madness
of his pride would have them credited to himself as to a divine
person.

Now when I see some brother Christian, any brother Christian,
ignorant of these things and confusing one thing with another, I
can look patiently upon such a man as he utters his opinion; and I
do not see how it can hurt him to be ignorant of the place or condition
of material things provided he does not hold any belief unworthy of
You, O Lord, Creator of all. But it does hurt him if he thinks that
this pertains to the essence of pious doctrine and dares to uphold too
obstinately things he does not know. Even this weakness in the first
beginnings of a man's faith is borne patiently by Charity, our mother,
while the new man is rising unto a perfect man, so as not to be carried
away with every wind of doctrine. But Manes had dared to set himself up as teacher, source, guide, and leader of all whom he could
convince in these matters, so that those who followed him believed
that they were following no mere man but Your Holy Spirit: once he
was caught out in error, surely such madness could be seen only as
detestable and utterly to be rejected? But I had not as yet clearly
discovered whether the changes in the length of days and nights, and
the alternation of night and day, and the eclipses of sun and moon,
and other things of which I read in the books of the astronomers,
could be explained along his lines: for if they could, even though
it might still remain unproven whether the things were so or not,
yet I was prepared to trust rather in his authority on account of his
reputation for sanctity.

VI

And for almost all those nine years in which without a settled mind
I listened to the Manichees, I had looked forward with unbounded
desire to the coming of this Faustus. For the others whom I had met,
when they failed to find answers to the questions of this sort I posed,
promised me Faustus: on his arrival and by conference with him
these things would be most lucidly explained, together with any
more important questions I might ask. When at last he came I found
him a pleasant man of pleasant speech, who rolled off the same kind
of things that the others had said with a great deal more charm.

But for my thirst of what use were the most attractive cup-bearer
and the most precious cups? My ears had already had their fill of

such stuff; it seemed to me no better merely because it was expressed better, nor true because eloquent. Nor did I feel that the soul must be wise because the face was attractive and the speech becoming. Obviously those who had promised him to me were not good judges of reality; and they thought him wise simply because they liked his speaking.

As it happens I have met just the opposite kind of man, who is suspicious of truth and unwilling to accept it if it is uttered in rich and ordered language. But You, O my God, had taught me in secret and marvellous ways. That it was You who taught me, I believe: for it is the truth, and there is no other teacher of truth save You, no matter where or when it may happen to shine. From You then I learned that a thing was not bound to be true because uttered eloquently, nor false because the utterance of the lips is ill-arranged; but that on the other hand a thing is not necessarily true because badly uttered, nor false because spoken magnificently. For it is with wisdom and folly as with wholesome and unwholesome food: just as either kind of food can be served equally well in rich dishes or simple, so plain or beautiful language may clothe either wisdom or folly indifferently.

Therefore the eagerness with which I had so long awaited the man was well repaid by his action and attitude in disputation, and by the apt and fluent language in which he clothed his ideas. I was pleased, and I praised and extolled him along with many another, indeed, more loudly than most. But I was disappointed that, with his flock thronging round him, I was not allowed to address him and put him the questions that troubled me and discuss them as man to man and with comment back and forth. At last I was able to find opportunity, and with some of my friends I sought his attention at a time when we could properly exchange ideas. I mentioned certain questions that concerned me and I found at once that the man was not learned in any of the liberal sciences save literature, and not especially learned even in that. He had read some of Cicero's speeches and a very few books of Seneca, some of the poets and such writings of his own sect as had been written in Latin and were not difficult; over and above that he had daily practice in oratory; and these combined to furnish his eloquence, which was rendered more pleasing and persuasive by the guidance of a good intelligence and a kind of grace that was natural to him. Is it not thus, as I remember it, Lord my God, Judge of my conscience? My heart and my memory are open before You, who were then acting in me by the hidden secret of Your Providence, and bringing my shameful errors before my face, that I might see them and hate them.

VII

For when I realized that he was unlearned in those matters in which I had thought he excelled, I began to despair of his being able to clarify and solve for me the questions that troubled me—though as I now realize he might have been able to hold the truth of piety even though he was a man of no learning, if he had not been a Manichean. For their books are packed with long-winded nonsense about the sky and the stars and the sun and the moon; and I now saw that he could not with any profundity show me, as I desired, as against the mathematical explanations I had read elsewhere, if the reality was still as the books of Manes stated it, or if at least some explanation equally good could be drawn from them. When I set these questions out for consideration and discussion, he was too modest to presume to undertake the task. He knew that he did not know these things, and he was not ashamed to admit it; he was not one of those talkative people—of whom I had suffered many—who would undertake to teach me, and say nothing. For he had a heart, which though it was not right towards God, was reasonably cautious in the matter of himself. He was not entirely ignorant of his own ignorance, and he did not want rashly to get caught up in a dispute which he could not hope to win and from which he could not gracefully retire. Even for this I liked him better: the modesty of a mind admitting incapacity is a finer thing than the knowledge I was in search of. And thus I found him upon all more difficult and abstruse questions.

The keenness with which I had studied the writings of Manes was thus somewhat blunted; and I was the more hopeless about their other doctors, now that, upon many matters which troubled me, the famous Faustus had shown so ill. But I began to see a good deal of him because of the very keen interest he had in literature, which at that time as professor of Rhetoric I was teaching young students at Carthage; we read either books he wanted (because he had heard of them), or such as I thought suitable to his intelligence. But all my effort and determination to make progress in the sect simply fell away through my coming to know this man. Not that I separated myself from them entirely; but simply, not finding anything better than the course upon which I had somehow or other stumbled, I decided to look no further for the time unless something more desirable should chance to appear. Thus Faustus, who had been a snare that brought death to many, did without his knowledge or will begin to unbind the snare that held me. For Thy hand, O my God, in the secret of Thy Providence did not desert my soul; from the blood of my mother's heart, sacrifice for me was offered Thee day and night by her tears, and Thou didst act with me in marvellous ways. For it was Thou, my God, who didst do it. For *with the Lord shall the steps of a man be directed* and *he shall like well his way*. How shall we attain salvation unless by Thy hand Thou dost remake what Thou didst make?

VIII

It was by Your action upon me that I was moved to go to Rome and teach there what I had taught in Carthage. How I was persuaded to this, I shall not omit to confess to You, because therein Your most profound depths and Your mercy ever present towards us are to be meditated upon and uttered forth. My reason for going to Rome was not the greater earnings and higher dignity promised by the friends who urged me to go—though at that time, these considerations certainly influenced my mind: the principal and practically conclusive reason, was that I had heard that youths there pursued their studies more quietly and were kept within a stricter limit of discipline. For instance, they were not allowed to come rushing insolently and at will into the school of one who was not their own master, nor indeed to enter it at all unless he permitted.

At Carthage the licence of the students is gross and beyond all measure. They break in impudently and like a pack of madmen play havoc with the order which the master has established for the good of his pupils. They commit many outrages, extraordinarily stupid acts, deserving the punishment of the law if custom did not protect them. Their state is the more hopeless because what they do is supposed to be sanctioned, though by Your eternal law it could never be sanctioned; and they think they do these things unpunished, when the very blindness in which they do them is their punishment, so that they suffer things incomparably worse than they do. When I was a student I would not have such habits in myself, but when I became a teacher I had to endure them in others; and so I decided to go to a place where, as I had been told by all who knew, such things were not done. But You, O my Hope and my Portion in the land of the living, forced me to change countries for my soul's salvation: You pricked me with such goads at Carthage as drove me out of it, and You set before me certain attractions by which I might be drawn to Rome —in either case using men who loved this life of death, one set doing lunatic things, the other promising vain things: and to reform my ways You secretly used their perversity and my own. For those who had disturbed my peace were blind in the frenzy of their viciousness, and those who urged me to go elsewhere savoured of earth. While I, detesting my real misery in the one place, hoped for an unreal happiness in the other.

Why I left the one country and went to the other, You knew, O God, but You did not tell either me or my mother. She indeed was in dreadful grief at my going and followed me right to the seacoast. There she clung to me passionately, determined that I should either go back home with her or take her to Rome with me, but I deceived her with the pretence that I had a friend whom I did not want to leave until he had sailed off with a fair wind. Thus I lied to my mother, and such a mother; and so got away from her. But this also You have mercifully forgiven me, bringing me from the waters of that sea, filled as I was with execrable uncleanness, unto the water of Your grace; so that when I was washed clean, the floods that poured from my mother's eyes, the tears with which daily she watered the ground towards which she bent her face in prayer for me, should cease to flow. She would not return home without me, but I managed with some difficulty to persuade her to spend the night in a place near the ship where there was an oratory in memory of St. Cyprian. That night I stole away without her: she remained praying and weeping. And what was she praying for, O my God, with all those tears but that You should not allow me to sail! But You saw deeper and granted the essential of her prayer: You did not do what she was at that moment asking, that You might do the thing she was always asking. The wind blew and filled our sails and the shore dropped from our sight. And the next morning she was frantic with grief and filled Your ears with her moaning and complaints because You seemed to treat her tears so lightly, when in fact You were using my own desires to snatch me away for the healing of those desires, and were justly punishing her own too earthly affection for me with the scourge of grief. For she loved to have me with her, as is the way of mothers, but far more than most mothers; and she did not realize what joys you would bring her from my going away. She did not realize it, and so she wept and lamented, and by the torments she suffered showed the heritage of Eve in her, seeking with sorrow what in sorrow she had brought forth. But when she had poured out all her accusation at my cruel deception, she turned once more to prayer to You for me. She went home and I to Rome.

IX

Rome welcomed me with the scourge of bodily illness, and I very nearly went to hell bearing all the weight of deadly sins which I had committed against You and myself and other men, over and above the bond of original sin whereby we all die in Adam. For You had not yet forgiven any of my sins in Christ, nor had He yet by His cross healed the enmity which I had contracted towards You by them. How, indeed, could they be healed by the cross of a phantom, which at that time I thought Him? The death of my own soul was as real, as the death of His body seemed to me false; and the life of my soul was as false—since on this matter it was in error—as the death of His body was real. My fever grew worse and I was very close to going off to perdition. For where should I have gone if I had departed then save to fire and torments such as my deeds deserved in the justice of Your ordinance? My mother was far away and knew nothing of my illness, but she prayed on for me. You who are present everywhere heard her where she was and had compassion on me where I was, so that I recovered the health of my body, though still far from health in my sacrilegious heart. For great as that peril had been I did not ask for Your baptism; and I was better as a boy in that I had begged it of my mother's piety, as I have already related and confessed. But I had grown rooted into my shame; and new in folly scorned Your healing precepts, who had saved me from double death in my sins. Had my mother's heart been pierced by *that* wound, it would never have been made whole. I have no words to express the love she had for me, and with how much more anguish she was now in spiritual travail of me than when she had borne me in the flesh. I cannot see how she could have been healed if my death in sin had come to pierce the deepest heart of her love. And where would then have been those urgent and ceaselessly repeated prayers? Nowhere but with You. But would You, O God of mercy, despise the contrite and humble heart of that chaste and pious widow, so generous in alms-giving, so ready in the service of Your saints, who let no day pass without attending the sacrifice at Your altar, and came twice a day with never an exception, morning and evening, to Your church, not to listen to idle tales and the gossip of the women but that she might hear You in Your discourses, and You her in her prayers? You could not despise and withhold Your help from the tears with which she begged of You not gold and silver nor any changing fleeting good, but the salvation of my soul—for it was by Your gift that she was what she was. Rather, Lord, You were ever at hand to hear her and do all in the order that You had predestinated. It could not be that You should deceive her in those visions and answers, those I have mentioned and others I have not mentioned. She laid them up in her faithful heart and again and again reminded You of them in her prayers, as of things written with Your own hand. Because Your mercy endures forever,

You deign, when You forgive any soul all its debts, to become Yourself a debtor by Your promises.

X

Thus You brought me out of that sickness and healed the son of Your handmaid in his body, that he might live on to receive a better and surer way of health. At Rome I again associated with those deceived and deceiving Holy Ones: not only with the Hearers, like the man in whose house I had fallen sick and recovered, but also with those whom they call the Elect. For I still held the view that it was not we that sinned, but some other nature sinning in us; and it pleased my pride to be beyond fault, and when I did any evil not to confess that I had done it, that You might heal my soul because it had sinned against You: I very much preferred to excuse myself and accuse some other thing that was in me but was not I. But in truth I was wholly I, it was my impiety that had divided me against myself. My sin was all the more incurable because I thought I was not a sinner; and my iniquity was most execrable in that I would rather have You, God Almighty, vanquished in me to my destruction than myself vanquished by You for my salvation.

You had not then as yet *set a watch before my mouth and a door round about my lips, that my heart might not incline to evil words, to make excuses in sins, with men that work iniquity:* and therefore was I still united with their Elect.

All the same because I despaired of finding any profit in that false doctrine, I began to hold slackly and carelessly even the ideas with which I had decided to rest content while I could find nothing better.

The notion began to grow in me that the philosophers whom they call Academics were wiser than the rest, because they held that everything should be treated as matter of doubt and affirmed that no truth can be understood by men. For so it seemed clear to me that they thought—and so they are commonly held to teach—though I did not yet understand their real meaning. And I did not neglect to dissuade my host from the excessive confidence that I saw he had in the fables with which the books of Manes are packed. All the same I was much more in their company than in the company of others who were not of their heresy. I did not defend it with my earlier keenness, yet the friendship of these men, of whom Rome shelters a great number, made me slower to seek any other: especially since I had no hope of being able to find the truth in Your church, O Lord of heaven and earth, Creator of all things visible and invisible. For they had turned me against it: and it seemed to me degrading to believe that You had the shape of our human flesh and were circumscribed within the bodily outlines of our limbs. When I desired to think of my God, I could not think of Him save as a bodily magnitude—for it seemed to me that what was not such was nothing at all: this indeed was the principal and practically the sole cause of my inevitable error.

Because of this I thought that the substance of evil was in some sense similar, and had its own hideous and formless bulk, either gross which they called earth, or thin and tenuous like the air: for they imagine it to be some malignant mind creeping over the earth. And because such poor piety as I had constrained me to hold that the good God could not have created any nature evil, I supposed that there were two opposing powers, each infinite, yet the evil one lesser and the good one greater; and from this abominable foundation other sacrilegious notions followed.

When my mind tried to find help in the Catholic faith, it was beaten back because the Catholic faith is not what I thought it was. It seemed to me more reverent, O my God, whom Your mercies in me glorify, to hold You infinite in all other parts even if I must confess You finite in that part where the power of evil was set against You, than to imagine You finitely contained in all Your parts in the shape of a human body. And it seemed better to believe that You had never created evil, than to believe that anything of the nature that I thought evil was should be from You: in my ignorance I thought of evil not simply as some kind of substance, but actually as bodily substance, because I had not learned to think of mind save as a more subtle body, extended in space [as bodies are]. I thought of our Saviour Himself, Your only-begotten Son, as brought forth for our salvation from the mass of Your most luminous substance: and I could believe nothing of him unless I could picture it in my own vain imagination. I argued that such a nature could not possibly be born of the virgin Mary, unless it were mingled with her flesh. And I could not see how that which I had thus figured to myself could be mingled and not defiled. Thus I feared to believe the Word made flesh lest I be forced to believe the Word defiled by flesh. I have no doubt that Your spiritual ones will smile at me, though kindly and lovingly, to read these confusions of my thought. But such I then was.

XI

Furthermore I thought it quite impossible to defend certain things which the Manichees had criticized in Your Scriptures: but I did by now quite honestly desire to discuss these things one by one with someone learned in Scripture and find out what he made of them.

For the speech of one Elpidius, who had spoken and disputed face to face against the Manichees, had already begun to affect me at Carthage, when he produced arguments from Scripture which were not easy to answer. And the answer they gave seemed to me feeble—indeed they preferred not to give it in public but only among ourselves in private—the answer being that the Scriptures of the New Testament had been corrupted by some persons unknown who wished to graft the law of the Jews upon the Christian faith; yet the Manicheans made no effort to produce uncorrupted copies. But I was held captive and stifled by these bodily masses, for I still thought corporeally; I panted under their weight for the clear pure air of Your truth, but still I could not breathe it.

XII

I began diligently to set about that for which I had come to Rome, namely the teaching of Rhetoric. First I gathered some few at my home, and by them I began to become known. And then I learned that Rome had its drawbacks which I had not had to suffer in Africa. For it is true that the riotous incursions of blackguardly youngsters did not happen here: but, so I was warned, "at a given moment a number of students plan together to cheat their master of his fees, and go off to some other master; for they are utterly faithless and hold justice cheap, compared with love of money." My heart hated them, and not with righteous hatred: for pretty surely I hated them more because of what I myself had to suffer from them than for the wrong they did to teachers generally. Such students are indeed depraved; they fornicate against You, O God, in loving the fleeting temptations of time and the filthy cash which soils the hand that holds it, and in embracing this passing world to the scorn of You who abide and ever call them, pardoning the adulterous soul of man when it returns to You. I still hate such vicious and perverse creatures; but I love them as subjects for amendment, souls who might be brought to love the lessons they learn more than money, and You, God, the Truth and Fullness of assured Good and most chaste Peace, more than the lessons. But at that time I disliked them for the harm they did me more than I wished them to become good for Your sake.

XIII

When therefore a message from Milan came to Rome, to the prefect, asking for a professor of Rhetoric for that city and arranging for public funds to cover his journey, I applied for the post with support

from men far gone in the follies of the Manichees—the purpose of my
journey being to be quit of them, though neither they nor I realized
it. The prefect Symmachus approved of a public oration I delivered
for the occasion, and sent me. So I came to Milan, to the bishop and
devout servant of God, Ambrose, famed among the best men of the
whole world, whose eloquence did then most powerfully minister to
*Thy people the fatness of Thy wheat and the joy of Thy oil and the
sober intoxication of Thy wine.* All unknowing I was brought by
God to him, that knowing I should be brought by him to God. That
man of God received me as a father, and as bishop welcomed my
coming. I came to love him, not at first as a teacher of the truth,
which I had utterly despaired of finding in Your church, but for his
kindness towards me. I attended carefully when he preached to the
people, not with the right intention, but only to judge whether his
eloquence was equal to his fame or whether it flowed higher or
lower than had been told me. His words I listened to with the greatest
care; his matter I held quite unworthy of attention. I enjoyed the
charm of his speaking, though for all his learning it was not so
pleasing and captivating as that of Faustus: I refer of course only to
the actual speaking: for the rest there was no comparison at all.
Faustus was simply straying about among the fallacies of the Manichees, Ambrose taught the doctrine of salvation most profitably. But
salvation is far from sinners, of the sort that I then was. Yet little by
little I was drawing closer, though I did not yet realize it.

XIV

Thus I did not take great heed to learn what he was saying but
only to hear how he said it: that empty interest was all I now had
since I despaired of man's finding the way to You. Yet along with the
words, which I admired, there also came into my mind the subject-
matter, to which I attached no importance. I could not separate them.
And while I was opening my heart to learn how eloquently he spoke,
I came to feel, though only gradually, how truly he spoke. First I
began to realize that there was a case for the things themselves, and
I began to see that the Catholic faith, for which I had thought nothing could be said in the face of the Manichean objections, could be
maintained on reasonable grounds: this especially after I had heard
explained figuratively several passages of the Old Testament which
had been a cause of death for me when taken literally. Many passages
of these books were expounded in a spiritual sense and I came to
blame my own hopeless folly in believing that the law and the
prophets could not stand against those who hated and mocked at

them. I did not yet feel that the Catholic way was to be followed, merely because it might have some learned men to maintain it and answer objections adequately and not absurdly; nor did I think that what I had so far held was to be condemned because both views were equally defensible. In fact the Catholic side was clearly not vanquished, yet it was not clearly victorious. I then bent my mind to see if I could by any clear proofs convict the Manicheans of error. If only I had been able to conceive of a substance that was spiritual, all their strong points would have been broken down and cast forth from my mind. But I could not.

Concerning the body of this world, and the whole of that nature which our bodily senses can attain to, I thought again and again and made many comparisons; and I still judged that the views of so many of the philosophers were more probable. So in what I thought to be the manner of the Academics—that is to say, doubting of all things and wavering between one and another—I decided that I must leave the Manichees; for in that time of doubt, I did not think I could remain in a sect to which I now preferred certain of the philosophers. Yet I absolutely refused to entrust the care of my sick soul to the philosophers, because they were without the saving name of Christ. I determined, then, to go on as a catechumen in the Catholic Church —the church of my parents—and to remain in that state until some certain light should appear by which I might steer my course.

BOOK SIX

AGED TWENTY-NINE

I–II   *Monica Comes to Milan*
    I   Monica's devotion to St. Ambrose
    II   Monica abandons an African devotional practice

III–V   *His Mind Still Searches*
    III   Ambrose too busy for private discussion; but Augustine learns that Catholic teaching is not what he had thought
    IV   He learns much from Ambrose's preaching but still remains uncertain
    V   Sees more clearly the provinces of faith and reason and the authority of Scripture

VI   *Disappointments in Worldly Affairs*
    VI   The incident of the drunken beggar

VII–X   *Alypius and Nebridius*
    VII   Alypius cured of his passion for the Games
    VIII   Alypius falls again into the same passion
    IX   How Alypius had earlier been accused of theft
    X   Alypius has three terms as Assessor; some account of Nebridius

XI–XVI   *The Problem of Continence*
    XI   Augustine sways this way and that, afraid above all that he can never achieve continence
    XII   Alypius begins to be attracted towards marriage by curiosity at the hold sex has upon Augustine
    XIII   Augustine engaged to be married to a girl two years under marriage age
    XIV   The plan for a community of friends
    XV   His mistress sent back to Africa: he takes another mistress
    XVI   Growing wretchedness

I

O GOD, my hope from my youth, where were You all this time, where had You gone? For was it not You who created me and distinguished me from the beasts of the field and made me wiser than the birds of the air? Yet I walked through dark and slippery places, and I went out of myself in the search for You and did not find the God of my heart. I had come into the depths of the sea and I had lost faith and all hope of discovering the truth. By this time my mother had come to me, following me over sea and land with the courage of piety and relying upon You in all perils. For they were in danger from a storm, and she reassured even the sailors—by whom travellers newly ventured upon the deep are ordinarily reassured—promising them safe arrival because thus You had promised her in a vision. She found me in a perilous state through my deep despair of ever discovering the truth. But even when I told her that if I was not yet a Catholic Christian, I was no longer a Manichean, she was not greatly exultant as at some unlooked-for good news, because she had already received assurance upon that part of my misery; she bewailed me as one dead certainly, but certainly to be raised again by You, offering me in her mind as one stretched out dead, that You might say to the widow's son: *"Young man, I say to thee arise"*: and he should sit up and begin to speak and You should give him to his mother. So her heart was not shaken with any tumult of exultation at hearing that what daily she had begged of You with tears had in so large part happened: for I was at least rescued from heresy, even if I had not yet attained the truth. In fact, because she was certain that You would give her what remained since You had promised her all, she answered me serenely and with a heart full of confidence that in Christ she believed that she would see me a faithful Catholic before she died. So much she said to me. But to You, O fount of mercy, she multiplied her prayers and her tears that You should hasten Your help and enlighten my darkness: and she hastened to church more zealously than ever and drank in the words of Ambrose as a fountain of water springing up into life everlasting. She loved that man as an angel of God because she had learned that it was by him that I had been brought so far as to the wavering state I was now

87

in; through which she took it for granted that I had to pass on my way from sickness to health, with some graver peril yet to come, analogous to what doctors call the crisis.

II

My mother had brought meal and bread and wine to certain oratories built to the memory of saints, as was her custom in Africa. But the sacristan prevented her. When she learned that the bishop himself had forbidden the practice, she received the prohibition so devoutly and obediently that I wondered at the ease with which she turned into a critic of her own former custom rather than of the present prohibition. For her soul was not a slave to wine-drinking, nor had she any love of wine to provoke her to hatred of the truth, like so many of both sexes who are as much sickened by a hymn of sobriety as drunkards would be if one poured water into their wine. But when my mother brought her basket with those accustomed dainties—of which she meant to eat a little and give away the rest —she never allowed herself more than one small cup diluted to her sober palate, and from this she would sip no more that was fitting. And if there were many oratories of departed saints to be honoured in that way, she took round with her the same cup to be used in each place: and this, not only diluted with water but by now luke-warm, she would share with others present in small sips, for her concern was with piety and not with the pleasure of the wine.

But when she found that the custom was forbidden by so famous a preacher and so pious a bishop even to those who used it soberly, lest it might be an occasion of gluttony to the heavier drinkers; and because in any event these funeral feasts in honour of our parents in the faith were too much like the superstitions of the heathens, she abandoned the practice quite willingly. In place of her basket filled with the fruits of the earth, she learned to offer at the shrines of the martyrs a breast full of prayers purer than any such gifts. Thus she was able to give what she could to the needy; and the communion of the Lord's Body was celebrated where the martyrs had been immolated and crowned in the likeness of His Passion.

But yet, O Lord my God, it does seem to me—and upon this matter my heart is in Your sight—that my mother might not so easily have borne the breaking of her custom if it had been forbidden by some other whom she did not love as she loved Ambrose. For on account of my salvation she loved him dearly; and he loved her on account of her most religious way of life, for she was fervent in spirit and ever doing good, and she haunted the church. So that when he saw me he

often broke out in her praises, congratulating me that I had such a
mother, and not realizing what sort of a son she had: for I doubted
all these things and did not believe that the way of life could be
discovered.

III

Nor did I then groan in prayer for Your help. My mind was intent
upon inquiry and unquiet for argumentation. I regarded Ambrose as
a lucky man by worldly standards to be held in honour by such important people: only his celibacy seemed to me a heavy burden. I
had no means of guessing, and no experience of my own to learn
from, what hope he bore within him, what struggles he might have
against the temptations that went with his high place, what was his
consolation in adversity, and on what joys of Your bread the hidden
mouth of his heart fed. Nor did he know how I was inflamed nor
the depth of my peril. I could not ask of him what I wished as I
wished, for I was kept from any face to face conversation with him by
the throng of men with their own troubles, whose infirmities he
served. The very little time he was not with these he was refreshing
either his body with necessary food or his mind with reading. When
he read, his eyes travelled across the page and his heart sought into the
sense, but voice and tongue were silent. No one was forbidden to
approach him nor was it his custom to require that visitors should
be announced: but when we came into him we often saw him reading
and always to himself; and after we had sat long in silence, unwilling
to interrupt a work on which he was so intent, we would depart
again. We guessed that in the small time he could find for the
refreshment of his mind, he would wish to be free from the distraction of other men's affairs and not called away from what he was
doing. Perhaps he was on his guard lest [if he read aloud]
someone listening should be troubled and want an explanation if
the author he was reading expressed some idea over obscurely, and
it might be necessary to expound or discuss some of the more difficult
questions. And if he had to spend time on this, he would get through
less reading than he wished. Or it may be that his real reason for
reading to himself was to preserve his voice, which did in fact readily
grow tired. But whatever his reason for doing it, that man certainly
had a good reason.

Anyhow I was given no opportunity of putting such questions as
I desired to that holy oracle of Yours, his breast, unless they were of
a sort to be heard briefly. But the agitation working in me required
that he should be fully at leisure if I were to pour it out before him;

and I never found him so. Still I heard him every Sunday preaching the word of truth to his congregation; and I became more and more certain that all those knots of cunning and calumny, which those who deceived me had tangled up against the holy books, could be untangled. I learned that the phrase "man created by You in Your own image" was not taken by Your spiritual children, whom of our Catholic mother You have made to be born anew by grace, to mean that You are bounded within the shape of a human body. And although I had not the vaguest or most shadowy notion how a spiritual substance could be, yet I was filled with shame—but joyful too—that I had been barking all these years not against the Catholic faith but against mere figments of carnal imaginations. I had been rash and impious in that I had spoken in condemnation of things which I should have learned more truly of by inquiry. For You, O highest and nearest, most hidden and most present, have not parts greater and smaller; You are wholly everywhere, yet nowhere limited within space, nor are You of any bodily form. And yet You have made man in Your own image, and man is in space from head to foot.

IV

Thus I was ignorant how this image of Yours could be; but I should have knocked at the door and proposed the question how it was to be believed, and not jeeringly opposed it as if it were believed in this or that particular way. The anxiety as to what I should hold as sure gnawed at my heart all the more keenly, as my shame increased at having been so long tricked and deceived by the promise of certainty, and at having with a rashness of error worthy of a child gone on spouting forth so many uncertainties as confidently as if I had known them for sure. That they were false, I saw clearly only later. Yet already I was certain that they were at least uncertain, and that I had taken them for certain, when in the blindness of my opposition I attacked Your Catholic church. I did not yet know that she was teaching the truth, but I had found that she did not teach the things of which I had so strongly accused her. So I was first confounded and then enlightened. And I rejoiced, O my God, that Your only church, the Body of Your only Son, in which the name of Christ had been put upon me while I was still an infant, had no taste for such puerile nonsense; nor in her sound doctrine had she the notion of somehow packing You, the Creator of all things, into any space—however mighty and ample yet bounded upon all sides—in the shape of a human body.

I was glad also that the old scriptures of the Law and the Prophets

were set before me now, no longer in that light in which they had
formerly seemed absurd, when I criticised Your holy ones for thinking
this or that which in plain fact they did not think. And it was a joy
to hear Ambrose who often repeated to his congregation, as if it were
a rule he was most strongly urging upon them, the text: *the letter
killeth, but the spirit giveth life.* And he would go on to draw aside
the veil of mystery and lay open the spiritual meaning of things which
taken literally would have seemed to teach falsehood. Nothing of
what he said struck me as false, although I did not as yet know
whether what he said was true. I held back my heart from accepting
anything, fearing that I might fall once more, whereas in fact the
hanging in suspense was more deadly. I wanted to be as certain of
things unseen as that seven and three make ten. For I had not reached
the point of madness which denies that even this can be known; but
I wanted to know other things as clearly as this, either such material
things as were not present to my senses, or spiritual things which I
did not know how to conceive save corporeally. By believing I might
have been cured; for then the eye of my mind would have been
clearer and so might in some way have been directed towards Your
truth which abides for ever and knows no defect. But as usually
happens, the man who has tried a bad doctor is afraid to trust even a
good one: so it was with the health of my soul, which could not be
healed save by believing, and refused to be healed that way for fear
of believing falsehood. Thus I was resisting Your hands, for You
first prepared for us the medicine of faith and then applied it to
the diseases of the world and gave it such great power.

V

From this time on I found myself preferring the Catholic doctrine,
realising that it acted more modestly and honestly in requiring things
to be believed which could not be proved—whether they were in
themselves provable though not by this or that person, or were not
provable at all—than the Manichees who derided credulity and made
impossible promises of certain knowledge, and then called upon men
to believe so many utterly fabulous and absurd things because they
could not be demonstrated. Next, Lord, with gentle and most merciful hand You worked upon my heart and rectified it. I began to
consider the countless things I believed which I had not seen, or
which had happened with me not there—so many things in the history
of nations, so many facts about places and cities which I had never
seen, so many things told me by friends, by doctors. by this man, by
that man: and unless we accepted these things, we should do nothing

at all in this life. Most strongly of all it struck me how firmly and unshakeably I believed that I was born of a particular father and mother, which I could not possibly know unless I believed it upon the word of others. Thus You brought me to see that those who believed Your Bible, which You have established among almost all peoples with such authority, were not to be censured, but rather those who did not believe it, and that I must give no heed to any who might say to me: "How do you know that those Scriptures were given to mankind by the Spirit of the One true and most true God?" For this point above all was to be believed; because no assault of fallacious questions which I had read in such multitude in the philosophers—who in any event contradicted each other—could constrain me not to believe both that You are, though what might be Your nature I did not know, and that the government of human affairs belongs to You.

But though I held these truths sometimes more strongly, sometimes less, yet I always believed both that You are and that You have a care of us: even if I did not know what I must hold as to Your substance, or what way leads to You—or leads back to You. Thus, since men had not the strength to discover the truth by pure reason and therefore we needed the authority of Holy Writ, I was coming to believe that You would certainly not have bestowed such eminent authority upon those Scriptures throughout the world, unless it had been Your will that by them men should believe in You and in them seek You.

Now that I heard them expounded so convincingly, I saw that many passages in these books which had at one time struck me as absurdities, must be referred to the profundity of mystery. Indeed the authority of Scripture seemed to be more to be revered and more worthy of devoted faith in that it was at once a book that all could read and read easily, and yet preserved the majesty of its mystery in the deepest part of its meaning: for it offers itself to all in the plainest words and the simplest expressions, yet demands the closest attention of the most serious minds. Thus it receives all within its welcoming arms, and at the same time brings a few direct to You by narrow ways: yet these few would be fewer still but for this twofold quality by which it stands so lofty in authority yet draws the multitude to its bosom by its holy lowliness. So I dwelt upon these things and You were near me, I sighed and You heard me, I was wavering uncertainly and You guided me, I was going the broad way of the world and You did not forsake me.

VI

I was all hot for honours, money, marriage: and You made mock of my hotness. In my pursuit of these, I suffered most bitter disap-

pointments, but in this You were good to me since I was thus prevented from taking delight in anything not Yourself. Look now into
my heart, Lord, by whose will I remember all this and confess it to
You. Let my soul cleave to You now that You have freed it from
the tenacious hold of death. At that time my soul was in misery, and
You pricked the soreness of its wound, that leaving all things it
might turn to You, who are over all and without whom all would
return to nothing, that it might turn to You and be healed. I was in
utter misery and there was one day especially on which You acted to
bring home to me the realisation of my misery. I was preparing an
oration in praise of the Emperor in which I was to utter any number of lies to win the applause of people who knew they were lies.
My heart was much wrought upon by the shame of this and inflamed
with the fever of the thoughts that consumed it. I was passing along
a certain street in Milan when I noticed a beggar. He was jesting and
laughing and I imagine more than a little drunk. I fell into gloom
and spoke to the friends who were with me about the endless sorrows
that our own insanity brings us: for here was I striving away, dragging
the load of my unhappiness under the spurring of my desires, and
making it worse by dragging it: and with all our striving, our one
aim was to arrive at some sort of happiness without care: the beggar
had reached the same goal before us, and we might quite well never
reach it at all. The very thing that he had attained by means of a few
pennies begged from passers-by—namely the pleasure of a temporary
happiness—I was plotting for with so many a weary twist and turn.

Certainly his joy was no true joy; but the joy I sought in my ambition was emptier still. In any event he was cheerful and I worried,
he had no cares and I nothing but cares. Now if anyone had asked
me whether I would rather be cheerful or fearful, I would answer:
"Cheerful": but if he had gone on to ask whether I would rather be
like that beggar or as I actually was, I would certainly have chosen
my own state though so troubled and anxious. Now this was surely
absurd. It could not be for any true reason. I ought not to have preferred my own state rather than his merely because I was the more
learned, since I got no joy from my learning, but sought only to
please men by it—not even to teach them, only to please them. Therefore did You break my bones with the rod of Your discipline.

Let my soul pay no heed to those who would say: "It makes a
difference what one is happy about. The beggar found joy in his
drunkenness, you sought joy in glory." But what glory, Lord? A
glory not in You. For my glory was no truer than his joy, and it turned
my head even more. That very night he would sleep off his drunkenness: but how often and often I had gone to bed with mine and

woken up with it, and would in the future go to bed with it and
wake up with it. It does indeed make a difference what one is happy
about: I know it, and I know that the happiness of a sure hope is
incomparably beyond all such vanity. And there was indeed a difference between him and me—for he was much the happier man: not
only because he was soaked in his merriment while I was eaten up
with cares, but also because he by wishing luck to all comers had at
least got wine, while I by lying was aiming only to get empty
praise.

I spoke much to this effect to the friends that were with me: and
I often observed that it was with them as it was with me, and I found
it very ill with me. So I worried and by worrying doubled the ill.
And when by chance prosperity smiled in my direction, I lacked the
spirit to seize it, for it fled away almost before I could get my hand
upon it.

VII

We were gloomy together with such thoughts, I and those who
were closest to me. I discussed the problem especially with Alypius
and Nebridius. Alypius was born in the same town as I. His parents
were of high rank there. He was younger than I, indeed he had
studied under me both when I began my teaching in our native town
and afterwards at Carthage. He was much attached to me because
he thought me kindly and learned, and I to him because of the
great bent towards virtue that was so marked in him so young. But
at Carthage the maelstrom of ill morals—and especially the passion for
idle spectacles—had sucked him in, his special madness being for
gladiatorial shows. When he first came into the grip of this wretched
craving, I had set up a school for the public and was teaching rhetoric.
He had not come to me as a pupil because of some difference that
had arisen between his father and me. I discovered that he was
quite fatally devoted to the Games, and I was much worried because
it seemed to me that so much promise was to be thrown away, or
had already been thrown away. But I had no way of advising him
or forcibly restraining him, neither the goodwill of a friend nor the
right of a master. For I took for granted that he would feel about me
as his father did. In fact he did not. He took his own line in the matter
rather than his father's, and fell into the way of greeting me when
we met and of coming sometimes into my school to listen awhile and
be off again.

But it had passed from my mind that I could do anything to prevent the waste of so good a mind in the blind and ruinous pursuit of the empty pastimes he was in. But You, Lord, who hold the helm of all that You have created, had not forgotten him—and indeed he was one day to be numbered amongst Your children as a high priest of Your sacrament. That his amendment might be obviously due to You, You brought it about through me, and without my being aware of it. For one day when I was sitting in my usual place with my students in front of me, he came in, greeted me, sat down and gave his attention to what was being discussed. I had in hand a passage that I was expounding: and it suddenly struck me that it could be very well illustrated by a comparison taken from the Games—a comparison which would make the point I was establishing clearer and more amusing, and which involved biting mockery of those who were slaves to that particular insanity. You know, O my God and his, that I was not thinking of Alypius or his need to be cured of that disease. But he applied it instantly to himself and thought I had said it solely on his account. Another might have taken it as a reason for being angry with me, but the youth was honest enough to take it as a reason for being angry with himself and for warmer attachment to me. You said long ago and caused it to be written in Your Book: *Rebuke a wise man and he will love you.*

As a matter of fact I had not been rebuking him, but You use all men with or without their knowledge for a purpose known to Yourself—and that purpose is just. Thus of my heart and tongue You made burning coals, to cauterize and heal a mind of such promise though it lay sick. Let him praise You not who does not realize Your mercies, which my soul's depths confess to You. As a result of what he had heard me say, he wrenched himself up out of the deep pit in which he had chosen to be plunged and in the darkness of whose pleasures he had been so woefully blinded. He braced his mind and shook it till all the filth of the Games fell away from it and he went no more.

Then he prevailed upon his unwilling father to let him be one of my students. His father did at last yield. Alypius began to take lessons from me again and so came to be involved with me in the same superstitions. He loved especially the pretence the Manichees made of continence, which he took to be quite genuine. But in fact it was a senseless and misleading continence, which seduced precious souls not yet able to reach the profound depth of virtue and easily deceived with the surface appearance of what was only an unreal counterfeit of virtue.

VIII

In pursuit of the worldly career whose necessity his parents were always dinning into his ears, he had gone before me to Rome to study Law: and there incredibly he had been carried away again by an incredible passion for gladiatorial shows. He had turned from such things and utterly detested them. But it happened one day that he met some friends and fellow-students coming from dinner: and though he flatly refused and vigorously resisted, they used friendly violence and forced him along with them to the amphitheater on a day of these cruel and murderous Games. He protested "Even if you drag my body to the place, can you force me to turn my mind and my eyes on the show? Though there, I shall not be there, and so I shall defeat both you and it."

Hearing this his companions led him on all the faster, wishing to discover whether he could do as he had said. When they had reached the Arena and had got such seats as they could, the whole place was in a frenzy of hideous delight. He closed up the door of his eyes and forbade his mind to pay attention to things so evil. If only he could have stopped his ears too! For at a certain critical point in the fight, the vast roar of the whole audience beat upon him. His curiosity got the better of him, and thinking that he would be able to treat the sight with scorn—whatever the sight might be—he opened his eyes and was stricken with a deeper wound in the soul than the man whom he had opened his eyes to see got in the body. He fell more miserably than the gladiator whose fall had set the crowd to that roar—a roar which had entered his ears and unlocked his eyes, so that his soul was stricken and beaten down. But in truth the reason was that its courage had so far been only audaciousness, and it was weak because it had relied upon itself when it should have trusted only in You. Seeing the blood he drank deep of the savagery. He did not turn away but fixed his gaze upon the sight. He drank in all the frenzy, with no thought of what had happened to him, revelled in the wickedness of the contest and was drunk with lust for blood. He was no longer the man who had come there but one of the crowd to which he had come, a fit companion for those who had brought him.

What more need I say? He continued to gaze, shouted, grew hot, and when he departed took with him a madness by which he was to be goaded to come back again, not only with those who at first took him there, but even more than they and leading on others. Yet out of all this You drew him with strong and merciful hand, teaching him to have confidence in You, not in himself. But this was long after.

IX

For the time, the matter was only laid up in his memory for his future healing. So also was an incident which had happened earlier while he was still a student in my school at Carthage. He was in the market-place at noon one day going over in his mind something that he had to say by heart (as students usually have to do) when You allowed him to be arrested as a thief by the officers in charge of the market. I imagine that You allowed this, O our God, for no other cause than that one who was to be so great should learn thus early that in judging cases man must not too easily be condemned by man through rash credulity. As he was walking by himself before the judgment-seat with his tablets and his pen, the real thief, a young man who was also a student, came along with an axe concealed under his clothes and quite unseen by Alypius went up to the leaden gratings which are over the silversmiths' shops and began to cut away the lead. When they heard the sound of the axe the silversmiths underneath began to call out and sent men to seize whomever they might find. The thief heard their voices and ran away leaving his axe behind for fear that he might be caught with it.

Now Alypius who had not seen the man arrive saw him depart, observed the speed of his departure, and wondering what it was all about went up to the place. He found the axe and stood looking at it with surprise. At this moment those who had been sent found him alone and carrying the weapon whose noise had startled them and brought them there. They seized him, dragged him off, and gathering the neighbouring shopkeepers made a great boast of having caught the thief in the act. They took him off to hand him over to the officers of the law. But his lesson stopped there. For at that point, Lord, You came to the aid of his innocence, of which indeed You were the only witness. For as he was being led off to imprisonment or torture, they were met by a certain architect, who had the principal charge of public buildings. They were particularly pleased to meet him just then, because they were themselves under suspicion of stealing the goods that were lost out of the market-place, and they felt that at last he would know who had done the stealing. But this man had often seen Alypius at the house of a certain Senator whom he himself frequently visited. He knew him at once and taking him by the hand drew him away from the crowd and enquired the cause of all the trouble. He heard what had happened and commanded the rabble who thronged about raging and threatening Alypius to come with him. They came to the house of the young man who had done

the deed. There was a boy outside the door who was quite ready to
tell the whole thing, being too young to fear that any harm would
come to his master from what he said: for he had gone with him to
the market place. Alypius remembered seeing the boy and told the
architect, who showed the hatchet to the boy and asked him whose
it was. "Ours" replied the boy immediately. He was questioned
further and disclosed everything. Thus the guilt was transferred to
the man who lived in that house, to the great confusion of the crowd
which had been hurling its taunts at Alypius. Alypius indeed, who
was later to be a dispenser of Your word and to investigate many cases
in Your Church, went off very much wiser for the experience.

X

I found him at Rome when I came there and he became my close
friend. He went with me to Milan, so that he might be still with
me, and might at the same time practice the Law he had studied,
but this rather to please his parents than of his own wish. He had
already sat three times as an Assessor, displaying an integrity that
caused others to marvel—whereas he marvelled that any should prefer money to honesty. His character was tested further, not only by
the temptation of bribery but also by the threat of danger to himself.
At Rome he had been Assessor to the Chancellor of the Italian Treasury. There was at the time a very powerful Senator, to whom many
were bound by favours received, while many stood in fear of him.
He wanted to have permission granted him for something forbidden
by the law. Ordinarily so powerful a man would have got it as a
matter of course. But Alypius refused. A bribe was offered: he treated
it with complete contempt. He was threatened and treated the threats
likewise. Everyone was amazed at so rare a spirit, in that he neither
courted the friendship nor feared the enmity of a man so important
and so well known for the innumerable means at his disposal for
advancing or damaging others. The Judge himself to whom Alypius
acted as Assessor, did not want to grant the permit, but would not
openly refuse it: he put the blame upon Alypius, claiming that Alypius would not let him do it: and in truth if he had tried, Alypius
would have left the court.

The only thing that did tempt him was his love of study: he
thought of having books copied for him at the reduced rates allowed
to Praetors. But considering the equity of the matter he came to a
better decision, holding justice which forbade it more valuable than
the power to do it. All that I have so far said is small: yet *he that is
faithful in that which is least, is faithful also in that which is greater;*

nor is that word void which proceeded from the mouth of Your Truth: *If then you have not been faithful in the unjust Mammon, who will trust you with that which is the true? and if you have not been faithful in that which is another's who will give you that which is your own?* Such then was the man who was so close a friend, and shared my wavering as to the course of life we should adopt.

I have mentioned Nebridius. He had left his native place near Carthage: he had left Carthage itself where he had mainly lived, had left his rich family estate and his house and his mother, for she would not come with him. All these things he had left and had come to Milan for no other reason than to be with me: for with a real passion for truth and wisdom, he was in the same anguish as I and the same uncertain wavering; and he continued his ardent search for the way of happiness and his close investigation of the most difficult questions. Thus there were together the mouths of three needy souls, bitterly confessing to one another their spiritual poverty and waiting upon You that You *might give them their food in due season.* And amidst the bitter disappointments which through Your mercy followed all our worldly affairs, darkness clouded our souls as we tried to see why we suffered these things. And we turned away in deepest gloom saying: *"How long shall these things be?"* This question was ever on our lips, but for all that we did not give up our worldly ways, because we still saw no certitude which it was worth changing our way of life to grasp.

XI

I was much exercised in mind as I remembered how long it was since that nineteenth year of my age in which I first felt the passion for true knowledge and resolved that when I found it I would give up all the empty hopes and lying follies of vain desires. And here I was going on for thirty, still sticking in the same mire, greedy for the enjoyment of things present though they ever eluded me and wasted my soul: and at every moment saying: "To-morrow I shall find it: it will be all quite clear and I shall grasp it. Faustus will come and explain everything. And those mighty Academics—is it true that nothing can be grasped with certainty for the directing of life? No: we must search the more closely and not despair. For now the things in the Scriptures which used to seem absurd are no longer absurd, but can be quite properly understood in another sense. I shall set my foot upon that step on which my parents placed me as a child, until I clearly find the truth. But where shall I search? When shall I search? Ambrose is busy. I am myself too busy to read. And in any event where can I find the books? Who has them, or when can I procure them? Can I borrow them from anyone? I must appoint set times, set apart certain hours for the health of my soul. A great hope has dawned: the Catholic faith does not teach the things I thought and vainly accused it of. Catholic scholars hold it blasphemy to believe God limited within the shape of a human body. Do I hesitate to knock, that other truths may be opened? My pupils occupy the morning hours, but what do I do with the rest? Why not do this? But if I do, when shall I have time to visit the powerful friends of whose influence I stand in need, or when prepare the lessons I sell to my pupils, or when refresh myself by relaxing my mind from too close pre-occupation with my heavy concerns?

"But perish all this. Let me dismiss this vanity and emptiness and give myself wholly to the search for truth. Life is a poor thing, death may come at any time: if it were to come upon me suddenly, in what state should I depart this life? And where am I to learn the things I have neglected? Or must I not rather suffer the punishment of my negligence? Or does death perhaps cut off and end all care along with our bodily sense? This too must be settled. But God forbid that it should be so. It is not for nothing or any mere emptiness that the magnificence of the authority of the Christian Faith is spread over all the world. Such great and wonderful things would never have been wrought for us by God, if the life of the soul were ended by the death of the body. Why then do I delay to drop my hopes of this world and give myself wholly to the search for God and true happiness?

"Yet stay a moment. After all, these worldly things are pleasant, they have their own charm and it is no small charm. The mind is not easily cut off from them merely because it would be base to go back to them. Again, it would not be too difficult to win some post of honour: and what more should I have to wish for? I have a body of powerful friends: even if I press on to nothing more ambitious, I could at least get a governorship. And then I could marry a wife, with some little money of her own, so that she would not increase my expenditure. And so I should have reached the limit of ambition. Many great men, well worthy of our imitation, have given themselves to the pursuit of wisdom even though they had wives."

These things went through my mind, and the wind blew one way and then another, and tossed my heart this way and that. Time was passing and I delayed to turn to the Lord. From day to day I postponed life in You, but I did not postpone the death that daily I was dying in myself. I was in love with the idea of happiness, yet I feared it where it was, and fled away from it in my search for it. The plain truth is that I thought I should be impossibly miserable if I had to forego the embraces of a woman: and I did not think of Your mercy as a healing medicine for that weakness, because I had never tried it. I thought that continency was a matter of our own strength, and I knew that I had not the strength: for in my utter foolishness I did not know the word of Your Scripture that none can be continent unless You give it. And truly You would have given it if with groaning of spirit I had assailed Your ears and with settled faith had cast my care upon You.

XII

It was Alypius indeed who kept me from marrying, with his unvarying argument that if I did we could not possibly live together with untroubled leisure in the pursuit of wisdom, as we had so long desired. For on that side of things he was quite extraordinarily chaste. Early in adolescence he had had the experience of sexual intercourse, but it took no hold upon him. Indeed he regretted having done it and despised it and from then on lived in complete continence. I brought up the example of those who had pursued wisdom in the married state, and served God faithfully, and faithfully kept and cherished their friends. But indeed I was far enough from their greatness of spirit. I was bound by this need of the flesh, and dragged with me the chain of its poisonous delight, fearing to be set free: and I rejected his words of wise counsel, pushing away the hand that would set me free as though it were hurting a sore place.

Moreover, through me the serpent began to speak to Alypius himself. By my tongue the devil wove fascinating snares and scattered them in his path for the entangling of his hitherto untrammeled feet. For he marvelled to see me, of whom he thought so much, stuck so fast in the grip of that particular lust as to affirm whenever we talked of it that I could not possibly lead a single life. I urged on my side, when I saw how puzzled he was, that there was a great difference between the snatched and furtive experience of sex which he had had as a boy—and now scarcely remembered and could therefore brush aside with no particular trouble—and the enjoyment of my permanent state. It only needed the honorable name of marriage, and he would have had no cause to wonder why I could not give up that way of life. The result was that he began to desire marriage himself, not through any lust for the pleasure of it but solely through curiosity: for as he explained, he wanted to discover what the thing was without which my life—which to him seemed so pleasing—would have seemed to me no life at all but torment. For his mind, itself free from the chain, marvelled at my enslavement; and from marvelling he came to a desire to try it. Thus he might well have entered upon the same experience and so fallen into the enslavement which at present he found so incomprehensible: for he was willing to make a covenant with death, and *he that loves danger shall fall into it*. Such honour as there is in marriage from the duty of well-ordered life together and the having of children, had very small influence with either of us. What held me so fiercely bound was principally the sheer habit of sating a lust that could never be satisfied, and what drew him who was not yet bound was curiosity about me. Thus we stood until You, O most High, not forsaking our dust but pitying our pitifulness, helped us by secret and wonderful ways.

XIII

Great effort was made to get me married. I proposed, the girl was promised me. My mother played a great part in the matter for she wanted to have me married and then cleansed with the saving waters of baptism, rejoicing to see me grow every day more fitted for baptism and feeling that her prayers and Your promises were to be fulfilled in my faith. By my request and her own desire she begged You daily with the uttermost intensity of her heart to show her in a vision something of my future marriage, but You would never do it. She did indeed see certain vain fantasies, under the pressure of her mind's preoccupation with the matter; and she told them to me, not, however, with the confidence she always had when You had shown things to her, but as if she set small store by them; for she said that there was a certain unanalysable savor, not to be expressed in words, by which she could distinguish between what You revealed and the dreams of her own spirit. Still she pushed on with the matter of my marriage, and the girl was asked for. She was still two years short of the age for marriage but I liked her and agreed to wait.

XIV

There was a group of us friends who had much serious discussion together, concerning the cares and troubles of human life which we found so hard to endure. We had almost decided to seek a life of peace, away from the throng of men. This peace we hoped to attain by putting together whatever we could manage to get, and making one common household for all of us: so that in the clear trust of friendship, things should not belong to this or that individual, but one thing should be made of all our possessions, and belong wholly to each one of us, and everybody own everything. It seemed that there might be perhaps ten men in this fellowship. Among us there were some very rich men, especially Romanianus, our fellow townsman, who had been a close friend of mine from childhood and had been brought to the court in Milan by the press of some very urgent business. He was strongest of all for the idea and he had considerable influence in persuasion because his wealth was much greater than anyone else's. We agreed that two officers should be chosen every year to handle the details of our life together, leaving the rest undisturbed. But then we began to wonder whether our wives would agree, for some of us already had wives and I meant to have one. So the whole plan, which we had built up so neatly, fell to pieces in our hands and was simply dropped. We returned to our old sighing and groaning and treading of this world's broad and beaten ways: for many thoughts were in our hearts, but *Thy counsel standeth forever.* And out of Thy counsel didst Thou deride ours and didst prepare Thine own things for us, meaning to *give us meat in due season* and *to open Thy hands and fill our souls with Thy blessing.*

XV

Meanwhile my sins were multiplied. She with whom I had lived so long was torn from my side as a hindrance to my forthcoming marriage. My heart which had held her very dear was broken and wounded and shed blood. She went back to Africa, swearing that she would never know another man, and left with me the natural son I had had of her. But I in my unhappiness could not, for all my manhood, imitate her resolve. I was unable to bear the delay of two years which must pass before I was to get the girl I had asked for in marriage. In fact it was not really marriage that I wanted. I was simply a slave to lust. So I took another woman, not of course as a wife; and thus my soul's disease was nourished and kept alive as vigorously as ever, indeed worse than ever, that it might reach the realm of matrimony in the company of its ancient habit. Nor was the wound healed that had been made by the cutting off of my former mistress. For there was first burning and bitter grief; and after that it festered, and as the pain grew duller it only grew more hopeless.

XVI

Praise be to Thee, glory to Thee, O fountain of mercies. I became more wretched and Thou more close to me. Thy right hand was ready to pluck me from the mire and wash me clean, though I knew it not.

So far nothing called me back from the depth of the gulf of carnal pleasure save fear of death and of the judgment to come, which, through all the fluctuations of my opinions, never left my mind. I discussed with my friends Alypius and Nebridius concerning the nature of good and evil, and Epicurus would certainly have won the palm in my judgment if I had not believed that after death there remained life for the soul and treatment according to its deserts, which Epicurus did not hold. And I put the question, supposing we were immortals and could live in perpetual enjoyment of the body without any fear of loss, why we should not then be happy, or what else should we seek. I did not realize that it belonged to the very heart of my wretchedness to be so drowned and blinded in it that I could not conceive that light of honor, and of beauty loved for its own sake, which the eye of the flesh does not see but only the innermost soul. I was so blind that I never came to ask myself what was the source of the pleasure I found in discussing these ideas (worthless as they were) with friends, and of my inability to be happy without friends, even in the sense of happiness which I then held, no matter how great the abundance of carnal pleasure. For truly I loved my friends, for their own sake, and I knew that I was in turn so loved by them. O, tortuous ways! Woe to my soul with its rash hope of finding something better if it forsook Thee! My soul turned and turned again, on back and sides and belly, and the bed was always hard. For Thou alone art her rest. And behold Thou art close at hand to deliver us from the wretchedness of error and establish us in thy way, and console us with Thy word: "Run, I shall bear you up and bring you and carry you to the end."

BOOK SEVEN

AGED THIRTY

I–II *Realisation That God Is Incorruptible*
    I   He sees that God must be incorruptible though he still conceives of God as in some way extended in space, e.g., as light "occupies" the atmosphere
    II Nebridius' argument which would have forced the Manichees to admit God corruptible

III–V *The Problem of the Origin of Evil*
    III He is now certain that he has a free will: but the problem how evil comes to be in his will is unsolved
    IV The truth of God's incorruptibility should have shown him the true nature of evil
    V Sees God as an infinite sea, and creation as a sponge penetrated by the sea, but still cannot see how evil gets into creation

VI *Finally Rejects Astrology*

VII–XVII *Beginning of Emancipation from Too Corporeal Thinking*
    VII He now holds certain Catholic truths but still cannot get the right order of lower things to God
    VIII God would not let his mind rest in error
    IX He reads some books of the Platonists from which he learns of the eternity and spirituality of the Word (though nothing of the Word made flesh)
    X He begins to see that extension in space is not necessary to being
    XI Things less than God neither absolutely are nor totally are not
    XII All things are good and all substances are from God
    XIII All things have their place in creation
    XIV Seeing God anew
    XV How all things are in God
    XVI Iniquity is not a substance
    XVII "At last I loved You and not some phantom instead of You"; but he has not the strength to hold his gaze fixed

XVIII–XXI *The Need for Christ*

XVIII Only Christ, the One Mediator, could have given him the strength, but he did not yet realize this

XIX What he thought of Christ at that time

XX It was well that he read the Platonists before reading the Scriptures

XXI He comes to St. Paul and comes to know Christ

I

NOW my evil sinful youth was over and I had come on into young manhood; but the older in years, the baser was my vanity, in that I could not conceive any other kind of substance than what these eyes are accustomed to see. I did not indeed, O God, think of You under the figure of a human body. From the moment I began to know anything of philosophy, I had rejected that idea; and I rejoiced to find the same rejection in the faith of our spiritual mother, Your Catholic Church. But what else to think You I did not know.

As a man, though so poor a man, I set myself to think of You as the supreme and sole and true God; and with all my heart I believed You incorruptible and inviolable and immutable, for though I did not see whence or how, yet I saw with utter certainty that what can be corrupted is lower than what cannot be corrupted, that the inviolable is beyond question better than the violable, and that what can suffer no change is better than what can be changed. My heart cried out passionately against all my imaginings; and I tried with this one truth to beat away all that circling host of uncleannesses from the eyes of my mind. But they were scarce gone for the space of a single glance. They came again close packed upon me, pressed upon my gaze and so clouded it that though I did not even then think of You under the shape of a human body, yet I could not but think of You as some corporeal substance, occupying all space, whether infused in the world, or else diffused through infinite space beyond the world. Yet even at this I thought of You as incorruptible and inviolable and immutable, and I still saw those as better than corruptible and violable and mutable. But whatever I tried to see as not in space seemed to me to be nothing, absolutely nothing, not even a void: for if a body were taken out of its place and the place remained without any body, whether of earth or water or air or sky, it would still be an empty place, a space-occupying nothingness.

Thus I was so gross of mind—not seeing even myself clearly—that whatever was not extended in space, either diffused or massed together or swollen out or having some such qualities or at least capable of having them, I thought must be nothing whatsoever. My mind was in search of such images as the forms my eye was accustomed to see; and I did not realize that the mental act by which I formed these images, was not itself a bodily image: yet it could not have formed them, unless it were something and something great. I conceived of You, Life of my life, as mighty everywhere and throughout infinite space, piercing through the whole mass of the world, and spread measureless and limitless every way beyond the world, so that the earth should have You and the sky should have You and all things should have You, and that they should be bounded in You but You nowhere bounded. For as the body of the air, which is above the earth, does not hinder the sun's light from passing through it, and that light penetrates it, yet does not break it or cut it but fills it wholly: so I thought that the body not only of the sky and air and sea but of the earth also was penetrable by You and easily to be pierced in all its parts, great and small, for the receiving of Your presence, while Your secret inspiration governed inwardly and outwardly all the things You had created.

This I held because I could think of nothing else. But it was false. For if it were so, a greater part of the earth would have contained a greater part of You, and a lesser a lesser; and all things should be filled with You in such a way that the body of an elephant should contain more of You than the body of a sparrow simply because it is larger and takes up so much more room; and so You would make Your parts present in the parts of the world piece by piece, little pieces in the little pieces, great masses in the great masses. That of course is not the truth of it. But You had not as yet enlightened my darkness.

II

But against the Manichees who deceived others because they were deceived themselves, and whose speech was dumbness because Your word did not sound from them, that argument was sufficient which long before, as far back as our Carthage days, had been proposed by Nebridius. I remember that when we heard it we were all powerfully struck by it. What would that imaginary brood of Darkness, which the Manichees were wont to set up as an opposing substance, have done against You if You had refused to fight with it. For if the answer was that it would have done You some damage, that would have been to make You violable and subject to corruption. But if the answer was that it could in no way have harmed You, then they would show no reason for Your fighting with it. But it was precisely the result of Your fighting that some part or member of You, some offspring of Your substance, was mingled with those contrary powers, those natures not created by You; and was so far corrupted by them and changed for the worse as to be turned from beatitude into misery and to need assistance to deliver it and make it clean. This was the human soul. It was enslaved, contaminated and corrupted; and to its aid came Your Word in its freedom and purity and integrity. But that Word was itself corruptible, because it was from one and the same substance [as the soul]. Thus if they affirmed You, whatever You are—that is Your substance by which You are—to be incorruptible, all these ideas of theirs must be false and execrable; but if they affirm You corruptible, that would on the face of it be false and to be abominated. Therefore this argument of Nebridius was sufficient against these men, and I should utterly have vomited them up from my overcharged breast, because they had no way of escape, without horrible sacrilege of heart and tongue, from what they held and said of You.

III

But though I said and firmly held that the Lord God was incorruptible and unalterable and in no way changeable, the true God who made not only our souls but our bodies also, and not only our souls and bodies but all things whatsoever, as yet I did not see, clear and unravelled, what was the cause of Evil. Whatever that cause might be, I saw that no explanation would do which would force me to believe the immutable God mutable; for if I did that I should have been the very thing I was trying to find [namely a cause of evil]. From now it was with no anxiety that I sought it, for I was sure that what the Manichees said was not true. With all my heart I rejected them, because I saw that while they inquired as to the source of evil, they were full of evil themselves, in that they preferred rather to hold that Your substance suffered evil than that their own substance committed it.

So I set myself to examine an idea I had heard—namely that our free-will is the cause of our doing evil, and Your just judgment the cause of our suffering evil. I could not clearly discern this. I endeavoured to draw the eye of my mind from the pit, but I was again plunged into it; and as often as I tried, so often was I plunged back. But it raised me a little towards Your light that I now was as much aware that I had a will as that I had a life. And when I willed to do or not do anything, I was quite certain that it was myself and no other who willed, and I came to see that the cause of my sin lay there.

But what I did unwillingly, it still seemed to me that I rather suffered than did, and I judged it to be not my fault but my punishment: though as I held You most just, I was quite ready to admit that I was being justly punished.

But I asked further: "Who made me? Was it not my God, who is not only Good but Goodness itself? What root reason is there for my willing evil and failing to will good, which would make it just for me to be punished? Who was it that set and ingrafted in me this root of bitterness, since I was wholly made by my most loving God? If the devil is the author, where does the devil come from? And if by his own perverse will he was turned from a good angel into a devil, what was the origin in him of the perverse will by which he became a devil, since by the all-good Creator he was made wholly angel?" By such thoughts I was cast down again and almost stifled; yet I was not brought down so far as the hell of that error, where no man confesses unto You, the error which holds rather that You suffer evil than that man does it.

IV

I now tried to discover other truths, as I had already come to realise that incorruptible is better than corruptible, so that You must be incorruptible, whatever might be Your nature. For no soul ever has been able to conceive or ever will be able to conceive anything better than You, the supreme and perfect Good. Therefore since the incorruptible is unquestionably to be held greater than the corruptible—and I so held it—I could now draw the conclusion that unless You were incorruptible there was something better than my God. But seeing the superiority of the incorruptible, I should have looked for You in that truth and have learned from it where evil is—that is learned the origin of the corruption by which Your substance cannot be violated. For there is no way in which corruption can affect our God, whether by His will or by necessity or by accident: for He is God, and what He wills is good, and Himself is Goodness; whereas to be corrupted is not good. Nor are You against Your will constrained to anything, for Your will is not greater than Your power. It would be greater, only if You were greater than Yourself: for God's will and God's power are alike God Himself. And what unlooked-for accident can befall You, since You know all things? No nature exists save because You know it. Why indeed should I multiply reasons to show that the substance which is God is not corruptible, since if it were, it would not be God?

V

I sought for the origin of evil, but I sought in an evil manner, and failed to see the evil that there was in my manner of enquiry. I ranged before the eyes of my mind the whole creation, both what we are able to see—earth and sea and air and stars and trees and mortal creatures; and what we cannot see—like the firmament of the Heaven above, and all its angels and spiritual powers: though even these I imagined as if they were bodies disposed each in its own place. And I made one great mass of God's Creation, distinguished according to the kinds of bodies in it, whether they really were bodies, or only such bodies as I imagined spirits to be. I made it huge, not as huge as it is, which I had no means of knowing, but as huge as might be necessary, though in every direction finite. And I saw You, Lord, in every part containing and penetrating it, Yourself altogether infinite: as if Your Being were a sea, infinite and immeasurable everywhere, though still only a sea: and within it there were some mighty but not infinite sponge, and that sponge filled in every part with the immeasurable sea. Thus I conceived Your Creation as finite, and filled utterly by Yourself, and You were Infinite. And I said: "Here is God, and here is what God has created; and God is good, mightily and incomparably better than all these; but of His goodness He created them good: and see how He contains and fills them.

"Where then is evil, and what is its source, and how has it crept into the Creation? What is its root, what is its seed? Can it be that it is wholly without being? But why should we fear and be on guard against what is not? Or if our fear of it is groundless, then our very fear is itself an evil thing. For by it the heart is driven and tormented for no cause; and that evil is all the worse, if there is nothing to fear yet we do fear. Thus either there is evil which we fear, or the fact that we fear is evil.

"Whence then is evil, since God who is good made all things good? It was the greater and supreme Good who made these lesser goods, but Creator and Creation are alike good. Whence then comes evil? Was there perhaps some evil matter of which He made this creation, matter which He formed and ordered, while yet leaving in it some element which He did not convert into good? But why? Could He who was omnipotent be unable to change matter wholly so that no evil might remain in it? Indeed why did He choose to make anything of it and not rather by the same omnipotence cause it wholly not to be? Could it possibly have existed against His will? And if it had so existed from eternity, why did He allow it so long to continue through the infinite spaces of time past, and then after so long a while choose to make something of it? If He did suddenly decide to act, surely the Omnipotent should rather have caused it to cease to be, that He Himself, the true and supreme and infinite Good, alone should be. Or, since it was not good that He who was good should frame and create something not good, could He not have taken away and reduced to nothing that matter which was evil, and provided good matter of which to create all things? For He would not be omnipotent if He could not create something good without the aid of matter which He had not created."

Such thoughts I revolved in my unhappy heart, which was further burdened and gnawed at by the fear that I should die without having found the truth. But at least the faith of Your Christ, Our Lord and Saviour, taught by the Catholic Church, stood firm in my heart, though on many points I was still uncertain and swerving from the norm of doctrine. Yet my mind did not forsake it, but drank of it more deeply with every day that passed.

VI

By now I had rejected the ridiculous prophesyings and blasphemous follies of the astrologers. Let Your own mercies, O my God, confess to You from the very depths of my soul. For who else recalls us from the death that all error is, except the Life which cannot die, and the Wisdom which illumines the minds that need it and needs no illumination from any other, by which the world is governed even to the wind-blown leaves of the trees? It was You then who provided the cure for the obstinacy with which I argued with Vindicianus, an old man of great mental acuteness, and with Nebridius a young man of very fine soul. Vindicianus maintained with great vehemence, Nebridius not quite so vehemently but repeatedly, that there was no art for foreseeing the future, but that human guesses sometimes chanced to fall out right: those who said a great deal would often say things that did in fact come to pass, although those who said them did not really know, but merely happened to say them in the course of saying so many things. Then by Your provision came a man to help me in this matter, one who was a fairly frequent consulter of the astrologers. He was not himself skilled in the art, but as I have said he followed it up with some curiosity. One thing he did know, which he said that he had heard from his father: but he did not realize how utterly destructive it was to any belief in their

art. This man, Firminus by name, an educated man and trained
in Rhetoric, consulted me as one very dear to him concerning certain
affairs of his own in which he placed very considerable worldly hopes,
wishing to know how I thought his constellations, as the astrologers call them, stood in the matter. I had now begun to turn towards
Nebridius' opinion, yet for all my own uncertainty I did not absolutely refuse to read the stars and tell him what I saw; but I added
that I was practically persuaded that the whole business was an
empty folly. Thereupon he told me that his father had been deeply
interested in the books of the astrologers and had had a friend as
keen as himself in studying them. They studied and conferred together upon these follies each with the same burning zeal: they
observed the moments at which the dumb animals about their houses
brought forth their young, and noted the position of the sky at those
moments, by way of getting experience in the art. And he said that
he had heard from his father that when his mother was pregnant
with him [Firminus], a female slave belonging to his father's friend
happened to be pregnant at the same time. This her master could
not be unaware of since he took such minute care to know about
the whelping of his very dogs. The friends had numbered the days
and hours and even the smallest parts of the hours, the one for his
wife and the other for his servant, with the most careful observation. And it chanced that both women brought forth their child at
the same instant. Thus they were compelled to cast the very same
horoscope even to the exact minute for both children, the one for
his son, the other for his slave. For when the women began to be
in labor, each man let the other know what was happening in his
own house, and they had messengers ready to send to each other
as soon as either should know that the child had been born—and
each of course would know instantly, since it was happening in his
own household; and the messengers sent by each, so my friend
said, met at a point equidistant from both houses, so that neither
could observe any position of the stars or any moment of time different from the other. Yet Firminus, born to wealth in his parents'
house, trod the pleasanter ways of life, grew in riches and was raised
to positions of honour; whereas the slave did not find the yoke of his
condition relaxed, but served his masters. So Firminus who knew
him told me.

I heard all this, and I believed it, because of the man who told
it. All my doubt was resolved and fell away. First I tried to win
Firminus from his interest, by telling him that if I had had to consult his stars and truly foretell his future, I should surely have had
to see in his horoscope that his parents had been people of standing

in their neighborhood, that his family was noble in his own city, that he was born free, that he was to have a sound education in the liberal arts. Whereas if the slave had consulted me upon the same constellations, for they were the very same, and asked me to foretell him the truth, then I ought to have seen in them that his family was low-born, his condition servile, and all sorts of other particulars very different and very far removed from the first child's. Thus looking at the same constellations I must utter different things if I were to tell the truth, and if I said the same things I should be foretelling falsely. Thus I saw it as obvious that such things as happened to be said truly from the casting of horoscopes were true not by skill but by chance; and such things as were false were not due to want of skill in the art but merely that luck had fallen the other way.

Having started upon this line of reasoning I began to consider what I should answer if any one of those fools who got their living by astrology and whom I was already longing to assail and overwhelm with ridicule, should simply reply that either Firminus had told me, or his father had told him, falsely: so I set myself to considering the case of those who are born twins, who usually emerge from the womb so close to each other that the small interval of time involved—however much influence they claim that it has in nature—cannot be estimated by any human observation so as to be set down in the tables which the astrologer has to inspect in order to pronounce the truth. It will not be the truth. For instance anyone inspecting those tables would have had to foretell the same future for Esau and Jacob, but the same things did not happen to them. Therefore he would either have had to foretell falsely, or else if he foretold truly then he would have had to see different things in the same horoscope. So again we see that any truth he spoke would have been by chance not skill. For You, O Lord, the most just ruler of the universe can so act by Your secret influence upon both those who consult and those who are consulted—neither of them knowing what they do—that when a man consults he hears what it behooves him to hear, given the hidden merits of souls, from the abyss of Your just judgment. Let no man say to You: What is this or why is this? He must not say it, he must not say it. For he is a man.

VII

Thus, O God my aid, from those chains You had freed me. But I was still seeking what might be the source of evil and I could see no answer. Yet with all the ebb and flow of my thought You did not let me be carried away from the faith by which I believed that You were, and that Your substance was unchangeable, and that You cared for men and would judge them; and that in Christ Your Son Our Lord, and in the Holy Scriptures which the authority of Your Catholic Church acknowledges, You had established the way of man's salvation unto that life which is to be after death. But with these truths held safe and inviolably rooted in my mind, I was still on fire with the question whence comes evil. What were the agonies, what the anguish of my heart in labour, O my God!

But though I knew it not, You were listening. And when in silence I sought so vehemently, the voiceless contritions of my soul were strong cries to Your mercy. You knew what I was suffering and no man knew it. For how little it was that my tongue uttered of it in the ears even of my closest friends! Could they hear the tumult of my soul, for whose utterance no time or voice of mine would have been sufficient? Yet into Your hearing came all that I cried forth in the anguish of my heart, and my desire was in Your sight, and the light of my eyes shone not for me. For that light was within, I looking outward. Nor was that light in space: but I was intent upon things that are contained in space, and in them I found no place to rest. The things of space neither so received me that I could say "It is enough, it is well," nor yet allowed me to return where I might find sufficiency and well-being. They were not good enough for me, I was not good enough for You: You are my true joy, and I am subject to You, and You have made subject to me the things below me that You have created. This was the right order and the middle way of salvation for me, that I should remain in Your image, and so in You should dominate my body. But when I rose against You in my pride and *ran upon my Lord with the thick neck of my shield,* those lower things became greater than I and pressed me under so that I could neither loosen their grip nor so much as breathe. Wherever I looked they bore in upon me, massed thick; and when I tried to think, the images of corporeal things barred me from turning back towards the truth, as though they said: "Where are you going, base and unclean?" All these things had grown out of my wound, for You humble the proud like one wounded; and I was separated from You by my own swollenness, as though my cheeks had swelled out and closed up my eyes.

VIII

But You, O Lord, abide forever, nor are You angry with us forever, for You have pity upon our dust and ashes. It was pleasing in Your sight to reshape what was deformed in me. And You kept stirring me with Your secret goad so that I should remain unquiet until You should become clear to the gaze of my soul. And from the secret hand of Your healing my swollenness abated, and the troubled and darkened sight of my mind was daily made better by the stinging ointment of sorrow.

IX

And first you willed to show me how You resist the proud and give grace to the humble, and with how great mercy You have shown men the way of humility in that the Word was made flesh and dwelt among men. Therefore You brought in my way by means of a certain man—an incredibly conceited man—some books of the Platonists translated from Greek into Latin. In them I found, though not in the very words, yet the thing itself and proved by all sorts of reasons: that *in the beginning was the Word and the Word was with God and the Word was God: the same was in the beginning with God; all things were made by Him and without him was made nothing that was made; in Him was life and the life was the light of men, and the light shines in darkness and the darkness did not comprehend* it. And I found in those same writings that the soul of man, though *it gives testimony of the light, yet is not itself the light;* but the Word, God Himself, is *the true light which enlightens every man that comes into this world; and that He was in the world and the world was made by Him, and the world knew Him not.* But I did not read in those books that *He came unto His own, and His own received Him not, but to as many as received Him He gave power to be made the sons of God, to them that believed in His name.*

Again I found in them that the Word, God, was *born not of flesh nor of blood, nor of the will of man nor of the will of the flesh, but of God;* but I did not find that *the Word became flesh.*

I found it stated, differently and in a variety of ways, that the Son *being in the form of the Father thought it not robbery to be equal with God,* because by nature He was God. But these books did not tell me that *He emptied Himself, taking the form of a servant, being made in the likeness of men, and in habit found as a man;* or that *He humbled Himself becoming obedient unto death, even to the death of the cross; for which cause God also hath exalted Him from the dead and given Him a name which is above all names, that in the name of Jesus every knee should bow of those that are in heaven, on earth, and under the earth; and that every tongue should confess that the Lord Jesus is in the glory of God the Father.*

Further I read there that Your only-begotten Son was before all

times and beyond all times and abides unchangeably, co-eternal with
You, and that *of His fullness souls receive*, that they may be blessed,
and that by participation in that wisdom which abides in them they
are renewed that they may be wise. But I did not read that *in due
time He died for the ungodly*, and that *Thou didst not spare Thy
only-begotten Son but delivered Him up for us all*. For *Thou hast
hid these things from the wise and hast revealed them to little ones,*
that *those who labor and are burdened should come to Him and He
should refresh them, because He is meek and humble of heart;* and
*the meek He directs in judgement, and the gentle He teaches His
ways, beholding our lowness and our trouble and forgiving all our
sins*. But those who wear the high boots of their sublimer doctrine
do not hear Him saying: *Learn of me for I am meek and humble of
heart and you shall find rest for your souls;* and *if they know God,
they have not glorified him as God or given thanks: but become vain
in their thoughts; and their foolish heart is darkened. Professing
themselves to be wise they become fools.*

Again I read in these books that they had *changed the glory of
Thy incorruption* into idols and divers images, *into the likeness of
the image of a corruptible man and of birds, and of four-footed
beasts, and of creeping things*—in fact into that Egyptian food for
which Esau had lost his birthright, since the people which was
Your firstborn worshipped the head of a four-footed beast instead
of You, turning in their heart back towards Egypt and bowing down
their soul, Your image, before the image of a calf that eats hay. I
found these things there and I did not feed upon them. For it
pleased You, O Lord, to take away the reproach of inferiority from
Jacob, so that the elder brother served the younger: and You have
called the Gentiles into Your inheritance. From the Gentiles indeed
I had come to You; and I fixed my mind upon the gold which You
willed that Your people should bring with them from Egypt: for
it was Yours, wherever it was. And You had said to the Athenians by
Your apostle that in You we live and move and are; as certain of
their own writers had said; and obviously it was from Athens that
these books came. But I did not fix my mind upon the idols of the
Egyptians which they served with the gold that was Yours, *changing
the truth of God into a lie and worshipping and serving a creature
rather that the Creator.*

X

Being admonished by all this to return to myself, I entered into
my own depths, with You as guide; and I was able to do it because

You were my helper. I entered, and with the eye of my soul, such as it was, I saw Your unchangeable Light shining over that same eye of my soul, over my mind. It was not the light of everyday that the eye of flesh can see, nor some greater light of the same order, such as might be if the brightness of our daily light should be seen shining with a more intense brightness and filling all things with its greatness. Your Light was not that, but other, altogether other, than all such lights. Nor was it above my mind as oil above the water it floats on, nor as the sky is above the earth; it was above because it made me, and I was below because made by it. He who knows the truth knows that Light, and he that knows the Light knows eternity. Charity knows it. O eternal truth and true love and beloved eternity! Thou art my God, I sigh to Thee by day and by night. When first I knew Thee, Thou didst lift me up so that I might see that there was something to see, but that I was not yet the man to see it. And Thou didst beat back the weakness of my gaze, blazing upon me too strongly, and I was shaken with love and with dread. And I knew that I was far from Thee in the region of unlikeness, as if I heard Thy voice from on high: "I am the food of grown men: grow and you shall eat Me. And you shall not change Me into yourself as bodily food, but into Me you shall be changed." And I learned that *Thou hast corrected man for iniquity and Thou didst make my soul shrivel up like a moth.* And I said "Is truth then nothing at all, since it is not extended either through finite spaces or infinite?" And Thou didst cry to me from afar: "I am who am." And I heard Thee, as one hears in the heart; and there was from that moment no ground of doubt in me: I would more easily have doubted my own life than have doubted that truth is: which is *clearly seen, being understood by the things that are made.*

XI

Then I thought upon those other things that are less than You, and I saw that they neither absolutely are nor yet totally are not: they are, in as much as they are from You: they are not, in as much as they are not what You are. For that truly is, which abides unchangeably. But *it is good for me to adhere to my God,* for if I abide not in Him, I cannot abide in myself. But He, in abiding in Himself, renews all things: and *Thou art my God for Thou hast no need of my goods.*

XII

And it became clear to me that corruptible things are good: if they were supremely good they could not be corrupted, but also if they were not good at all they could not be corrupted: if they were supremely good they would be incorruptible, if they were in no way good there would be nothing in them that might corrupt. For corruption damages; and unless it diminished goodness, it would not damage. Thus either corruption does no damage, which is impossible or—and this is the certain proof of it—all things that are corrupted are deprived of some goodness. But if they were deprived of all goodness, they would be totally without being. For if they might still be and yet could no longer be corrupted, they would be better than in their first state, because they would abide henceforth incorruptibly. What could be more monstrous than to say that things could be made better by losing all their goodness? If they were deprived of all goodness, they would be altogether nothing: therefore as long as they are, they are good. Thus whatsoever things are, are good; and that evil whose origin I sought is not a substance, because if it were a substance it would be good. For either it would be an incorruptible substance, that is to say, the highest goodness; or it would be a corruptible substance, which would not be corruptible unless it were good. Thus I saw and clearly realized that You have made all things good, and that there are no substances not made by You. And because all the things You have made are not equal, they have a goodness [over and above] as a totality: because they are good individually, and they are very good all together, for our God has made all things very good.

XIII

To You, then, evil utterly is not—and not only to You, but to Your whole creation likewise, evil is not: because there is nothing over and above Your Creation that could break in or derange the order that You imposed upon it. But in certain of its parts there are some things which we call evil because they do not harmonize with other things; yet these same things do harmonize with still others and thus are good; and in themselves they are good. All these things which do not harmonize with one another, do suit well with that lower part of creation which we call the earth, which has its cloudy and windy sky in some way apt to it. God forbid that I should say: "I wish that these things were not"; because even if I saw only them, though I should want better things, yet even for them alone I should praise You: for that You are to be praised, things of earth show—*dragons, and all deeps, fire, hail, snow, ice, and stormy winds, which fulfill Thy word; mountains and all hills, fruitful trees and all cedars; beasts and all cattle, serpents and feathered fowl; kings of the earth and all*

*people, princes and all judges of the earth; young men and maidens,
old men and young, praise Thy name.* And since from the heavens,
O our God, *all Thy angels praise Thee in the high places, and all
Thy hosts, sun and moon, all the stars and lights, the heavens of
heavens, and the waters that are above the heavens, praise thy name*
—I no longer desired better, because I had thought upon them all
and with clearer judgement I realized that while certain higher
things are better than lower things, yet all things together are better
than the higher alone.

XIV

There is no sanity in those whom anything in creation displeases,
any more than there was in me when I was displeased with many
things that You had made. Because my soul did not dare to be displeased with my God, it would not allow that what displeased it
was Yours. Thus it strayed off into the error of holding two substances, and it found no rest but talked wildly. Turning from that
error it had made for itself a god occupying the infinite measures
of all space, and had thought this god to be You, and had placed it in
its heart, and thus had once again become the temple of its own
idol, a temple abominable to You. But You caressed my head, though
I knew it not, and closed my eyes that they should not see vanity;
and I ceased from myself a little and found sleep from my madness.
And from that sleep I awakened in You, and I saw You infinite in
a different way; but that sight was not with the eyes of flesh.

XV

And I looked upon other things, and I saw that they owed
their being to You, and that all finite things are in You: but
in a different manner, being in You not as in a place, but because
You are and hold all things in the hand of Your truth, and all
things are true inasmuch as they are: nor is falsehood anything,
save that something is thought to be which is not. And I observed
that all things harmonized not only with their places but also with
their times; and that You, who alone are eternal, did not begin to
work after innumerable spaces of time had gone by: since all the
spaces of time, spaces past, spaces to come, could neither go nor
come if You did not operate and abide.

XVI

My own experience had shown me that there was nothing extraordinary in the same bread being loathsome to a sick palate and

agreeable to a healthy, and in light being painful to sore eyes which
is a joy to clear. Your justice displeases the wicked: but so do the
viper and the smaller worms: yet these You have created good, and
suited to the lower parts of Your creation—to which lower parts
indeed the wicked themselves are well suited, insofar as they are
unlike You, though they become suited to the higher parts as they
grow more like You. So that when I now asked what is iniquity, I
realized that it was not a substance but a swerving of the will which
is turned towards lower things and away from You, O God, who
are the supreme substance: so that it casts away what is most inward
to it and swells greedily for outward things.

XVII

And I marvelled to find that at last I loved You and not some
phantom instead of You; yet I did not stably enjoy my God, but was
ravished to You by Your beauty, yet soon was torn away from You
again by my own weight, and fell again with torment to lower things.
Carnal habit was that weight. Yet the memory of You remained
with me and I knew without doubt that it was You to whom I should
cleave, though I was not yet such as could cleave to You: *for the corruptible body is a load upon the soul, and the earthly habitation
presses down the mind that muses upon many things.* I was altogether certain that Your *invisible things are clearly seen from the
creation of the world, being understood by the things that are made:*
so too are Your everlasting power and Your Godhead. I was now
studying the ground of my admiration for the beauty of bodies,
whether celestial or of earth, and on what authority I might rightly
judge of things mutable and say: "This ought to be so, that not so."
Enquiring then what was the source of my judgement, when I did
so judge I had discovered the immutable and true eternity of truth
above my changing mind. Thus by stages I passed from bodies to the
soul which uses the body for its perceiving, and from this to the
soul's inner power, to which the body's senses present external things,
as indeed the beasts are able; and from there I passed on to the
reasoning power, to which is referred for judgement what is received
from the body's senses. This too realised that it was mutable in me,
and rose to its own understanding. It withdrew my thought from
its habitual way, abstracting from the confused crowds of fantasms
that it might find what light suffused it, when with utter certainty
it cried aloud that the immutable was to be preferred to the mutable,
and how it had come to know the immutable itself: for if it had not
come to some knowledge of the immutable, it could not have known

it as certainly preferable to the mutable. Thus in the thrust of a trembling glance my mind arrived at That Which Is. Then indeed I saw clearly Your *invisible things which are understood by the things that are made;* but I lacked the strength to hold my gaze fixed, and my weakness was beaten back again so that I returned to my old habits, bearing nothing with me but a memory of delight and a desire as for something of which I had caught the fragrance but which I had not yet the strength to eat.

XVIII

So I set about finding a way to gain the strength that was necessary for enjoying You. And I could not find it until I embraced the *Mediator between God and man, the man Christ Jesus, who is over all things, God blessed forever,* who was calling unto me and saying: *I am the Way, the Truth, and the Life;* and who brought into union with our nature that Food which I lacked the strength to take: for *the Word was made flesh* that Your Wisdom, by which You created all things, might give suck to our souls' infancy. For I was not yet lowly enough to hold the lowly Jesus as my God, nor did I know what lesson His embracing of our weakness was to teach. For Your Word, the eternal Truth, towering above the highest parts of Your creation, lifts up to Himself those that were cast down. He built for Himself here below a lowly house of our clay, that by it He might bring down from themselves and bring up to Himself those who were to be made subject, healing the swollenness of their pride and fostering their love: so that their self-confidence might grow no further but rather diminish, seeing the deity at their feet, humbled by the assumption of our coat of human nature: to the end that weary at last they might cast themselves down upon His humanity and rise again in its rising.

XIX

But I realised none of this at that time. I thought of Christ my Lord as of a man of marvellous wisdom, whom no other could possibly equal; and I saw his miraculous birth from a virgin—with the example it gave that temporal things are to be despised for the sake of immortality—as a mark of divine care for us, which surely merited for Him complete authority as our master. But the mystery contained in the truth that the Word was made flesh, I could not even faintly glimpse. From what had come down in writing about him—that he ate and drank, slept, walked, was glad, was sad, preached—I had

gathered that his body did not cleave to Your Word save through
a human mind and soul. This anyone knows who grasps the immutability of Your Word, as I now grasped it in my own fashion and
indeed held it unwaveringly. For at one moment to be moving the
limbs by the will, at another keeping them still; now feeling some
particular emotion, now not feeling it; now uttering wisdom in
human speech, now silent—all these are properties of a mutable soul
and a mutable mind. If Scripture told falsely of Christ on this matter,
all of it would be involved in the peril of falsehood, and there would
be no sure faith for mankind left in it. Taking then what was
written there as truth, I saw Christ as complete man: not the body
of a man only, or an animating soul without a rational mind, but
altogether man; and I thought he was to be preferred to all others
not as the very Person of Truth but because of the great excellence of
his human nature and his more perfect participation in wisdom.

Alypius, on the other hand, imagined that Catholics believed
that in Christ God was clothed in flesh—meaning that there was
the godhead and a body in Him, but no soul. He thought they
held that He had not a human mind. And since it seemed quite clear
to him that what had been handed down to us concerning Christ
could not have been done save by a creature both vital and rational,
he was slower in his movement towards the Christian faith itself. But
once he realized that this was the error of the Apollinarian heretics, he
liked the Catholic faith better and accepted it. But I admit that it was
only some time later that I learned how, in the truth that the Word
was made flesh, Catholic doctrine is distinguished from the error of
Photinus. In fact the refutation of heretics serves to bring into
clearer light what Your church holds and what sound doctrine is.
*For there must be also heresies: that they who are approved may be
made manifest among the weak.*

XX

Now that I had read the books of the Platonists and had been set
by them towards the search for a truth that is incorporeal, I came
to see Your *invisible things which are understood by the things that
are made.* I was at a standstill, yet I *felt* what through the darkness
of my mind I was not able actually to see; I was certain that You
are and that You are infinite, but not as being diffused through space
whether finite or infinite: that You truly are and are ever the same,
not in any part or by any motion different or otherwise; and I knew
that all other things are from You from the simple fact that they are
at all. Of these things I was utterly certain, yet I had not the strength

to enjoy You. I talked away as if I knew a great deal; but if I had
not sought the way to You in Christ our Saviour, I would have come
not to instruction but to destruction. For I had begun to wish to
appear wise, and this indeed was the fulness of my punishment; and
I did not weep for my state, but was badly puffed up with my knowledge. Where was that charity which builds us up upon the foundation of humility, which is Christ Jesus? Or when would those books
have taught me that? Yet I think it was Your will that I should come
upon these books before I had made study of the Scriptures, that
it might be impressed on my memory how they had affected me:
so that, when later I should have become responsive to You through
Your Books with my wounds healed by the care of Your fingers, I
might be able to discern the difference that there is between pre-
sumption and confession, between those who see what the goal is
but do not see the way, and [those who see] the Way which leads
to that country of blessedness, which we are meant not only to know
but to dwell in. If I had been first formed by Your Holy Scriptures so that You had grown sweet to me through their familiar
use, and had come later upon these books of the Platonists, they
might have swept me away from the solid ground of piety; and even
if I had remained firm in that disposition which for my health Scripture had taught me, I might perhaps have thought that the same
disposition could have been acquired from those books if a man
studied them alone.

XXI

So now I seized greedily upon the adorable writing of Your Spirit,
and especially upon the apostle Paul. And I found that those difficulties, in which it had once seemed to me that he contradicted
himself and that the text of his discourse did not agree with the
testimonies of the law and the prophets, vanished away. In that
pure eloquence I saw One Face, and I learned to rejoice with trembling. I found that whatever truth I had read in the Platonists was
said here with praise of Your grace: that he who sees should *not so
glory as if he had not received*—and received, indeed, not only what
he sees but even the power to see, *for what has he that he has not
received?* And further, that he [who sees] is not only taught to *see*
You who are always the same, but is also strengthened to take hold of
You; and that he who cannot see You from afar off, may yet walk
on that way by which he may come and see and take hold. For though
a man be *delighted with the law of God according to the inward man,*
what shall he do about that *other law in his members, fighting against*

*the law of his mind and captivating him in the law of sin that is in
his members?* For *Thou art just, O Lord,* but *we have sinned, we
have committed iniquity, we have done wickedly* and Thy hand has
grown heavy upon us and we are justly delivered over to that first
sinner, the ruler of death, because he has turned our will to the
likeness of his will, whereby he stood not in Thy truth. But what
shall unhappy man do? *Who shall deliver him from the body of
this death,* save *the grace of God by Jesus Christ our Lord* whom
Thou hast begotten coeternally with Thee and *possessed in the beginning of Thy ways; in whom the prince of this world found nothing
worthy of death yet killed Him; and the handwriting was blotted
out of the decree which was contrary to us.*

The writings of the Platonists contain nothing of all this. Their
pages show nothing of the face of that love, the tears of confession,
Your sacrifice, an afflicted spirit, a contrite and humbled heart, the
salvation of Your people, the espoused city, the promise of the Holy
Spirit, the chalice of our redemption. In them no one sings: *Shall
not my soul be submitted unto God? From Him is my salvation: for
He is my God, my salvation, and my defense: I shall be no more
moved.* And we hear no voice calling: *Come unto me, all you that
labour.* They scorned to learn from Him, *because He is meek and
humble of heart. For Thou hast hidden these things from the wise
and prudent and hast revealed them to the little ones.* It is one thing
to see the land of peace from a wooded mountaintop, yet not find
the way to it and struggle hopelessly far from the way, with hosts of
those fugitive deserters from God, under their leader the Lion and
the Dragon, besetting us about and ever lying in wait; and quite
another to hold to the way that leads there, a way guarded by the
care of our heavenly General, where there are no deserters from the
army of heaven to practice their robberies—for indeed they avoid
that way as a torment. Marvellously these truths graved themselves
in my heart when I read that latest of Your apostles and looked upon
Your works and trembled.

BOOK EIGHT

AGED THIRTY–ONE

I–IV   *The Conversion of Victorinus*
      I   Augustine hindered from embracing Christ by his sexual passions
     II   Simplicianus tells him of Victorinus' conversion
  III–IV   Why there is special rejoicing over special converts

V–XII   *Augustine's Conversion*
     V   How sexual passion held him
    VI   Ponticianus visits Augustine and Alypius and tells the story of the two officials converted by the Life of St. Antony
   VII   Augustine contrasts himself with these officials
  VIII   He longs to be converted but his will still wavers
   IX   Why does the will not obey the mind's orders?
    X   The Manichees are wrong in thinking such conflicts in the will an evidence of two natures in man
   XI   He almost resolves, but his ancient lusts still solicit him
  XII   The child's voice calling "Take and Read": Romans XIII, 13: he and Alypius resolve upon conversion

I

LET ME, O my God, remember with thanks to Thee and confess Thy mercies upon me. Let my bones be pierced through with Thy love, and let them say: *Who is like unto Thee, O Lord? Thou hast broken my bonds, I will sacrifice to Thee the sacrifice of praise.* How Thou hast broken them I shall tell and all who adore Thee will say as they listen: Blessed be the Lord in heaven and on earth, great and wonderful is His name.

Your words had rooted deep in my heart and I was fenced about on all sides by You. Of Your eternal life I was now certain, though I saw it *in a dark manner and as through a glass.* All my former doubt about an incorruptible substance from which every substance has its being was taken from me. My desire now was not to be more sure of You but more steadfast in You.

But in my temporal life all was uncertain; my heart had to be purged of the old leaven. The way, our Saviour himself, delighted me; but I still shrank from actually walking a way so strait. Then by You it came into my mind, and the idea appealed strongly to me, to go to Simplicianus whom I knew to be Your good servant, for Your grace shone in him. I had heard that from his youth he had lived in great love of You. He was now grown old; and it seemed to me that from a long lifetime spent in so firm a following of Your way he must have experienced much and learned much. And truly so it was. I hoped that if I conferred with him about my problems he might from that experience and learning show me the best way for one affected as I was to walk in Your path.

For I saw the Church full; and one went this way, and one that. But I was unhappy at the life I led in the world, and it was indeed a heavy burden, for the hope of honour and profit no longer inflamed my desire, as formerly, to help me bear so exacting a servitude. These things delighted me no longer in comparison with Your sweetness and the beauty of Your house which I loved. But what still held me tight bound was my need of woman: nor indeed did the apostle forbid me to marry, though he exhorted to a better state, wishing all men to be as he was himself. But I in my weakness was for choosing the softer place, and this one thing kept me from taking a sure line upon others. I was weary and wasted with the cares that were eating into me, all because there were many things which I was unwilling to suffer but had to put up with for the sake of living with a wife, a way of life to which I was utterly bound. I had heard from the mouth of Truth itself that *there are eunuchs who have made themselves eunuchs for the kingdom of heaven;* but Christ had said, *He that can take it, let him take it.* Certainly *all men are vain in whom there is not the knowledge of God and who cannot, by these good things that are seen, find Him that is.* Now I was no longer in that sort of vanity; I had gone beyond it and in the testimony of the whole creation I had found You, our Creator, and Your Word who is with You and one God with You, by whom You created all things. But there is another sort of godlessness, that of the men who *knowing God have not glorified Him as God or given thanks.* Into this also I had fallen, but Your right hand upheld me and taking me out of it, placed me where I might find health. For You have said to man: *Behold, the fear of the Lord is wisdom;* and again: *Be not desirous to seem wise, for those who affirm themselves to be wise become fools.* I had now found the pearl of great price, and I ought to have sold all I had and bought it. But I hesitated still.

II

So I went to Simplicianus, who had begotten Ambrose, now bishop, into Your grace, and whom indeed Ambrose loved as a father. I told him all the wanderings of my error. But when I told him that I had read certain books of the Platonists which had been translated into Latin by Victorinus, one time professor of Rhetoric in Rome—who had, so I heard, died a Christian—he congratulated me for not having fallen upon the writings of other philosophers which are full of vain deceits, according to the elements of this world, whereas in the Platonists God and his Word are everywhere implied. Then to draw me on to the humility of Christ, hidden from the wise and revealed to little ones, he began to speak of Victorinus himself whom he had known intimately when he was in Rome. Of Victorinus he told me what I shall now set down, for the story glorifies Your grace and it should be told to Your glory. For here was an old man deeply learned, trained in all the liberal sciences, a man who had read and weighed so many of the philosophers' writings, the teacher of so many distinguished senators, a man who on account of the brilliance of his teaching had earned and been granted a statue in the Roman forum—an honour the citizens of this world think so great. He had grown old in the worship of idols, had taken part in their sacrilegious rites, for almost all the Roman nobility at that time was enthusiastic for them and was ever talking of "prodigies and the monster gods of every kind, and of the jackal-headed Anubis—who all had once fought against the Roman deities Neptune and Venus and Minerva" and had been beaten: yet Rome was on its knees before these gods it had conquered. All this Victorinus with his thunder of eloquence had gone on championing for so many years even into old age: yet he thought it no shame to be the child of Your Christ, an infant at Your font, bending his neck under the yoke of humility and his forehead to the ignominy of the Cross.

O Lord, Lord, who dost *bow down Thy heavens and descend, dost touch the mountains and they smoke,* by what means didst Thou find thy way into that breast? He read, so Simplicianus said, Holy Scripture; he investigated all the Christian writings most carefully and minutely. And he said not publicly but to Simplicianus privately and as one friend to another: "I would have you know that I am now a Christian." Simplicianus answered: "I shall not believe it nor count you among Christians unless I see you in the Church of Christ." Victorinus asked with some faint mockery: "Then is it the walls that make Christians?" He went on saying that he was a Christian, and Simplicianus went on with the same denial, and Victorinus always repeated his retort about the walls. The fact was that he feared to offend his friends, important people and wor-shippers of these demons; he feared that their enmity might fall heavily upon him from the height of their Babylon-dignity as from the cedars of Lebanon which the Lord had not yet brought down. But when by reading in all earnestness he had drawn strength, he grew afraid that Christ might deny him before His angels if he were ashamed to confess Christ before men. He felt that he was guilty of a great crime in being ashamed of the sacraments of the lowliness of Your Word, when he had not been ashamed of the sacrilegious rites of those demons of pride whom in his pride he had worshipped. So he grew proud towards vanity and humble towards truth. Quite suddenly and without warning he said to Simpli-cianus, as Simplicianus told me: "Let us go to the Church. I wish to be made a Christian." Simplicianus, unable to control his joy, went with him. He was instructed in the first mysteries of the faith, and not long after gave in his name that he might be regenerated by baptism, to the astonishment of Rome and the joy of the Church. The proud saw it and were enraged, ground their teeth and were livid with envy: but the Lord God was the hope of his servant, so that he had no regard for vanities and lying follies.

Finally when the hour had come for his profession of faith—which at Rome was usually made by those who were about to enter into Your grace in a set form of words learned and memorized and spoken from a platform in the sight of the faithful—Simplicianus told me that the priests offered Victorinus to let him make the profession in private, as the custom was with such as seemed likely to find the ordeal embarrassing. But he preferred to make profession of salvation in the sight of the congregation in church. For there had been no salvation in the Rhetoric he had taught, yet he had professed it publicly. Obviously therefore he should be in less fear of Your meek flock when he was uttering Your word, since he had had no fear of the throng of the deluded when uttering his own. When therefore he had gone up to make his profession all those who knew him began whispering his name to one another with congratulatory murmurs. And indeed who there did not know him? And from the lips of the rejoicing congregation sounded the whisper, "Victorinus, Victorinus." They were quick to utter their exultation at seeing him and as quickly fell silent to hear him. He uttered the true faith with glorious confidence, and they would gladly have snatched him to their very heart. Indeed, they did take him to their heart in their love and their joy: with those hands they took him.

III

O loving God, what is it in men that makes them rejoice more for the salvation of a soul that was despaired of or one delivered from a major peril, than if there had always been hope or the peril had been less? Even You, O Merciful Father, rejoice more *upon one sinner doing penance than upon ninety and nine just who need not penance.* It is with special joy that we hear how the lost sheep is brought home upon the exultant shoulders of the shepherd and how the coin is put back into Your treasury while the neighbors rejoice with the woman who found it. And the joy we feel at mass in Your church brings tears as we hear of that younger son who was dead and made alive again, who had been lost and was found. You rejoice in us and in Your angels who stand fast in holy charity. For You are ever the same because You ever know, and in the one way of knowing, all those things which are not always existent nor always the same.

What is it in the soul, I ask again, that makes it delight more to have found or regained the things it loves than if it had always had them? Creatures other than man bear the same witness, and all things are filled with testimonies acclaiming that it is so. The victorious general has his triumph; but he would not have been victorious if he had not fought; and the greater danger there was in the battle, the greater rejoicing in the triumph. The storm tosses the sailors and threatens to wreck the ship; all are pale with the threat of death. But the sky grows clear, the sea calm, and now they are as wild with exultation as before with fear. A friend is sick and his pulse threatens danger; all who want him well feel as if they shared his sickness. He begins to recover, though he cannot yet walk as strongly as of old: and there is more joy than there was before, when he was still well and could walk properly. Note too that men procure the actual pleasures of human life by way of pain—I mean not only the pain that comes upon us unlooked for and beyond our will, but unpleasantness planned and willingly accepted. There is no pleasure in eating or drinking, unless the discomfort of hunger and thirst come before. Drunkards eat salty things to develop a thirst so great as to be painful, and pleasure arises when the liquor quenches the pain of the thirst. And it is the custom that promised brides do not give themselves at once lest the husband should hold the gift cheap unless delay had set him craving.

We see this in base and dishonourable pleasure, but also in the pleasure that is licit and permitted, and again in the purest and most honourable friendship. We have seen it in the case of him who had been dead and was brought back to life, who had been lost and was found. Universally the greater joy is heralded by greater pain. What does this mean, O Lord my God, when Thou art an eternal joy to Thyself, Thou Thyself art joy itself, and things about Thee ever rejoice in Thee? What does it mean that this part of creation thus alternates between need felt and need met, between discord and harmony? Is this their mode of being, this what Thou didst give them, when from the heights of heaven to the lowest earth, from the beginning of time to the end, from the angel to the worm, from the first movement to the last, Thou didst set all kinds of good things and all Thy just works each in its place, each in its season? Alas for me, how high art Thou in the highest, how deep in the deepest! And Thou dost never depart from us, yet with difficulty do we return to Thee.

IV

Come, Lord, work upon us, call us back, set us on fire and clasp us close, be fragrant to us, draw us to Thy loveliness: let us love, let us run to Thee. Do not many from a deeper pit of blindness than Victorinus come back to Thee, enlightened by that light in which they receive from Thee the power to be made Thy sons? But because they are not so well-known, there is less rejoicing over them even by those who do know them. For when many rejoice together, the joy of each one is richer: they warm themselves at each other's flame. Further in so far as they are known widely, they guide many to salvation and are bound to be followed by many. So that even those who have gone before rejoice much on their account, because the rejoicing is not only on their account. It would be shameful if in Your tabernacle the persons of the rich should be welcome before the poor, or the nobly born before the rest: since *Thou hast rather chosen the weak things of the world to confound the strong, and hast chosen the base things of the world and the things that are contemptible, and things that are not, in order to bring to nought things that are.* It was by Paul's tongue that You uttered these words. Yet when Paulus the proconsul came under the light yoke of Christ and became a simple subject of the great King, his pride brought low by the apostle's spiritual might, even that least of Your apostles now desired to be called Paul, in place of his former name of Saul, for the glory of so great a victory. Victory over the enemy is greater when we win from him a man whom he holds more strongly and through whom he holds more people. He has a firmer hold on the eminent by reason of their noble rank, and through them he holds very many people by reason of their authority. Therefore the heart of Victorinus was all the more welcome because the devil had held it as an impregnable fortress; and the tongue of Victorinus because it was a strong sharp weapon with which the devil had slain many. It was right for Your sons to rejoice with more abounding joy because our King had bound the strong man, and they saw his vessels taken from him and cleansed and made available unto Your honour and *profitable to the Lord unto every good work.*

V

Now when this man of Yours, Simplicianus, had told me the story of Victorinus, I was on fire to imitate him: which indeed was why he had told me. He added that in the time of the emperor Julian, when a law was made prohibiting Christians from teaching Literature and Rhetoric, Victorinus had obeyed the law, preferring to give up his own school of words rather than Your word, by which You make eloquent the tongues of babes. In this he seemed to me not only courageous but actually fortunate, because it gave him the chance to devote himself wholly to You. I longed for the same chance, but I was bound not with the iron of another's chains, but by my own iron will. The enemy held my will; and of it he made a chain and bound me. Because my will was perverse it changed to lust, and lust yielded to become habit, and habit not resisted became necessity. These were like links hanging one on another—which is why I have called it a chain—and their hard bondage held me bound hand and foot. The new will which I now began to have, by which I willed to worship You freely and to enjoy You, O God, the only certain Joy, was not yet strong enough to overcome that earlier will rooted deep through the years. My two wills, one old, one new, one carnal, one spiritual, were in conflict and in their conflict wasted my soul.

Thus, with myself as object of the experiment, I came to understand what I had read, how the *flesh lusts against the spirit and the spirit against the flesh.* I indeed was in both camps, but more in that which I approved in myself than in that which I disapproved. For in a sense it was now no longer I that was in this second camp, because in large part I rather suffered it unwillingly than did it with my will. Yet habit had grown stronger against me by my own act, since I had come willingly where I did not now will to be. Who can justly complain when just punishment overtakes the sinner? I no longer had the excuse which I used to think I had for not yet forsaking the world and serving You, the excuse namely that I had no certain knowledge of the truth. By now I was quite certain; but I was still bound to earth and refused to take service in Your army; I feared to be freed of all the things that impeded me, as strongly as I ought to have feared the being impeded by them. I was held down as agreeably by this world's baggage as one often is by sleep; and indeed the thoughts with which I meditated upon You were like the efforts of a man who wants to get up but is so heavy with sleep that he simply sinks back into it again. There is no one who wants to be asleep always—for every sound judgment holds that it is best to be awake—yet a man often postpones the effort of shaking himself awake when he feels a sluggish heaviness in the limbs, and settles pleasurably into another doze though he knows he should not,

because it is time to get up. Similarly I regarded it as settled that it
would be better to give myself to Your love rather than go on yielding to my own lust; but the first course delighted and convinced my
mind, the second delighted my body and held it in bondage. For
there was nothing I could reply when You called me: *Rise, thou
that sleepest and arise from the dead: and Christ shall enlighten thee;*
and whereas You showed me by every evidence that Your words were
true, there was simply nothing I could answer save only laggard
lazy words: "Soon," "Quite soon," "Give me just a little while." But
"soon" and "quite soon" did not mean any particular time; and "just
a little while" went on for a long while. It was in vain that *I delighted in Thy law according to the inner man, when that other
law in my members rebelled against the law of my mind and led me
captive in the law of sin that was in my members.* For the law of sin is
the fierce force of habit, by which the mind is drawn and held even
against its will, and yet deservedly because it had fallen wilfully
into the habit. *Who then should deliver me from the body of this
death, but Thy grace only, through Jesus Christ Our Lord?*

VI

Now, O Lord, my Helper and my Redeemer, I shall tell and
confess to Your name how You delivered me from the chain of that
desire of the flesh which held me so bound, and the servitude of
worldly things. I went my usual way with a mind ever more anxious,
and day after day I sighed for You. I would be off to Your church
as often as my business, under the weight of which I groaned, left
me free. Alypius was with me, at liberty from his legal office after
a third term as Assessor and waiting for private clients, to whom he
might sell his legal advice—just as I sold skill in speaking, if indeed
this can be bought. Nebridius had yielded to our friendship so far
as to teach under Verecundus, a great friend of all of us, a citizen
and elementary school teacher of Milan, who had earnestly asked
and indeed by right of friendship demanded from our company the
help he badly needed. Nebridius was not influenced in the matter
by any desire for profit, for he could have done better had he chosen,
in a more advanced school; but he was a good and gracious friend
and too kindly a man to refuse our requests. But he did it all very
quietly, for he did not want to draw the attention of those persons
whom the world holds great; he thus avoided distraction of mind,
for he wanted to have his mind free and at leisure for as many hours
as possible to seek or read or hear truths concerning wisdom.

On a certain day—Nebridius was away for some reason I cannot recall—there came to Alypius and me at our house one Ponticianus, a fellow countryman of ours, being from Africa, holder of an important post in the emperor's court. There was something or other he wanted of us and we sat down to discuss the matter. As it happened he noticed a book on a gaming table by which we were sitting. He picked it up, opened it, and found that it was the apostle Paul, which surprised him because he had expected that it would be one of the books I wore myself out teaching. Then he smiled a little and looked at me, and expressed pleasure but surprise too at having come suddenly upon that book, and only that book, lying before me. For he was a Christian and a devout Christian; he knelt before You in church, O our God, in daily prayer and many times daily. I told him that I had given much care to these writings. Whereupon he began to tell the story of the Egyptian monk Antony, whose name was held in high honour among Your servants, although Alypius and I had never heard it before that time. When he learned this, he was the more intent upon telling the story, anxious to introduce so great a man to men ignorant of him, and very much marvelling at our ignorance. But Alypius and I stood amazed to hear of Your wonderful works, done in the true faith and in the Catholic Church so recently, practically in our own times, and with such numbers of witnesses. All three of us were filled with wonder, we because the deeds we were now hearing were so great, and he because we had never heard them before.

From this story he went on to the great groups in the monasteries, and their ways all redolent of You, and the fertile deserts of the wilderness, of all of which we knew nothing. There was actually a monastery at Milan, outside the city walls. It was full of worthy brethren and under the care of Ambrose. And we had not heard of it. He continued with his discourse and we listened in absolute silence. It chanced that he told how on one occasion he and three of his companions—it was at Treves, when the emperor was at the chariot races in the Circus—had gone one afternoon to walk in the gardens close by the city walls. As it happened they fell into two groups, one of the others staying with him, and the other two likewise walking their own way. But as those other two strolled on they came into a certain house, the dwelling of some servants of Yours, poor in spirit, of whom is the kingdom of God. There they found a small book in which was written the life of Antony. One of them began to read it, marvelled at it, was inflamed by it. While he was actually reading he had begun to think how he might embrace such a life, and give up his worldly employment to serve You alone. For the two men were both state officials. Suddenly the man who was doing the reading was filled with a love of holiness and angry at himself with righteous shame. He looked at his friend and said to him: "Tell me, please, what is the goal of our ambition in all these labours of ours? What are we aiming at? What is our motive in being in the public service? Have we any higher hope at court than to be friends of the emperor? And at that level, is not everything uncertain and full of perils? And how many perils must we meet on the way to this greater peril? And how long before we are there? But if I should choose to be a friend of God, I can become one now." He said this, and all troubled with the pain of the new life coming to birth in him, he turned back his eyes to the book. He read on and was changed inwardly, where You alone could see; and the world dropped away from his mind, as soon appeared outwardly. For while he was reading and his heart thus tossing on its own flood, at length he broke out in heavy weeping, saw the better way and chose it for his own. Being now Your servant he said to his friend, "Now I have broken from that hope we had and have decided to serve God; and I enter upon that service from this hour, in this place. If you have no will to imitate me, at least do not try to dissuade me."

The other replied that he would remain his companion in so great a service for so great a prize. So the two of them, now Your servants, built a spiritual tower at the only cost that is adequate, the cost of leaving all things and following You. Then Ponticianus and the man who had gone walking with him in another part of the garden came looking for them in the same place, and when they found them suggested that they should return home as the day was now declining. But they told their decision and their purpose, and how that will had arisen in them and was now settled in them; and asked them not to try to argue them out of their decision, even if they would not also join them. Ponticianus and his friend, though not changed from their former state, yet wept for themselves, as he told us, and congratulated them in God and commended themselves to their prayers. Then with their own heart trailing in the dust they went off to the palace, while the other two, with their heart fixed upon heaven, remained in the hut. Both these men, as it happened, were betrothed, and when the two women heard of it they likewise dedicated their virginity to You.

VII

This was the story Ponticianus told. But You, Lord, while he was speaking, turned me back towards myself, taking me from behind

my own back where I had put myself all the time that I preferred
not to see myself. And You set me there before my own face that
I might see how vile I was, how twisted and unclean and spotted
and ulcerous. I saw myself and was horrified; but there was no
way to flee from myself. If I tried to turn my gaze from myself, there
was Ponticianus telling what he was telling; and again You were
setting me face to face with myself, forcing me upon my own sight,
that I might see my iniquity and loathe it. I had known it, but I
had pretended not to see it, had deliberately looked the other way
and let it go from my mind.

But this time, the more ardently I approved those two as I heard
of their determination to win health for their souls by giving themselves up wholly to Your healing, the more detestable did I find myself in comparison with them. For many years had flowed by—a dozen
or more—from the time when I was nineteen and was stirred by
the reading of Cicero's Hortensius to the study of wisdom; and here
was I still postponing the giving up of this world's happiness to
devote myself to the search for that of which not the finding only
but the mere seeking is better than to find all the treasures and
kingdoms of men, better than all the body's pleasures though they
were to be had merely for a nod. But I in my great worthlessness—
for it was greater thus early—had begged You for chastity, saying:
"Grant me chastity and continence, but not yet." For I was afraid
that You would hear my prayer too soon, and too soon would heal
me from the disease of lust which I wanted satisfied rather than extinguished. So I had gone wandering in my sacrilegious superstition
through the base ways of the Manicheans: not indeed that I was
sure they were right but that I preferred them to the Christians,
whom I did not inquire about in the spirit of religion but simply
opposed through malice.

I had thought that my reason for putting off from day to day
the following of You alone to the contempt of earthly hopes was
that I did not see any certain goal towards which to direct my course.
But now the day was come when I stood naked in my own sight
and my conscience accused me: "Why is my voice not heard? Surely
you are the man who used to say that you could not cast off vanity's
baggage for an uncertain truth. Very well: now the truth is certain, yet you are still carrying the load. Here are men who have been
given wings to free their shoulders from the load, though they did
not wear themselves out in searching nor spend ten years or more
thinking about it."

Thus was I inwardly gnawed at. And I was in the grip of the
most horrible and confounding shame, while Ponticianus was telling

his story. He finished the tale and the business for which he had come; and he went his way, and I to myself. What did I not say against myself, with what lashes of condemnation did I not scourge my soul to make it follow me now that I wanted to follow You! My soul hung back. It would not follow, yet found no excuse for not following. All its arguments had already been used and refuted. There remained only trembling silence: for it feared as very death the cessation of that habit of which in truth it was dying.

VIII

In the midst of that great tumult of my inner dwelling place, the tumult I had stirred up against my own soul in the chamber of my heart, I turned upon Alypius, wild in look and troubled in mind, crying out: "What is wrong with us? What is this that you heard? The unlearned arise and take heaven by force, and here are we with all our learning, stuck fast in flesh and blood! Is there any shame in following because they have gone before us, would it not be a worse shame not to follow at once?" These words and more of the same sort I uttered, then the violence of my feeling tore me from him while he stood staring at me thunderstruck. For I did not sound like myself. My brow, cheeks, eyes, flush, the pitch of my voice, spoke my mind more powerfully than the words I uttered. There was a garden attached to our lodging, of which we had the use, as indeed we had of the whole house: for our host, the master of the house, did not live there. To this garden the storm in my breast somehow brought me, for there no one could intervene in the fierce suit I had brought against myself, until it should reach its issue: though what the issue was to be, You knew, not I: but there I was, going mad on my way to sanity, dying on my way to life, aware how evil I was, unaware that I was to grow better in a little while. So I went off to the garden, and Alypius close on my heels: for it was still privacy for me to have him near, and how could he leave me to myself in that state? We found a seat as far as possible from the house. I was frantic in mind, in a frenzy of indignation at myself for not going over to Your law and Your covenant, O my God, where all my bones cried out that I should be, extolling it to the skies. The way was not by ship or chariot or on foot: it was not as far as I had gone when I went from the house to the place where we sat. For I had but to will to go, in order not merely to go but to arrive: I had only to will to go—but to will powerfully and wholly, not to turn and twist a will half-wounded this way and that, with the part that would rise struggling against the part that would keep to the earth.

In the torment of my irresolution, I did many bodily acts. Now men sometimes will to do bodily acts but cannot, whether because they have not the limbs, or because their limbs are bound or weakened with illness or in some other way unable to act. If I tore my hair, if I beat my forehead, if I locked my fingers and clasped my knees, I did it because I willed to. But I might have willed and yet not done it, if my limbs had not had the pliability to do what I willed. Thus I did so many things where the will to do them was not at all the same thing as the power to do them: and I did not do what would have pleased me incomparably more to do—a thing too which I could have done as soon as I willed to, given that willing means willing *wholly*. For in that matter, the power was the same thing as the will, and the willing *was* the doing. Yet it was not done, and the body more readily obeyed the slightest wish of the mind, more readily moved its limbs at the mind's mere nod, than the mind obeyed itself in carrying out its own great will which could be achieved simply by willing.

IX

Why this monstrousness? And what is the root of it? Let Your mercy enlighten me, that I may put the question: whether perhaps the answer lies in the mysterious punishment that has come upon men and some deeply hidden damage in the sons of Adam. Why this monstrousness? And what is the root of it? The mind gives the body an order, and is obeyed at once: the mind gives itself an order and is resisted. The mind commands the hand to move and there is such readiness that you can hardly distinguish the command from its execution. Yet the mind is mind, whereas the hand is body. The mind commands the mind to will, the mind is itself, but it does not do it. Why this monstrousness? And what is the root of it? The mind I say commands itself to will: it would not give the command unless it willed: yet it does not do what it commands. The trouble is that it does not totally will: therefore it does not totally command. It commands in so far as it wills; and it disobeys the command in so far as it does not will. The will is commanding itself to be a will—commanding itself, not some other. But it does not in its fullness give the command, so that what it commands is not done. For if the will were so in its fullness, it would not command itself to will, for it would already will. It is therefore no monstrousness, partly to will, partly not to will, but a sickness of the soul to be so weighted down by custom that it cannot wholly rise even with the support of truth. Thus there are two wills in us, because neither of them is entire: and what is lacking to the one is present in the other.

X

Let them perish from thy presence, O God, as perish vain talkers and seducers of the soul, who observing that there are two wills at issue in our coming to a decision proceed to assert [as the Manichees do] that there are two minds in us of different natures, one good, one evil. For they are evil themselves in holding such evil opinions; and they will become good only if they perceive truth and come to it as your Apostle says to them: *You were heretofore darkness but now light in the Lord.* But these men though they want to be light, want to be light in themselves and not in the Lord, imagining the nature of the soul to be the same as God. Thus they become not light but deeper darkness, since in their abominable arrogance they have gone further from You, *the true Light that enlightens every man that comes into this world.* Take heed what you say and blush for shame: *draw near unto Him and be enlightened, and your faces shall not be ashamed.* When I was deliberating about serving the Lord my God, as I had long meant to do, it was I who willed to do it, I who was unwilling. It was I. I did not wholly will, I was not wholly unwilling. Therefore I strove with myself and was distracted by myself. This distraction happened to me though I did not want it, and it showed me not the presence of some second mind, but the punishment of my own mind. Thus it was not I who caused it but *the sin that dwells in me,* the punishment of a sin freely committed by Adam, whose son I am.

For if there be as many contrary natures in man as there are wills in conflict with one another, then there are not two natures in us but several. Take the case of a man trying to make up his mind whether he would go to the Manichees' meeting-house or to the theatre. The Manichees would say: "Here you have two natures, one good, bringing him to the meeting-house, the other evil, taking him away. How else could you have this wavering between two wills pulling against each other?" Now I say that both are bad, the will that would take him to the Manichees and the will that would take him to the theatre. But they hold that the will by which one comes to them is good. Very well! Supposing one of us is trying to decide and wavering between two wills in conflict, whether to go to the theatre or to *our* church, will not the Manichees be in some trouble about an answer? For either they must admit, which they do not want to, that a good will would take a man to our church as they think it is a good will that brings those who are receivers of their sacrament and belong to them to their church; or they must hold that there are two evil natures and two evil wills at conflict in one man, and what they are always saying will not be true—namely that there is one good will and one evil will. Otherwise, they must be converted to the truth and not deny that when a man is taking a decision there is one soul drawn this way and that by diverse wills.

Therefore, when they perceive that there are two wills in conflict in man, they must not say that there are two opposing minds in conflict, one good, one bad, from two opposing substances and two opposing principles. For You, O God of truth, refute them and disprove them and convict them of error: as in the case where both wills are bad, when, for instance, a man is deliberating whether he shall kill another man by poison or by dagger; whether he should seize this or that part of another man's property, when he cannot seize both; whether he should spend his money on lust or hoard his money through avarice; whether he should go to the games or the theatre if they happen both to come on the same day. Let us add a third possibility to this last man, whether he should go and commit a theft from someone else's house, if the occasion should arise: and indeed a fourth, whether he should go and commit adultery, if the chance occurs at the same time. If all four things come together at the same point of time, and all are equally desired, yet all cannot be done, then they tear the mind by the conflicting pull of four wills—or even more, given the great mass of things which can be desired. Yet the Manichees do not hold such a multitude of different substances.

The same reasoning applies to wills that are good. For I ask them whether it is good to find delight in the reading of the Apostle, and good to find delight in the serenity of a Psalm, and good to discuss the Gospel. To each of these they answer that it is good: but, if all these things attract us at the same moment, are not different wills tugging at the heart of man while we deliberate which we should choose? Thus they are all good, yet they are all in conflict until one is chosen, and then the whole will is at rest and at one, whereas it had been divided into many. Or again, when eternity attracts the higher faculties and the pleasure of some temporal good holds the lower, it is one same soul that wills both, but not either with its whole will; and it is therefore torn both ways and deeply troubled while truth shows the one way as better but habit keeps it to the other.

XI

Thus I was sick at heart and in torment, accusing myself with a new intensity of bitterness, twisting and turning in my chain in the hope that it might be utterly broken, for what held me was so small a thing! But it still held me. And You stood in the secret places of my soul, O Lord, in the harshness of Your mercy redoubling the scourges of fear and shame lest I should give way again and that small slight tie which remained should not be broken but should grow again to full strength and bind me closer even than before. For I kept saying within myself: "Let it be now, let it be now," and by the mere words I had begun to move towards the resolution. I almost made it, yet I did not quite make it. But I did not fall back into my original state, but as it were stood near to get my breath. And I tried again and I was almost there, and now I could all but touch it and hold it: yet I was not quite there, I did not touch it or hold it. I still shrank from dying unto death and living unto life. The lower condition which had grown habitual was more powerful than the better condition which I had not tried. The nearer the point of time came in which I was to become different, the more it struck me with horror; but it did not force me utterly back nor turn me utterly away, but held me there between the two.

Those trifles of all trifles, and vanities of vanities, my one-time mistresses, held me back, plucking at my garment of flesh and murmuring softly: "Are you sending us away?" And "From this moment shall we not be with you, now or forever?" And "From this moment shall this or that not be allowed you, now or forever?" What were they suggesting to me in the phrase I have written "this or that," what were they suggesting to me, O my God? Do you in your mercy keep from the soul of Your servant the vileness and uncleanness they were suggesting. And now I began to hear them not half so loud; they no longer stood against me face to face, but were softly muttering behind my back and, as I tried to depart, plucking stealthily at me to make me look behind. Yet even that was enough, so hesitating was I, to keep me from snatching myself free, from shaking them off and leaping upwards on the way I was called: for the strong force of habit said to me: "Do you think you can live without them?"

But by this time its voice was growing fainter. In the direction

towards which I had turned my face and was quivering in fear of
going, I could see the austere beauty of Continence, serene and indeed joyous but not evilly, honourably soliciting me to come to her
and not linger, stretching forth loving hands to receive and embrace
me, hands full of multitudes of good examples. With her I saw
such hosts of young men and maidens, a multitude of youth and
of every age, gray widows and women grown old in virginity, and
in them all Continence herself, not barren but the fruitful mother
of children, her joys, by You, Lord, her Spouse. And she smiled
upon me and her smile gave courage as if she were saying: "Can
you not do what these men have done, what these women have
done? Or could men or women have done such in themselves, and
not in the Lord their God? The Lord their God gave me to them.
Why do you stand upon yourself and so not stand at all? Cast yourself upon Him and be not afraid; He will not draw away and let
you fall. Cast yourself without fear, He will receive you and heal
you."

Yet I was still ashamed, for I could still hear the murmuring of
those vanities, and I still hung hesitant. And again it was as if she
said: "Stop your ears against your unclean members, that they may
be mortified. They tell you of delights, but not of such delights
as the law of the Lord your God tells." This was the controversy
raging in my heart, a controversy about myself against myself. And
Alypius stayed by my side and awaited in silence the issue of such
agitation as he had never seen in me.

XII

When my most searching scrutiny had drawn up all my vileness
from the secret depths of my soul and heaped it in my heart's sight,
a mighty storm arose in me, bringing a mighty rain of tears. That
I might give way to my tears and lamentations, I rose from Alypius:
for it struck me that solitude was more suited to the business of
weeping. I went far enough from him to prevent his presence from
being an embarrassment to me. So I felt, and he realized it. I suppose I had said something and the sound of my voice was heavy
with tears. I arose, but he remained where we had been sitting, still
in utter amazement. I flung myself down somehow under a certain
fig tree and no longer tried to check my tears, which poured forth
from my eyes in a flood, *an acceptable sacrifice to Thee*. And much
I said not in these words but to this effect: *"And Thou, O Lord, how
long? How long, Lord; wilt Thou be angry forever? Remember not our*

former iniquities." For I felt that I was still bound by them. And I continued my miserable complaining: "How long, how long shall I go on saying tomorrow and again tomorrow? Why not now, why not have an end to my uncleanness this very hour?"

Such things I said, weeping in the most bitter sorrow of my heart. And suddenly I heard a voice from some nearby house, a boy's voice or a girl's voice, I do not know: but it was a sort of sing-song, repeated again and again, "Take and read, take and read." I ceased weeping and immediately began to search my mind most carefully as to whether children were accustomed to chant these words in any kind of game, and I could not remember that I had ever heard any such thing. Damming back the flood of my tears I arose, interpreting the incident as quite certainly a divine command to open my book of Scripture and read the passage at which I should open. For it was part of what I had been told about Antony, that from the Gospel which he happened to be reading he had felt that he was being admonished as though what he read was spoken directly to himself: *Go, sell what thou hast and give to the poor and thou shalt have treasure in heaven; and come follow Me.* By this experience he had been in that instant converted to You. So I was moved to return to the place where Alypius was sitting, for I had put down the Apostle's book there when I arose. I snatched it up, opened it and in silence read the passage upon which my eyes first fell: *Not in rioting and drunkenness, not in chambering and impurities, not in contention and envy, but put ye on the Lord Jesus Christ and make not provision for the flesh in its concupiscences.* [*Romans* xiii, 13.] I had no wish to read further, and no need. For in that instant, with the very ending of the sentence, it was as though a light of utter confidence shone in all my heart, and all the darkness of uncertainty vanished away. Then leaving my finger in the place or marking it by some other sign, I closed the book and in complete calm told the whole thing to Alypius and he similarly told me what had been going on in himself, of which I knew nothing. He asked to see what I had read. I showed him, and he looked further than I had read. I had not known what followed. And this is what followed: *"Now him that is weak in faith, take unto you."* He applied this to himself and told me so. And he was confirmed by this message, and with no troubled wavering gave himself to God's good-will and purpose—a purpose indeed most suited to his character, for in these matters he had been immeasurably better than I.

Then we went in to my mother and told her, to her great joy. We related how it had come about: she was filled with triumphant exultation, and praised You who are mighty beyond what we ask or conceive: for she saw that You had given her more than with all her pitiful weeping she had ever asked. For You converted me to Yourself so that I no longer sought a wife nor any of this world's promises, but stood upon that same rule of faith in which You had shown me to her so many years before. Thus You changed her mourning into joy, a joy far richer than she had thought to wish, a joy much dearer and purer than she had thought to find in grand-children of my flesh.

BOOK NINE

AGED THIRTY–TWO

I–VII   *Reception into the Church*
1 The joy of conversion
II Decision to abandon his professorship of Rhetoric
III Verecundus unhappy, Nebridius happy: both die baptised
IV Vacation in the country; he reads Psalm IV; is cured of toothache
V Ambrose advises him to read Isaias
VI He is baptised with his son Adeodatus and Alypius
VII Of chanting and how Ambrose had brought it to Milan

VIII–XIII *The Death of Monica*
VIII They start back for Africa; account of Monica's child-hood
IX How she lived at peace with her husband and finally won him to Christianity
X The window at Ostia: conversation upon Beatitude
XI Monica dies
XII His grief, and his fear lest his grief may be weakness
XIII He knows she was not sinless but is confident of her salvation: yet he prays for her soul and asks our prayers

I

O LORD, *I am Thy servant: I am Thy servant and the son of Thy handmaid. Thou hast broken my bonds. I will sacrifice to Thee the sacrifice of praise.* Let my heart and my tongue praise Thee, and *let all my bones say, O Lord, who is like to Thee?* Let them say and do Thou answer me and say to my soul: *I am Thy salvation.* Who am I and what kind of man am I? What evil has there not been in my deeds, or if not in my deeds, in my words, or if not in my words, then in my will? But You, Lord, are good and merciful, and Your right hand had regard to the profundity of my death and drew out the abyss of corruption that was in the bottom of my heart. By Your gift I had come totally not to will what I willed but to will what You willed. But where in all that long time was my free will, and from what deep sunken hiding-place was it suddenly summoned forth in the moment in which I bowed my neck to Your easy yoke and my shoulders to Your light burden, Christ Jesus, my Helper and my Redeemer? How lovely I suddenly found it to be free from the loveliness of those vanities, so that now it was a joy to renounce what I had been so afraid to lose. For You cast them out of me, O true and supreme Loveliness, You cast them out of me and took their place in me, You who are sweeter than all pleasure, yet not to flesh and blood; brighter than all light, yet deeper within than any secret; loftier than all honour, but not to those who are lofty to themselves. Now my mind was free from the cares that had gnawed it, from aspiring and getting and weltering in filth and rubbing the scab of lust. And I talked with You as friends talk, my glory and my riches and my salvation, my Lord God.

II

And I thought it would be good in Your sight if I did not dramatically snatch my tongue's service from the speech-market but quietly withdrew; but that in any event withdraw I must, so that youths—not students of Your law or Your peace but of lying follies and the conflicts of the law—should no longer buy at my mouth the tools of their madness. Fortunately it happened that there were only a few

days left before the Vintage Vacation; and I decided to endure them
so that I might leave with due deliberation, seeing that I had been
redeemed by You and was not going to put myself up for sale again.
Our purpose therefore was known to You, but not to men other
than our own friends. We had agreed among ourselves not to spread
the news abroad at all, although, in our ascent from *the valley of
tears* and our singing of the *song of degrees,* You had given us *sharp
arrows* and *burning coals* against *cunning tongues* that might argue
against us with pretended care for our interest, might destroy us
saying that they loved us: as men consume food saying that they
love it.

You had pierced our hearts with the arrow of Your love, and our
minds were pierced with the arrows of Your words. To burn away
and utterly consume our slothfulness so that we might no more be
sunk in its depths, we had the depths of our thought filled with
the examples of Your servants whom You had changed from darkness to light and from death to life; and these inflamed us so
powerfully that any false tongue of contradiction did not extinguish
our flame but set us blazing more fiercely. But because for Your
name, which You have sanctified throughout the earth, our decision
would find many to praise it, I was afraid that it would look like
ostentation if I did not wait for the approaching vacation but immediately resigned from a profession which everyone knew I practiced: for the faces of all about would be turned on my act, in that
I had not chosen to wait for the vacation when it was so close, and
it would be widely said that I had done it to make myself seem important. And what would it have profited me to have people discussing
and arguing about my purpose and to have our good ill-spoken of?

Furthermore that very summer, under the too heavy labor of teaching, my lungs had begun to give way and I breathed with difficulty;
the pain in my breast showed that they were affected and they no
longer let me talk with any strength for too long at a time. At first
this had disturbed me, because it made it practically a matter of necessity that I should lay down the burden of teaching, or at least give
it up for the time if I was to be cured and grow well again. But when
the full purpose of giving myself leisure to meditate on how You
are the Lord arose in me and became a settled resolve—as you know,
O my God—I actually found myself glad to have this perfectly truth-
ful excuse to offer parents who might be offended and for their
children's sake would never willingly have let me give up teaching.
So I was full of joy, and I put up with the space of time that still
had to run—I fancy it was about twenty days. But to bear the time
took considerable fortitude. Desire for money, which formerly had

helped me to bear the heavy labor of teaching, was quite gone; so that I should have [had nothing to help me bear it and so] found it altogether crushing if patience had not taken the place of covetousness. Some of Your servants, my brethren, may think that I sinned in this, since having enrolled with all my heart in Your service, I allowed myself to sit for so much as an hour in the chair of untruthfulness. It may be so. But, most merciful Lord, have You not pardoned and remitted this sin, along with others most horrible and deadly, in the holy water of baptism?

III

Meanwhile Verecundus was worrying himself ill over the good that had come to us. He saw himself losing our company by reason of his own chains, which bound him very tight. He was not yet a Christian, though his wife was, and indeed she was the strongest obstacle of all in the way of his setting out upon that journey on which we had started. For he said that he would not be a Christian in any other way, than the way that was beyond his power. But he very generously offered that as long as we were in the country, we might stay in his house. You will reward him, O Lord, with the reward of the just, for You have already given him the lot of the just. At a time when we were away in Rome he was seized with some bodily illness, and in the course of it became a Christian and was baptized, and so departed this life. Thus you had mercy not only upon him, but upon us too: otherwise, thinking of the wonderful kindness our friend had shown us, we should have been tormented with unbearable sorrow if we had not been able to number him in Your flock. Thanks be to our God! We are Yours, as Your exhortations and consolations prove. You are faithful to Your promises, and you will repay Verecundus for his country house at Cassiciacum, where we rested in You from the world's troubles, with the loveliness and eternal freshness of Your paradise: for You forgave him his sins upon earth in the mountain of abundance, Your mountain, the mountain of richness.

At the time, however, Verecundus was very much perturbed; but Nebridius altogether joyful. For although before he was a Christian he had fallen into that same pit of deadly error and believed the true body of Your Son to be a phantasm, he had emerged from that error; and though he had not yet received any sacraments of Your church, he was a most zealous seeker of the truth. Not long after our conversion and regeneration by Your baptism, You took him from this life, by then a baptized Catholic and serving You in Africa in perfect

chastity among his own people, for he had made his whole family
Christian. And now he lives in Abraham's bosom. Whatever is
meant by that bosom, there my Nebridius lives, my most beloved
friend, Your son by adoption and no longer a freed-man only. There
he lives. For what other place is there for such a soul? There he
lives, in the place of which he asked me, an ignorant poor creature,
so many questions. He no longer puts his bodily ear to my lips, but
the lips of his spirit to Your fountain, drinking his fill of wisdom,
all that his thirst requires, happy without end. Nor do I think he
is so intoxicated with the draught of that wisdom as to forget me,
since You, O Lord, of whom he drinks are mindful of us.

There then we were, consoling the unhappy Verecundus, for our
friendship was not impaired by conversion, and exhorting him to
fidelity in his state, namely the married life. As for Nebridius, we
were merely waiting for him to follow us. He was so close that he
might well follow, and he was indeed on the point of doing so when
at last those days of waiting for the vacation came to an end. For
they seemed long and many to me, because of the longing I had
for that freedom and leisure in which I might sing to You from the
depths of my heart: *My heart hath said to Thee: I have sought Thy
face. Thy face, O Lord, will I still seek.*

IV

And now the day was come on which I was to be set free from the
teaching of Rhetoric in fact, as I was already free in mind. And so
it came about. You delivered my tongue as You had already delivered
my heart, and I rejoiced and praised You, and so went off with my
friends to the country-house. The amount of writing I did there—
the writing was now in your service but during this breathing-space
still smacked of the school of pride—my books exist to witness, with
the record they give of discussions either with my friends there
present or with Yourself when I was alone with You; and there are
my letters to show what correspondence I had with Nebridius while
he was away. But when shall I have the time to relate all Your great
acts of goodness towards me, especially at that time, since I must
hasten to tell of matters greater still?

For my memory reminds me, and pleasant it is, O Lord, to confess
to You, what inner goads you used to tame me, and how you brought
me low, *making low the mountains and hills of my thoughts, making
straight what was crooked, and plain what was rough.* And I remember too how You subdued my heart's brother Alypius to the name of
Jesus Christ Your only-begotten Son, Our Lord and Saviour, which

at first he thought it would be in some sense lowering to put into my writings. For he would have had them redolent of the high cedars of the schools, which the Lord had now broken down, rather than of the health-giving herbs of the Church which are of such avail against the bites of serpents.

When I read the Psalms of David, songs of faithfulness and devotion in which the spirit of pride has no entry, what cries did I utter to You, O my God, I but a novice in your true love, a catechumen keeping holiday in a country-house with that other catechumen Alypius: though my mother also was with us, a woman in sex, with the faith of a man, with the serenity of great age, the love of a mother, the piety of a Christian. What cries did I utter to You in those Psalms and how was I inflamed towards You by them, and on fire to set them sounding through all the world, if I could, against the pride of man! But in truth they are already sung throughout the world and *there is none who can hide himself from Thy heat.* I thought of the Manichees with indignation and a burning anguish of sorrow. I pitied them because they did not know our sacraments and our healing, but were insanely set against the medicine that would have cured their insanity. I wished that they might be somewhere close at hand— without my knowing that they were there—and could see my face and hear my words, when in that time of leisure I read the Fourth Psalm; and that they could see what that Psalm did in me: *When I called upon Thee, Thou, God of my justice, didst hear me; when I was in distress, Thou hast enlarged me: have mercy on me, O Lord, and hear my prayer.* Would that they could have heard me—without my knowing that they heard me, lest they might think it was on their account I was speaking as I spoke when I recited these words: and indeed I would not have said those things or said them in the same way, if I had realized that I was being heard and seen by them: nor, if I *had* said them, would they have understood how I was speaking with myself and to myself in Your presence from the natural movement of my spirit.

I was in fear and horror, and again I was on fire with hope and exultation in your mercy, O Father. And all these emotions found expression in my eyes and in my voice when Your Holy Spirit turned to us and said: *O ye sons of men, how long will ye be dull of heart? Why do you love vanity so much and seek after lying?* For I myself had loved vanity and sought after lying. *And Thou, Lord,* hadst already *made Thy holy one wonderful,* raising Him from the dead and setting Him at Thy right hand, whence He should send from on high His promise, the Paraclete, the Spirit of Truth. And He had already sent Him, though I knew it not. He had sent Him

because already He was magnified and risen from the dead and
ascended into heaven. For till then the Spirit was not yet given,
because Jesus was not yet glorified. And the prophet cried aloud:
*How long will you be dull of heart? Why do you love vanity and
seek after lying? Know ye also that the Lord hath made His holy
one wonderful?* He cries out "How long," he cries out "Know ye."
And I so long was ignorant and loved vanity and sought after
lying.

I heard these things and trembled to hear them, for they were
spoken to such as I remembered myself to have been. For in those
phantasms which I had taken for truth were vanity and lying. And
I cried out many things strongly and earnestly in the grief I felt at
what I remembered. If only those could have heard me who still
loved vanity and sought after lying. Perchance they would have
been troubled, and have vomited up their error; and You would have
heard them when they cried to You: for He who intercedes with
You for us died for us with a true death of the body.

I read, *Be angry and sin not.* And by this I was much moved, O
my God, for I had by then learned to be angry with myself for the
past, that I might not sin in what remained of life: and to be angry
with good reason, because it was not some other nature of the race
of darkness that had sinned in me, as the Manichees say: and they
are not angry at themselves, but treasure up to themselves wrath
against the day of wrath and of the revelation of the just judgement
of God.

The good I now sought was not in things outside me, to be seen
by the eye of flesh under the sun. For those that find their joy outside them easily fall into emptiness and are spilled out upon the
things that are seen and the things of time, and in their starved
minds lick shadows. If only they could grow weary of their own
hunger and say: *Who shall show us good things?* And we should
say and they should hear: *The light of Thy countenance is sealed
upon us,* O Lord. For we are not *the Light that enlightens every man*
but we are enlightened by Thee that *as we were heretofore darkness
we are now light in Thee.* If they could but see the Light interior
and eternal: for now that I had known it, I was frantic that I could
not make them see it even were they to ask: *Who shall show us
good things?* For the heart they would bring me would be in their
eyes, eyes that looked everywhere but at You. But there, where
I had been angry with myself, in my own room where I had been
pierced, where I had offered my sacrifice, slaying the self that I had
been, and, in the newly-taken purpose of newness of life, hoping in
You—there You began to make me feel Your love and to give *gladness*

in my heart. I cried out as I read this aloud and realized it within: and I no longer wished any increase of earthly goods, in which a man wastes time and is wasted by time, since in the simplicity of the Eternal I had other corn and wine and oil.

It was with a deep cry of my heart that I uttered the next verse: *O in peace! O in the selfsame! O* how he has said: *I will sleep and I will rest.* For who shall stand against us *when the saying that is written will come to pass: Death is swallowed up in victory?* You supremely are that selfsame, for You are not changed and in You is that rest in which all cares are forgotten, since there is no other besides You, and we have not to seek other things which are not what You are: but You, Lord, alone have *made me dwell in hope.* All these things I read and was on fire; nor could I find what could be done with those deaf dead, of whom indeed I had myself been one for I had been a scourge, a blind raging snarler against the Scriptures, which are all honeyed with the honey of heaven and all luminous with Your light: and now I was fretting my heart out over the enemies of these same Scriptures.

When shall I recall and set down all that belongs to those days in the country? I have not forgotten, nor shall I pass in silence, the bite of Your scourge and the wonderful swiftness of Your mercy. During those days You sent me the torture of toothache, and when it had grown so agonizing that I could not speak, it came into my heart to ask all my friends there present to pray for me to You, the God of every kind of health. I wrote this down on my tablet and gave it to them to read. As soon as we had gone on our knees in all simplicity, the pain went. But what was the pain or how did it go? I admit that I was terrified, O my Lord, my God, for as far back as my earliest infancy I had never experienced any such thing. Thus in that depth I recognized the act of Your will, and I gave praise to Your name, rejoicing in faith. But this faith would not let me feel safe about my past sins, since Your baptism had not yet come to remit them.

V

When the Vintage Vacation was over I gave the people of Milan notice that they must find someone else to sell the art of words to their students, because I had chosen to serve You, and because owing to my difficulty in breathing and the pain in my lungs I could not continue my teaching. And in a letter I told Your bishop, the holy Ambrose, of my past errors and my present purpose, that he might advise me which of Your Scriptures I should especially read to pre-

pare me and make me more fit to receive so great a grace. He told me
to read Isaias the prophet, I imagine because he more clearly foretells
the gospel and the calling of the gentiles than the other Old Testament writers; but I did not understand the first part of his book,
and thinking that it would be all of the same kind, put it aside meaning to return to it when I should be more practised in the Lord's
way of speech.

VI

When the time had come to give in my name for baptism, we
left the country and returned to Milan. Alypius had decided to be
born again in You at the same time, for he was already endowed
with the humility that Your sacraments require, and had brought
his body so powerfully under control that he could tread the
icy soil of Italy with bare feet, which required unusual fortitude.
We also took with us the boy Adeodatus, carnally begotten by me
in my sin. You had made him well. He was barely fifteen, yet he
was more intelligent than many a grave and learned man. In this
I am but acknowledging to You Your own gifts, O Lord my God,
Creator of all and powerful to reshape our shapelessness: for I had
no part in that boy but the sin. That he had been brought up by
us in Your way was because You had inspired us, no other. I do
but acknowledge to You Your own gifts. There is a book of mine
called De Magistro: it is a dialogue between him and me. You know,
O God, that all the ideas which are put into the mouth of the other
party to the dialogue were truly his, though he was but sixteen. I
had experience of many other remarkable qualities in him. His great
intelligence filled me with a kind of awe: and who but You could be
the maker of things so wonderful? But You took him early from this
earth, and I think of him utterly without anxiety, for there is nothing
in his boyhood or youth or anywhere in him to cause me to fear. We
took him along with us, the same age as ourselves in Your grace, to
be brought up in Your discipline: and we were baptised, and all
anxiety as to our past life fled away. The days were not long enough
as I meditated, and found wonderful delight in meditating, upon
the depth of Your design for the salvation of the human race. I
wept at the beauty of Your hymns and canticles, and was powerfully moved at the sweet sound of Your Church's singing. Those
sounds flowed into my ears, and the truth streamed into my heart:
so that my feeling of devotion overflowed, and the tears ran from
my eyes, and I was happy in them.

VII

It was only a little while before that the church of Milan had begun to practise this kind of consolation and exultation, to the great joy of the brethren singing together with heart and voice. For it was only about a year, or not much more, since Justina, the mother of the boy emperor Valentinian, was persecuting Your servant Ambrose in the interests of her own heresy: for she had been seduced by the Arians. The devoted people had stayed day and night in the church, ready to die with their bishop, Your servant. And my mother, Your handmaid, bearing a great part of the trouble and vigil, had lived in prayer. I also, though still not warmed by the fire of Your Spirit, was stirred to excitement by the disturbed and wrought-up state of the city. It was at this time that the practice was instituted of singing hymns and psalms after the manner of the Eastern churches, to keep the people from being altogether worn out with anxiety and want of sleep. The custom has been retained from that day to this, and has been imitated by many, indeed in almost all congregations throughout the world.

At this time You revealed to Your bishop Ambrose in a vision the place where the bodies of the martyrs Protasius and Gervasius lay hid, which You had for so many years kept incorrupt in the treasury of Your secret knowledge that You might bring them forth at the proper moment to check a woman's fury—the woman being the ruler of the Empire! For when they were discovered and dug up and with due honour brought to Ambrose's basilica, not only were people cured who had been tormented by evil spirits—and the devils themselves forced to confess it—but also there was a man, a citizen well known to the city, who had been blind for many years: he asked what was the cause of the tumultuous joy of the people, and when he heard, he sprang up and asked his guide to lead him into the place. When he arrived there he asked to be allowed to touch with his handkerchief the place on which lay the saints, whose death is precious in Your sight. He did so, put the handkerchief to his eyes, and immediately they were opened. The news spread abroad, Your praises glowed and shone, and if the mind of that angry woman was not brought to the sanity of belief, it was at least brought back from the madness of persecution. Thanks be to my God! From what and towards what have You led my memory, that it should confess to You these great things which I had altogether forgotten? Yet even then, *when the odor of Thy ointments was so sweet smelling,* I did not *run after Thee:* and for this I wept all the more now when

I heard Your hymns and canticles, as one who had then sighed for You and now breathed in You, breathed so far as the air allows in this our house of grass.

VIII

You, Lord, who make men of one mind to dwell in one house brought to our company a young man of our own town, Evodius. He had held office in the civil service, had been converted and baptised before us, had resigned from the state's service, and given himself to Yours. We kept together, meaning to live together in our devout purpose. We thought deeply as to the place in which we might serve You most usefully. As a result we started back for Africa. And when we had come as far as Ostia on the Tiber, my mother died. I pass over many things, for I must make haste. Do You, O my God, accept my confessions and my gratitude for countless things of which I say nothing. But I will not omit anything my mind brings forth concerning her, Your servant, who brought me forth—brought me forth in the flesh to this temporal light, and in her heart to light eternal. Not of her gifts do I speak but of Your gifts in her. For she did not bring herself into the world or educate herself in the world: it was You who created her, nor did her father or mother know what kind of being was to come forth from them. It was the scepter of Your Christ, the discipline of your Only-Begotten, that brought her up in holy fear, in a Catholic family which was a worthy member of Your church. Yet it was not the devotion of her mother in her upbringing that she talked most of, but of a certain aged servant, who had indeed carried my mother's father on her back when he was a baby, as little ones are accustomed to be carried on the backs of older girls. Because of this, because also of her age and her admirable character, she was very much respected by her master and mistress in their Christian household. As a result she was given charge of her master's daughters. This charge she fulfilled most conscientiously, checking them sharply when necessary with holy severity and teaching them soberly and prudently. Thus, except at the times when they ate—and that most temperately—at their parents' table, she would not let them even drink water, no matter how tormenting their thirst. By this she prevented the forming of a bad habit, and she used to remark very sensibly: "Now you drink water because you are not allowed to have wine; but when you are married, and thus mistresses of food-stores and wine-cellars, you will despise water, but the habit of drinking will still remain." By this kind of teaching and the authority of her commands she moderated

the greediness that goes with childhood and brought the little girls'
thirst to such a control that they no longer wanted what they ought
not to have.

Yet, as Your servant told me, her son, there did steal upon my
mother an inclination to wine. For when, in the usual way, she
was sent by her parents, as a well-behaved child, to draw wine from
the barrel, she would dip the cup in, but before pouring the wine
from the cup into the flagon, she would sip a little with the very
tip of her lips, only a little because she did not yet like the taste
sufficiently to take more. Indeed she did it not out of any craving
for wine, but rather from the excess of childhood's high spirits,
which tend to boil over in absurdities, and are usually kept in check
by the authority of elders. And so, adding to that daily drop a little
more from day to day—for he that despises small things, falls little
by little—she fell into the habit, so that she would drink off greedily
cups almost full of wine. Where then was that wise old woman with
her forceful prohibitions? Could anything avail against the evil in
us, unless Your healing, O Lord, watched over us? When our father
and mother and nurses are absent, You are present, who created us,
who call us, who can use those placed over us for some good unto
the salvation of our souls. What did You do then, O my God? How
did You cure her, and bring her to health? From another soul You
drew a harsh and cutting sarcasm, as though bringing forth a sur-
geon's knife from Your secret store, and with one blow amputated
that sore place. A maidservant with whom she was accustomed to go
to the cellar, one day fell into a quarrel with her small mistress
when no one else chanced to be about, and hurled at her the most
biting insult possible, calling her a drunkard. My mother was pierced
to the quick, saw her fault in its true wickedness, and instantly
condemned it and gave it up. Just as the flattery of a friend can pervert, so the insult of an enemy can sometimes correct. Nor do You,
O God, reward men according to what You do by means of them,
but according to what they themselves intended. For the girl being
in a temper wanted to enrage her young mistress, not to amend her,
for she did it when no one else was there, either because the time
and place happened to be thus when the quarrel arose, or because
she was afraid that elders would be angry because she had not told
it sooner. But You, O Lord, Ruler of heavenly things and earthly,
who turn to Your own purposes the very depths of rivers as they
run and order the turbulence of the flow of time, did by the folly of
one mind bring sanity to another; thus reminding us not to attribute
it to our own power if another is amended by our word, even if we
meant to amend him.

IX

My mother, then, was modestly and soberly brought up, being rather made obedient to her parents by You than to You by her parents. When she reached the age for marriage, and was bestowed upon a husband, she served him as her lord. She used all her effort to win him to You, preaching You to him by her character, by which You made her beautiful to her husband, respected and loved by him and admirable in his sight. For she bore his acts of unfaithfulness quietly, and never had any jealous scene with her husband about them. She awaited Your mercy upon him, that he might grow chaste through faith in You. And as a matter of fact, though generous beyond measure, he had a very hot temper. But she knew that a woman must not resist a husband in anger, by deed or even by word. Only, when she saw him calm again and quiet, she would take the opportunity to give him an explanation of her actions, if it happened that he had been roused to anger unreasonably. The result was that whereas many matrons with much milder husbands carried the marks of blows to disfigure their faces, and would all get together to complain of the way their husbands behaved, my mother—talking lightly but meaning it seriously—advised them against their tongues: saying that from the day they heard the matrimonial contract read to them they should regard it as an instrument by which they became servants; and from that time they should be mindful of their condition and not set themselves up against their masters. And they often expressed amazement—for they knew how violent a husband she had to live with—that it had never been heard, and there was no mark to show, that Patricius had beaten his wife or that there had been any family quarrel between them for so much as a single day. And when her friends asked her the reason, she taught them her rule, which was as I have just said. Those who followed it, found it good and thanked her; those who did not, went on being bullied and beaten.

Her mother-in-law began by being angry with her because of the whispers of malicious servants. But my mother won her completely by the respect she showed, and her unfailing patience and mildness. She ended by going to her son, telling him of the tales the servants had bandied about to the destruction of peace in the family between herself and her daughter-in-law, and asking him to punish them for it. So he, out of obedience to his mother and in the interests of order in the household and peace among his womenfolk, had the servants beaten whose names he had been given, as she had asked when giving them. To which she added the promise that anyone

must expect a similar reward from her own hands who should think
to please her by speaking ill of her daughter-in-law. And as no one
had the courage to do so, they lived together with the most notable
degree of kindness and harmony.

This great gift also, O my God, my Mercy, You gave to Your good
servant, in whose womb You created me, that she showed herself,
wherever possible, a peacemaker between people quarreling and
minds at discord. For swelling and undigested discord often belches
forth bitter words when in the venom of intimate conversation with
a present friend hatred at its rawest is breathed out upon an absent
enemy. But when my mother heard bitter things said by each of the
other, she never said anything to either about the other save what
would help to reconcile them. This might seem a small virtue, if
I had not had the sorrow of seeing for myself so many people who—
as if by some horrible widespreading infection of sin—not only tell
angry people the things their enemies said in anger, but even add
things that were never said at all. Whereas, on the contrary, ordinary
humanity would seem to require not merely that we refrain from
exciting or increasing wrath among men by evil speaking, but that
we study to extinguish wrath by kind speaking. Such a one was
she: and You were the master who taught her most secretly in the
school of her heart.

The upshot was that towards the very end of his life she won her
husband to You; and once he was a Christian she no longer had
to complain of the things she had had to bear with before he was a
Christian. Further, she was a servant of Your servants. Such of them
as knew her praised and honoured and loved You, O God, in
her; for they felt Your presence in her heart, showing itself in the
fruit of her holy conversation. She had been *the wife of one husband,
had requited her parents, had governed her house* piously, *was well
reported of for good works*. She had *brought up her children,* being
in labour of them as often as she saw them swerving away from You.
Finally of all of us Your servants, O Lord—since by Your gift You
suffer us to speak—who before her death were living together after
receiving the grace of baptism, she took as much care as if she had
been the mother of us all, and served us as if she had been the
daughter of us all.

X

When the day was approaching on which she was to depart this
life—a day that You knew though we did not—it came about, as I
believe by Your secret arrangement, that she and I stood alone lean-

ing in a window, which locked inwards to the garden within the house where we were staying, at Ostia on the Tiber; for there we were away from everybody, resting for the sea-voyage from the weariness of our long journey by land. There we talked together, she and I alone, in deep joy; and *forgetting the things that were behind and looking forward to those that were before,* we were discussing in the presence of Truth, which You are, what the eternal life of the saints could be like, *which eye has not seen nor ear heard, nor has it entered into the heart of man.* But with the mouth of our heart we panted for the high waters of Your fountain, the fountain of the life which is with You: that being sprinkled from that fountain according to our capacity, we might in some sense meditate upon so great a matter.

And our conversation had brought us to this point, that any pleasure whatsoever of the bodily senses, in any brightness whatsoever of corporeal light, seemed to us not worthy of comparison with the pleasure of that eternal Light, not worthy even of mention. Rising as our love flamed upward towards that Selfsame, we passed in review the various levels of bodily things, up to the heavens themselves, whence sun and moon and stars shine upon this earth. And higher still we soared, thinking in our minds and speaking and marvelling at Your works: and so we came to our own souls, and went beyond them to come at last to that region of richness unending, where You feed Israel forever with the food of truth: and there life is that Wisdom by which all things are made, both the things that have been and the things that are yet to be. But this Wisdom itself is not made: it is as it has ever been, and so it shall be forever: indeed "has ever been" and "shall be forever" have no place in it, but it simply is, for it is eternal: whereas "to have been" and "to be going to be" are not eternal. And while we were thus talking of His Wisdom and panting for it, with all the effort of our heart we did for one instant attain to touch it; then sighing, and leaving the first fruits of our spirit bound to it, we returned to the sound of our own tongue, in which a word has both beginning and ending. For what is like to your Word, Our Lord, who abides in Himself forever, yet grows not old and makes all things new!

So we said: If to any man the tumult of the flesh grew silent, silent the images of earth and sea and air: and if the heavens grew silent, and the very soul grew silent to herself and by not thinking of self mounted beyond self: if all dreams and imagined visions grew silent, and every tongue and every sign and whatsoever is transient—for indeed if any man could hear them, he should hear them saying with one voice: We did not make ourselves, but He made us who abides forever: but if, having uttered this and so set us to listening to Him who made them, they all grew silent, and in their silence He alone spoke to us, not by them but by Himself: so that we should hear His word, not by any tongue of flesh nor the voice of an angel nor the sound of thunder nor in the darkness of a parable, but that we should hear Himself whom in all these things we love, should hear Himself and not them: just as we two had but now reached forth and in a flash of the mind attained to touch the eternal Wisdom which abides over all: and if this could continue, and all other visions so different be quite taken away, and this one should so ravish and absorb and wrap the beholder in inward joys that his life should eternally be such as that one moment of understanding for which we had been sighing—would not this be: *Enter Thou into the joy of Thy Lord?* But when shall it be? Shall it be when *we shall all rise again* and *shall not all be changed?*

Such thoughts I uttered, though not in that order or in those actual words; but You know, O Lord, that on that day when we talked of these things the world with all its delights seemed cheap to us in comparison with what we talked of. And my mother said: "Son, for my own part I no longer find joy in anything in this world. What I am still to do here and why I am here I know not, now that I no longer hope for anything from this world. One thing there was, for which I desired to remain still a little longer in this life, that I should see you a Catholic Christian before I died. This God has granted me in superabundance, in that I now see you His servant to the contempt of all worldly happiness. What then am I doing here?"

XI

What answer I made, I do not clearly remember; within five days or not much longer she fell into a fever. And in her sickness, she one day fainted away and for the moment lost consciousness. We ran to her but she quickly returned to consciousness, and seeing my brother and me standing by her she said as one wondering: "Where was I?" Then looking closely upon us as we stood wordless in our grief, she said: "Here you will bury your mother." I stayed silent and checked my weeping. But my brother said something to the effect that he would be happier if she were to die in her own land and not in a strange country. But as she heard this she looked at him anxiously, restraining him with her eye because he savored of earthly things, and then she looked at me and said: "See the way he talks." And then she said to us both: "Lay this body wherever it may be. Let no care of it disturb you: this only I ask of you that you should remember me at the altar of the Lord wherever you may be." And when she had uttered this wish in such words as she could manage, she fell silent as her sickness took hold of her more strongly.

But as I considered Your gifts, O unseen God, which You send into the hearts of Your faithful to the springing up of such wonderful fruits, I was glad and gave thanks to You, remembering what I had previously known of the care as to her burial which had always troubled her: for she had arranged to be buried by the body of her husband. Because they had lived together in such harmony, she had wished—so little is the human mind capable of rising to the divine— that it should be granted her, as an addition to her happiness and as something to be spoken of among men, that after her pilgrimage beyond the sea the earthly part of man and wife should lie together under the same earth. Just when this vain desire had begun to vanish from her heart through the fullness of Your goodness, I did not know; but I was pleased and surprised that it had now so clearly vanished: though indeed in the conversation we had had together at the window, when she said: "What am I still doing here?" there had appeared no desire to die in her own land. Further I heard afterwards that in the time we were at Ostia, she had talked one day to some of my friends, as a mother talking to her children, of the contempt of this life and of the attraction of death. I was not there at the time. They marvelled at such courage in a woman—but it was You who had given it to her—and asked if she was not afraid to leave her body so far from her own city. But she said: "Nothing is far from God, and I have no fear that He will not know at the end of the world from what place He is to raise me up." And so on the ninth day of her illness, in the fifty-sixth year of her life and the thirty-third of mine, that devout and holy soul was released from the body.

XII

I closed her eyes; and an immeasurable sorrow flowed into my heart and would have overflowed in tears. But my eyes under the mind's strong constraint held back their flow and I stood dry-eyed. In that struggle it went very ill with me. As she breathed her last, the child Adeodatus broke out into lamentation and we all checked him and brought him to silence. But in this very fact the childish element in me, which was breaking out into tears, was checked and brought to silence by the manlier voice of my mind. For we felt that it was not fitting that her funeral should be solemnized with moaning and weeping and lamentation, for so it is normal to weep when death is seen as sheer misery or as complete extinction. But she had not died miserably, nor did she wholly die. Of the one thing we were sure by reason of her character, of the other by the reality of our faith.

What then was it that grieved my heart so deeply? Only the newness of the wound, in finding the custom I had so loved of living with her suddenly snapped short. It was a joy to me to have this one testimony from her: when her illness was close to its end, meeting with expressions of endearment such services as I rendered, she called me a dutiful loving son, and said in the great affection of her love that she had never heard from my mouth any harsh or reproachful word addressed to herself. But what possible comparison was there, O my God who made us, between the honour I showed her and the service she had rendered me?

Because I had now lost the great comfort of her, my soul was wounded and my very life torn asunder, for it had been one life made of hers and mine together. When the boy had been quieted and ceased weeping, Evodius took up the psalter and began to chant —with the whole house making the responses—the psalm *Mercy and judgment I will sing to Thee, O Lord*. And when they heard what was being done, many of the brethren and religious women came to us; those whose office it was were making arrangement for the burial, while, in another part of the house where it could properly be done I discoursed, with friends who did not wish to leave me by myself, upon matters suitable for that time. Thus I used truth as a kind of fomentation to bring relief to my torment, a torment known to You, but not known to those others: so that listening closely to me they thought that I lacked all feeling of grief. But in Your ears, where none of them could hear, I accused the emotion in me as weakness; and I held in the flood of my grief. It was for the moment a little diminished, but returned with fresh violence, not with any pouring of tears or change of countenance: but I knew what I was crushing down in my heart. I was very much ashamed that these human emotions could have such power over me—though it belongs to the due order and the lot of our earthly condition that they should come to us—and I felt a new grief at my grief and so was afflicted with a twofold sorrow.

When the body was taken to burial, I went and returned without tears. During the prayers which we poured forth to you when the sacrifice of our redemption was offered for her—while the body, as the custom there is, lay by the grave before it was actually buried— during those prayers I did not weep. Yet all that day I was heavy with grief within and in the trouble of my mind I begged of You in my own fashion to heal my pain; but You would not—I imagine because You meant to impress upon my memory by this proof how strongly the bond of habit holds the mind even when it no longer feeds upon deception. The idea came to me to go and bathe, for I had heard that the bath—which the Greeks call αλανεῖον—is so called because it drives anxiety from the mind. And this also I acknowledge to Your mercy, O Father of orphans, that I bathed and was the same man after as before. The bitterness of grief had not sweated out of my heart. Then I fell asleep, and woke again to find my grief not a little relieved. And as I was in bed and no one about, I said over those true verses that Your servant Ambrose wrote of You:

> Deus creator omnium
> polique rector vestiens
> diem decoro lumine,
> noctem sopora gratia,
>
> artus solutos ut quies
> reddat laboris usui
> mentesque fessas allevet
> luctusque solvat anxios.

And then little by little I began to recover my former feeling about Your handmaid, remembering how loving and devout was her conversation with You, how pleasant and considerate her conversation with me, of which I was thus suddenly deprived. And I found solace in weeping in Your sight both about her and for her, about myself and for myself. I no longer tried to check my tears, but let them flow as they would, making them a pillow for my heart: and it rested upon them, for it was Your ears that heard my weeping, and not the ears of a man, who would have misunderstood my tears and despised them. But now, O Lord, I confess it to You in writing, let him read it who will and interpret it as he will: and if he sees it as sin that for so small a portion of an hour I wept for my mother, now dead and departed from my sight, who had wept so many years for me that I should live ever in Your sight—let him not scorn me but rather, if he is a man of great charity, let him weep for my sins to You, the Father of all the brethren of Your Christ.

XIII

Now that my heart is healed of that wound, in which there was perhaps too much of earthly affection, I pour forth to You, O our

God, tears of a very different sort for Your handmaid—tears that flow
from a spirit shaken by the thought of the perils there are for every
soul that dies in Adam. For though she had been made alive in
Christ, and while still in the body had so lived that Your name was
glorified in her faith and her character, yet I dare not say that
from the moment of her regeneration in baptism no word issued
from her mouth contrary to Your Command. Your Son, who is
Truth, has said: *Whosoever shall say to his brother, Thou fool, shall
be in danger of hell fire;* and it would go ill with the most praise-
worthy life lived by men, if You were to examine it with Your
mercy laid aside! But because You do not enquire too fiercely into
our sins, we have hope and confidence of a place with You. Yet
if a man reckons up before You the merits he truly has, what is he
reckoning except Your own gifts? If only men would know themselves to be but men, so that he that glories would glory in the Lord!

Thus, my Glory and my Life, God of my heart, leaving aside for
this time her good deeds, for which I give thanks to Thee in joy,
I now pray to Thee for my mother's sins. Grant my prayer through
the true Medicine of our wounds, who hung upon the cross and who
now sitting at Thy right hand makes intercession for us. I know that
she dealt mercifully, and from her heart forgave those who tres-
passed against her: do Thou also forgive such trespasses as she may
have been guilty of in all the years since her baptism, forgive them,
Lord, forgive them, I beseech Thee: enter not into judgment with
her. Let Thy mercy be exalted above Thy justice for Thy words
are true and Thou hast promised that the merciful shall obtain
mercy. That they should be merciful is Thy gift who *hast mercy on
whom Thou wilt, and wilt have compassion on whom Thou wilt.*

And I believe that Thou hast already done what I am now asking;
but be not offended, Lord, at the things my mouth would utter. For
on that day when her death was so close, she was not concerned
that her body should be sumptuously wrapped or embalmed with
spices, nor with any thought of choosing a monument or even for
burial in her own country. Of such things she gave us no command,
but only desired to be remembered at Thy altar, which she had
served without ever missing so much as a day, on which she knew
that the holy Victim was offered, *by whom the handwriting is
blotted out of the decree that was contrary to us,* by which offering
too the enemy was overcome who, reckoning our sins and seeking
what may be laid to our charge, found nothing in Him, in whom
we are conquerors. Who shall restore to Him His innocent blood?
Who shall give Him back the price by which He purchased us and
so take us from Him? To this sacrament of our redemption Thy

handmaid had bound her soul by the bond of faith. Let none wrest her from Thy protection; let neither the lion nor the dragon bar her way by force or craft. For she will not answer that she owes nothing, lest she should be contradicted and confuted by that cunning accuser: but she will answer that her debts have been remitted by Him, to whom no one can hand back the price which He paid for us, though He owed it not.

So let her rest in peace, together with her husband, for she had no other before nor after him, but served him, in patience bringing forth fruit for Thee, and winning him likewise for Thee. And inspire, O my Lord my God, inspire Thy servants my brethren, Thy sons my masters, whom I serve with heart and voice and pen, that as many of them as read this may remember at Thy altar Thy servant Monica, with Patricius, her husband, by whose bodies Thou didst bring me into this life, though how I know not. May they with loving mind remember these who were my parents in this transitory light, my brethren who serve Thee as our Father in our Catholic mother, and those who are to be fellow-citizens with me in the eternal Jerusalem, which Thy people sigh for in their pilgrimage from birth until they come there: so that what my mother at her end asked of me may be fulfilled more richly in the prayers of so many gained for her by my Confessions than by my prayers alone.

BOOK TEN

CONCLUDES AUGUSTINE'S CONFESSION

I–V   *Why He Makes This Confession*
    I   Prayer that his heart may see God and himself
    II   How he confesses to God
    III Why he confesses to men (a) his past sins (b) his present state
    IV   What profit to the reader?
    V   Confession difficult because a man does not know himself wholly

VI–VII   *What Is God?*
    VI   Creation's answer
    VII By what faculty does he come to know God?

VIII–XXV   *Analysis of Memory*

XXVI–XXIX   *Prayer*
    XXVI   Listening to God
    XXVII   "Late have I loved Thee"
    XXVIII This life contrasted with Beatitude
    XXIX   "Grant what Thou dost command, and command what Thou wilt"

XXX–XLI   *Augustine's Present State*
    XXX   "The lust of the flesh": sexual temptation: why so much more powerful in sleep
    XXXI   Eating and drinking
    XXXII   Sweet scents
    XXXIII The pleasures of the ear: hymns and canticles
    XXXIV   The pleasures of sight
    XXXV   "The lust of the eyes": knowing for knowing's sake: idle curiosity
    XXXVI   "The pride of life": pleasure in the fear and love men have for him
    XXXVII How can he test himself on this matter?
    XXXVIII Love of praise does tempt him
    XXXIX   Of those who do not concern themselves with others' approval but win their own

XL His mind traverses all things in search of God and at times he reaches "a kind of delight which, could it ever be made permanent in me, would be hard to distinguish from the life to come"

XLI God would not be possessed along with a lie

XLII–XLIII *The True Mediator*

XLII Men who seek the mediation of spirits are deceived by the devil

XLIII How Christ alone is the Mediator

I

LET ME KNOW THEE who knowest me, *let me know Thee even as I am known*. O Thou, the Power of my soul, enter into it and fit it for Thyself, that Thou mayest have it and possess it without spot or wrinkle. This is my hope, this is my prayer, and in this hope do I rejoice when I rightly rejoice. But as for the other things of this life, the more we weep for them the less they deserve our tears, and the less we weep for them, the more we should weep. For behold Thou lovest the truth, and *he that does the truth comes to the light*. I wish to do it in confession, in my heart before Thee, in my writing before many witnesses.

II

And even if I would not confess to You, what could be hidden in me, O Lord, from You to whose eyes the deepest depth of man's conscience lies bare? I should only be hiding You from myself, not myself from You. But now that my groaning is witness that I am displeasing to myself, You shine unto me and I delight in You and love You and yearn for You, so that I am ashamed of what I am and renounce myself and choose You and please neither You nor myself save in You. To You then, O Lord, I am laid bare for what I am. And I have said with what profit I confess to You. For my confession is not by bodily words, or bodily cries, but with the words of the soul and the upward cry of my thought, which Your ear knows. For when I am wicked, confession to You simply means being displeased at myself; when I am good, confession to You means simply not attributing my goodness to myself: for You, O Lord, bless the just man, but first You turn him from ungodliness to justice. And so my confession, O my God, in Your sight is made silently: and yet not silently, for if it makes no sound, yet it cries aloud in my heart. For whatever good I utter to men, You have heard from me before I utter it; and whatever good You hear from me, You have first spoken to me.

III

What therefore have I to do with men that they should hear my confessions, as if it were they who would cure all that is evil in me?

Men are a race curious to know of other men's lives, but slothful
to correct their own. Why should they wish to hear from me what
I am, when they do not wish to hear from You what they are
themselves? And when they hear me confessing of myself, how do
they know whether I speak the truth, since *no man knows the things
of a man but the spirit of a man that is in him?* Whereas if they
hear from You something about themselves, they cannot say: "The
Lord is lying." For to hear from You about themselves is simply to
know themselves. And who, knowing himself, can say: "It is false,"
unless himself is lying? But because charity believes all things—that
is, all things spoken by those whom it binds to itself and makes
one—I, O Lord, confess to You that men may hear, for though I
cannot prove to them that my confession is true, yet those will
believe me whose ears charity has opened to me.

But do You, O my inmost Physician, make clear to me what
profit I gain by it. When the confessions of my past sins—which
You have forgiven and covered up, giving me joy in You, changing
my life by faith and Your sacrament—are read and heard, they stir
up the heart. It no longer lies in the lethargy of despair and says
"I cannot," but keeps wakeful in the love of Your mercy and the
loveliness of Your grace, by which every weak man is made strong,
since by it he is made conscious of his weakness. As for the good,
it rejoices them to hear of sins committed in the past by men now
free from them: not because these things are sins, but because they
were and no longer are.

But again, O Lord my God, to whom daily my conscience makes
confession, relying more in the hope of Your mercy than in its own
innocence, with what profit, I beseech You, do I confess unto men
in Your sight by this book, not what I once was, but what I now
am? I have seen and spoken of that other profit. But as to what I now
am while I am writing my Confessions, there are many who desire
to know—both people who know me personally, and people who do
not, but have heard something from me or about me. Yet they have
not their ear at my heart, where I am what I am. They wish, therefore, to hear from my own confession what I am inwardly, where
they cannot pierce with eye or ear or mind. They desire to know
and are prepared to believe, but will they know? The charity by
which they are good, tells them that in my confession I do not lie
about myself; and this charity in them believes me.

IV

But for what profit do they wish to hear it? Do they desire to rejoice
with me when they hear how close by Your grace I have come to

You, and to pray for me when they hear how far I am held from You by my own weight? To such shall I show myself. For it is no small fruit, O Lord my God, that many should give thanks to You for me and many should pray to You for me. Let the mind of my brethren love that in me which You teach to be worthy of love, and grieve for that in me which You teach to be worthy of grief. So let the mind of my brethren act—not the mind of strangers nor the children of strangers, *whose mouth has spoken vanity, and whose right hand is the right hand of iniquity*—but the mind of my brethren who rejoice for what they see good in me and are grieved for what they see ill, but whether they see good or ill still love me. To such shall I show myself: let their breath come faster for my good deeds: let them sigh for my ill. For my good deeds are Your act and Your gift, my ill deeds are my own faults and Your punishments. Let their breath come faster for the one, let them sigh for the other, and let the hymn of praise and the weeping rise up together in Your sight from Your censers which are the hearts of my brethren. And do Thou, Lord, delighted with the odour of Thy holy temple, *have mercy upon me according to Thy great mercy*, and for Thy Name's sake; and in no point deserting what Thou hast begun, supply what is imperfect in me.

This then is the fruit of my confession—the confession not of what I have been, but of what I am—in that I confess not only before You, with inward exultation yet trembling, with inward sorrow yet with hope as well: but also in the ears of the believing sons of men, companions of my joy and sharers of my mortality, my fellow citizens, fellow pilgrims: those who have gone before, and those who are to come after, and those who walk the way of life with me. These are Your servants, my brethren, whom You have chosen that they should be Your sons, my masters whom You have commanded me to serve if I am to live with You and in You. And this Your word to me would be a lesser thing, if it merely commanded me by word and did not go before me in the doing. Thus I do it, in deed and in word, I do it under Your wings, for the peril would be too great were not my soul under Your wings and subject to You, and my infirmity known to You. I am but a little one, yet my Father lives forever and my Protector is sufficient for me. For He is the same who begot me and who watches over me: and You are all my good, You the almighty who are with me even before I am with You. To such then as You command me to serve will I show, not what I was, but what I now am, what I continue to be. But I do not judge myself. Thus therefore let me be heard.

V

For You, O Lord, are my judge, because though *no man knows the things of a man, save the spirit of a man that is in him,* yet there is something of man that the very spirit of man that is in him does not know. But You, Lord, know all of him, for You made him. As for me, although I despise myself in Your sight, and hold myself but dust and ashes, yet I know something of You which I do not know of myself. It is true that *now we see through a glass in a dark manner and not yet face to face;* so that as long as I am on pilgrimage and not with You, I am more present to myself than to You; yet I know that You cannot in any way suffer violence, whereas I do not know which temptations I myself can resist and which I cannot. But there is hope, because You are *faithful and will not suffer us to be tempted above that which we are able: but will also make issue with temptation, that we may be able to bear it.* I will confess therefore what I know of myself and what I do not know; for what I know of myself I know through the shining of Your light; and what I do not know of myself, I continue not to know until my darkness shall be made as noonday in Your countenance.

VI

It is with no doubtful knowledge, Lord, but with utter certainty that I love You. You have stricken my heart with Your word and I have loved You. And indeed heaven and earth and all that is in them tell me wherever I look that I should love You, and they cease not to tell it to all men, so that there is no excuse for them. For *You will have mercy on whom You will have mercy, and You will show mercy to whom You will show mercy:* otherwise heaven and earth cry their praise of You to deaf ears.

But what is it that I love when I love You? Not the beauty of any bodily thing, nor the order of seasons, not the brightness of light that rejoices the eye, nor the sweet melodies of all songs, nor the sweet fragrance of flowers and ointments and spices: not manna nor honey, not the limbs that carnal love embraces. None of these things do I love in loving my God. Yet in a sense I do love light and melody and fragrance and food and embrace when I love my God—the light and the voice and the fragrance and the food and embrace in the soul, when that light shines upon my soul which no place can contain, that voice sounds which no time can take from me, I breathe that fragrance which no wind scatters, I eat the food which is not lessened by eating, and I lie in the embrace which satiety never comes to sunder. This it is that I love, when I love my God.

And what is this God? I asked the earth and it answered: "I am not He"; and all things that are in the earth made the same confession. I asked the sea and the deeps and the creeping things, and they answered: "We are not your God; seek higher." I asked the winds that blow, and the whole air with all that is in it answered: "Anaximenes was wrong; I am not God." I asked the heavens, the sun, the moon, the stars, and they answered: "Neither are we God whom you seek." And I said to all the things that throng about the gateways of the senses: "Tell me of my God, since you are not He. Tell me something of Him." And they cried out in a great voice: "He made us." My question was my gazing upon them, and their answer was their beauty. And I turned to myself and said: "And you, who are you?" And I answered: "A man." Now clearly there is a body and a soul in me, one exterior, one interior. From which of these two should I have enquired of my God? I had already sought Him by my body, from earth to heaven, as far as my eye could send its beams on the quest. But the interior part is the better, seeing that all my body's messengers delivered to it, as ruler and judge, the answers that heaven and earth and all things in them made when they said: "We are not God," and, "He made us." The inner man knows these things through the ministry of the outer man: I the inner man knew them, I, I the soul, through the senses of the body. I asked the whole frame of the universe about my God and it answered me: "I am not He, but He made me."

Is not the face of the earth clearly seen by all whose senses function properly? Then why does it not give the same answer to all? Animals great and small see it, but cannot interrogate it. For reason does not preside in them to judge upon the evidence their senses bring. But man can interrogate it, and so should be able clearly to see *the invisible things of God understood by things which are made;* but they love these last too much and become subject to them, and subjects cannot judge. All these things refuse to answer those who ask, unless they ask with power to judge. If one man merely sees the world, while another not only sees but interrogates it, the world does not change its speech—that is, its outward appearance which speaks —in such a way as to appear differently to the two men; but presenting exactly the same face to each, it says nothing to the one, but gives answer to the other: or rather it gives its answer to all, but only those understand who compare its voice as it comes through their senses, with the truth that is within them. For truth says to me: "Your God is not heaven or earth or any corporeal thing." So their

very nature tells us. For clearly there is less bulk in the part than
in the whole. And I tell you, my soul, you are better, since you vivify
the whole bulk of the body: you give the body life, which no body
can give to a body. But your God is the Life of your life.

VII

I ask again what it is that I love when I love my God? Who is
He that is above the topmost point of my soul? By that same soul
I shall ascend to Him. I shall mount beyond the power by which
I am united to my body, and by which I fill its whole structure with
life. Not by that can I find my God: for by that *the horse and the
mule which have no understanding* could equally find Him, for there
is in them the same power giving life to their bodies. There is
another faculty, by which not only do I give life to my body but
sense perception likewise, a faculty which the Lord created for me
when He commanded the eye not to hear and the ear not to see,
but gave me the eye to see by and the ear to hear by, and gave to
all the other senses their respective places and functions: which, in
their diversity, I the one soul act by. But this faculty also I must
mount beyond: for this also the horse and the mule have. They perceive by means of the body.

VIII

I shall mount beyond this power of my nature, still rising by
degrees towards Him who made me. And so I come to the fields
and vast palaces of memory, where are stored the innumerable images
of material things brought to it by the senses. Further there is stored
in the memory the thoughts we think, by adding to or taking from
or otherwise modifying the things that sense has made contact with,
and all other things that have been entrusted to and laid up in
memory, save such as forgetfulness has swallowed in its grave. When
I turn to memory, I ask it to bring forth what I want: and some
things are produced immediately, some take longer as if they had
to be brought out from some more secret place of storage; some pour
out in a heap, and while we are actually wanting and looking for
something quite different, they hurl themselves upon us in masses
as though to say: "May it not be we that you want?" I brush them
from the face of my memory with the hand of my heart, until at
last the thing I want is brought to light as from some hidden place.
Some things are produced just as they are required, easily and in
right order; and things that come first give place to those that follow,
and giving place are stored up again to be produced when I want
them. This is what happens, when I say anything by heart.

In the memory all the various things are kept distinct and in their right categories, though each came into the memory by its own gate. For example, light and all the colors and shapes of bodies come in by the eyes, all the kinds of sound by the ears, all scents by the nostrils, all tastes by the mouth; and by a sense that belongs to the whole body comes in what is hard and what is soft, what is hot or cold, rough or smooth, heavy or light, whether outside the body or inside. All these things the vast recesses, the hidden and unsearchable caverns, of memory receive and store up, to be available and brought to light when need arises: yet all enter by their own various gates to be stored up in memory. Nor indeed do the things themselves enter: only the images of the things perceived by the senses are there for thought to remember them.

And even though we know by which senses they were brought in and laid up in the memory, who can tell how these images were formed? Even when I am in darkness and in silence, I can if I will produce colors in my memory, and distinguish black from white and any other colors if I choose; and sounds do not break in and disturb the image I am considering that came in through the eye, since the sounds themselves were already there and lie stored up apart. For I can summon them too, if I like, and they are immediately present; and though my tongue is at rest and my throat silent I can sing as I will; nor do the images of the colors, although they are as truly present, interfere or interrupt when I call from the storehouse some other thing which came in by the ear. Similarly all other things that were brought in by the other senses and stored up in the memory can be called up at my pleasure: I distinguish the scent of lilies from the scent of violets, though at that instant I smell nothing; and I like honey better than wine, some smooth thing better than rough, though I am not tasting or handling but only remembering.

All this I do inside me, in the huge court of my memory. In my memory are sky and earth and sea, ready at hand along with all the things that I have ever been able to perceive in them and have not forgotten. And in my memory too I meet myself—I recall myself, what I have done, when and where and in what state of mind I was when I did it. In my memory are all the things I remember to have experienced myself or to have been told by others. From the same store I can weave into the past endless new likenesses of things either experienced by me or believed on the strength of things experienced; and from these again I can picture actions and events and hopes for the future; and upon them all I can meditate as if they were present. "I shall do this or that," I say to myself in the vast recess of my mind with its immeasurable store of images of things so great: and this or that follows. "O, if only this or that could be!" or again, "May God prevent this or that!" Such things I say within myself, and when I speak of them the images of all the things I mention are to hand from the same storehouse of memory, and if the images were not there I could not so much as speak of the things.

Great is this power of memory, exceedingly great, O my God, a spreading limitless room within me. Who can reach its uttermost depth? Yet it is a faculty of my soul and belongs to my nature. In fact I cannot totally grasp all that I am. Thus the mind is not large enough to contain itself: but where can that part of it be which it does not contain? Is it outside itself and not within? How can it not contain itself? [How can there be any of itself that is not *in* itself?] As this question struck me, I was overcome with wonder and almost stupor. Here are men going afar to marvel at the heights of mountains, the mighty waves of the sea, the long courses of great rivers, the vastness of the ocean, the movements of the stars, yet leaving themselves unnoticed and not seeing it as marvellous that when I spoke of all these things, I did not see them with my eyes, yet I could not have spoken of them unless these mountains and waves and rivers and stars which I have seen, and the ocean of which I have heard, had been inwardly present to my sight: in my memory, yet with the same vast spaces between them as if I saw them outside me. When I saw them with my eyes, I did not by seeing them swallow them into me; nor are they themselves present in me, but only their images; and I know by what sense of my body each one of them was impressed upon my mind.

IX

These are not the only thoughts to which the immense capaciousness of memory gives rise. In memory also are all such things as we have learned of the liberal sciences and have not forgotten, lying there as if in a more inward place, which yet is no place; and of these I have not the images but the things themselves. For what grammar is or the art of disputation, how many kinds of questions there are—whatever I know of such matters is in my memory not as though I retained the image and left the thing outside, or as though it had sounded in my mind then passed away, like a voice heard by the ear which leaves something by which it can be recalled as though it were sounding, though it sounds no more; or like an odor which, though it passes and is borne away on the wind, affects the sense of smell and so impresses on the memory some image of itself which we can recall and recreate; or like food which certainly has no taste as far as the belly is concerned, yet has a kind of taste in the memory; or like something that has touched the body and been felt and can still be imagined in memory although no longer in contact with us. In these cases the things themselves are not brought into the memory; it is only their images which are seized with such marvellous speed, and stored away marvellously as if in cabinets, and as marvellously brought forth again when we remember.

X

Now when I hear that there are three kinds of questions: whether a thing is, what it is, of what sort it is: I do indeed retain the images of the sounds of which those words are composed, and I know that they passed through the air with a certain noise and now no longer are. But the things themselves which the sounds signified I could not come at by any bodily sense nor see them at all save by my mind; and what I stored in my memory was not their images but the truths themselves. But how they got into me, it is for them to tell if they can. For I run my mind over all the doorways of my body, but I cannot find any door by which they could have come in. For my eyes say: "If they were coloured, we reported them to you"; my ears say: "If they sounded, we gave you notice of them"; the nostrils say: "If they had any smell, they went in through us"; the sense of taste says: "Unless there was any taste in them, there is no use in my being asked"; the sense of touch says: "If the thing is not a body, I did not handle it, and if I did not handle it, I did not report it to you." Very well then, whence and how did they get into my memory? I do not know. For when I first learned them I was not trusting some other man's mind, but recognized them in my own; and I saw them as true and committed them to my mind as if placing them where I could get at them again whenever I desired. Thus they must have been in my mind even before I learned them, though they were not in my memory. Then where were they, or how did it come that when I heard them spoken I recognized them and said: "It is so, it is true," unless they *were* in my memory already, but so far back, thrust away as it were in such remote recesses, that unless they had been drawn forth by some other man's teaching, I might perhaps never have managed to think of them at all?

XI

Thus we find that to learn those things which do not come into us as images by the senses, but which we know within ourselves without images and as they actually are, is in reality only to take things that the memory already contained, but scattered and unarranged, and by thinking bring them together, and by close attention have them placed within reach in that same memory: so that things which had formerly lain there scattered and not considered, now come easily and familiarly to us. And my memory carries an immense number of things of this sort, which have already been discovered and, as I have said, placed within reach—the things we are said to have learned and to know. Yet if I ceased to give thought to them for quite a short space of time, they would sink again and fall away into the more remote recesses of the memory, and I should have to think them out afresh and put them together again from the same place— for there is nowhere else for them to have gone—if I am to know them: in other words they must be collected out of dispersion, and indeed the verb *to cogitate* is named from this drawing together. For *cogito* (I think) has the same relation to *cogo* (I put together) as *agito* to *ago* and *factito* to *facio*. But the mind of man has claimed the word *cogitate* completely for its own: not what is put together anywhere else but only what is put together in the mind is called cogitation.

XII

The memory also contains the innumerable principles and laws of numbers and dimensions; and none of these have been impressed upon it by any bodily sense, seeing that they have neither colour nor sound nor scent nor taste nor feel. I have heard the sounds of the words by which they are expressed when we discuss them, but the sounds are not the same as the truths themselves. For the sounds are of one kind in Greek, quite different in Latin, but the things themselves are neither Greek nor Latin nor of any other language. I have seen the lines drawn by architects, some of them as fine as a spider's web; but the truths are different, they are not the images of such things as the eye of my body has shown me. To know them is to recognize them interiorly without any concept of any kind of body whatsoever. With all my bodily senses I have perceived the numbers we use in counting; but the basic numbers *by* which we count are not the same as these, nor images of these; but really are. Let whoever does not see these truths laugh at me for talking thus: while he laughs at me I shall be sorry for him.

XIII

All these things I have in my memory, and how I learned them I have in my memory. And I have also heard and have in my memory notions that have been falsely urged against them; and though the notions are false yet it is not false that I remember them. I recall distinguishing between the truths and the fallacious objections: and to see myself now making the distinction is different from remembering the times I made it in the past. Thus I remember that I formerly saw them so, and I lay up in my memory how I see and understand them now, so that I may remember later that I understood them at the present time. And I remember that I remembered just as, if later I recall that I was now able to remember these things, it will be by the power of memory that I shall recall it.

XIV

My memory also contains the feelings of my mind, not in the mode in which the mind itself has them when it is experiencing them, but in a different mode, proper to the power of memory. For I remember that in the past I was cheerful, but I am not cheerful now; and I remember past sadness yet am not sad. I remember past fears without fear, and past desire without desire. Sometimes the thing is exactly contrary—when I am joyful I remember past sorrow, and in present sorrow remember past joy. Now this would not be remarkable if my memories were only of the body: for the mind is one thing and the body another, and it would not be strange if my mind's joy were not affected by remembering the body's past pain. But the mind and the memory are not two separate things—for when we tell another to remember something we say: "See that you have it in mind"; and when we forget something, we say: "It was not in my mind" or "It escaped my mind." Thus we call the memory mind. Since this is so, how comes it that when I am joyful yet remember past sorrow, so that the mind has joy and the memory sorrow, my mind is joyful because there is joy in it, but my memory is not sorrowful because there is sorrow in it? Surely no one would say that the memory does not belong to the mind. Perhaps one might say that the memory is like the mind's stomach, and joy and sorrow like nice or nasty food; when joy and sorrow are committed to the memory it is as though they had passed into the stomach, where they can lie but not be tasted. It is of course ridiculous to see it like this, yet some sort of resemblance there is.

But note again: when I name these four movements of the mind—desire, joy, fear, sadness—I draw them from my memory; and any discussion I can make of them by defining, or by dividing each according to its own genus and species, I find in my memory what to say and it is from my memory that I bring it forth: yet I am not perturbed by their emotional quality when in memory I call them back; and before I recalled them and meditated upon them,

they were there, otherwise it would not have been possible for me
to fetch them forth. Perhaps therefore just as food is brought up
from the stomach by chewing the cud, so things are brought up
from the memory by remembering. But if that is so, why is not
the pleasure of the joy or the pain of the sorrow felt in the mouth
of his thinking by the man who thus remembers them? Or is this
the point of dissimilarity which makes the resemblance incomplete?
Indeed would any one be willing to speak of sorrow or fear, if as often
as we named them we had to feel sorrow or fear? Yet we could not
speak of them unless we found in our memory not only the sound of
their names according to images impressed upon it by the senses of the
body, but also the notions of the things themselves, which notions we
did not receive by any gate of the body; it was the mind, aware of
them through the experience of its own passions, which committed
them to the memory; or, as often happens, the memory of itself
retained them, although the mind did not commit them to it.

XV

But whether all this is by images or not, it is not easy to say. For
I mention a stone or the sun, when the things themselves are not present to my senses, yet images of the things are present in my memory.
When I name some pain of the body, it is not present, since I am
not in pain; yet unless there were some image of it in my memory,
I should not know what to say of it or how to differentiate it in
thought from pleasure. I name bodily health, when I am in bodily
health, and the thing itself is present in me; all the same, unless there
were some image of it in my memory, I could not possibly recall what
the sound of the name signified; nor would sick people know what
was meant by the word health, in the absence of the thing itself from
the body, unless some image were preserved by the power of memory.
I name the numbers we use in counting: and it is not their images
that are in my memory but themselves. I mention the sun's image, and
this too is in my memory: yet it is not the image of its image that I
recall but the image itself: that is what is present when I remember
it. I name memory and I recognize what I am naming, but where do
I recognize it except in my memory? Can the memory possibly be
present to itself by its image and not rather by its own being?

XVI

I can also name forgetfulness and know what I mean by the word;
but how should I recognize the thing itself unless I remembered it?
I am not speaking of the sound of the word, but of the thing the

sound signifies; for if I had forgotten the thing, I should be unable to remember what the sound stood for. When I remember memory my memory itself is present to itself by itself; but when I remember forgetfulness, then memory and forgetfulness are present together —forgetfulness which I remember, memory by which I remember. But what is forgetfulness except absence of memory? How then can that be present for me to remember, which when it is present means that I cannot remember? If what we remember we hold in our memory, and if unless we remembered forgetfulness, we should not on hearing the word recognize what is meant by it, then forgetfulness is contained in the memory. Therefore that is present, to keep us from forgetting it, which when it is present we do forget. Are we to understand from this that when we remember forgetfulness, it is not present to the memory in itself but by its image: because if it were present in itself it would cause us not to remember but to forget? Who can analyze this, or understand how it can be?

Assuredly, Lord, I toil with this, toil within myself: I have become to myself a soil laborious and of heavy sweat. For I am not now considering the parts of the heavens, or measuring the distances of the stars, or seeking how the earth is held in space; it is I who remember, I, my mind. It is not remarkable if things that I am not are far from my knowledge: but what could be closer to me than myself? Yet the power of memory in me I do not understand, though without memory I could not even name myself. What am I to say, when I see so clearly that I remember forgetfulness? Am I to say that something I remember is not in my memory? Or am I to say that forgetfulness is in my memory to keep me from forgetting? Either would be absurd. Is there a third possibility? Could I say that the image of forgetfulness is retained in my memory, not forgetfulness itself, when I remember it? But how could I say this since if the image of a thing is imprinted on the memory, the thing itself must first have been present, for the image to be able to be imprinted? Thus I remember Carthage and such other places as I have been in; I remember the faces of men I have seen and things reported by the other senses; I remember the health or sickness of the body. For when these were present, the memory received their images from them, and these remained present to be gazed on and thought about by the mind when in their absence I might choose to remember them. It follows that if forgetfulness is retained in the memory by means of an image and not in itself, then itself must at some time have been present for its image to be received. But when it was present, how did it write its image in my memory since by its presence it destroys what it finds noted there? At any rate whatever the manner of it, however incomprehensible and inexplicable, I am certain that I do remember forgetfulness, although by forgetfulness what we remember is effaced.

XVII

Great is the power of memory, a thing, O my God, to be in awe of, a profound and immeasurable multiplicity; and this thing is my mind, this thing am I. What then am I, O my God? What nature am I? A life powerfully various and manifold and immeasurable. In the innumerable fields and dens and caverns of my memory, innumerably full of innumerable kinds of things, present either by their images as are all bodies, or in themselves as are our mental capacities, or by certain notions or awarenesses, like the affections of the mind—for even when the mind is not experiencing these, the memory retains them, although whatever is in the memory is in the mind too—in and through all these does my mind range, and I move swiftly from one to another and I penetrate them as deeply as I can, but find no end. So great is the force of memory, so great the force of life even while man lives under sentence of death here.

What am I to do now, O my true Life, my God? I shall mount beyond this my power of memory, I shall mount beyond it, to come to You, O lovely Light. What have You to say to me? In my ascent by the mind to You who abide above me, I shall mount up beyond that power of mine called memory, longing to attain to touch You at the point where that contact is possible and to cleave to You at the point where it is possible to cleave. For the beasts and the birds have memory, or else they could never find their dens or their nests or all the other things their way of life needs; indeed without memory they would be unable to have a way of life. So I must pass beyond memory to come to Him who separated me from the four footed beasts and made me wiser than the birds of the air. I shall pass beyond memory to find You, O truly good and certain Loveliness, and where shall I find You? If I find You beyond my memory, then shall I be without memory of You. And how shall I find You if I am without memory of You?

XVIII

The woman who had lost a groat sought it with a light. But she would not have found it if she had not remembered it. For when it was found, how should she have known whether it was what she sought, if she had not remembered it? I remember that I have often lost things and looked for them and found them again and I know this, that when I was looking for any such and someone asked me:

"Is this it? Is that it?" I kept on saying "No," until the thing I was looking for was produced. But unless I had remembered it, whatever it was, even if it had been offered to me I should not have found it because I should not have recognized it. It is always thus when we seek and find anything we have lost. For if a thing is absent from the eye but not from the memory—as any visible body may be—its image is held within us and is sought for until the thing itself is restored to our sight. And when it has been found, it is recognized by the image within us. We do not say that we have found what was lost unless we recognize it, nor can we recognize it unless we remember it. It was only lost to the eyes; it was preserved in the memory.

XIX

When then the memory itself loses anything, as happens when we forget something and try to recall it, where are we to look for it save in the memory? And if the memory chances to offer us something else instead, we reject it until we come upon the thing we are looking for. And when we come upon it we say: "This is it"; but we could not say this unless we recognized it, and we could not recognize it unless we remembered it. Yet certainly we had forgotten it. May it be that the whole of it had not escaped and that by the part which we still held we looked for the other part, because the memory—feeling that it did not have all that was accustomed to go together, and moving haltingly because of the loss of what it was used to—was demanding to have the missing part restored? Thus if we see or think about some man known to us, but have forgotten his name and are trying to remember it, if some other name occurs to us we do not accept it because it was not our habit to think of that name with that man; thus we go on rejecting until the name occurs with which the mind is satisfied, because it had been used to associating it with the man. But where does that name come back from except from the memory? For even when it is through being reminded by something else that we recognize someone's name, it is still by memory that we do it, for we do not hold it as some new thing learned, but by memory we are sure that this is what the name was. But were the name utterly blotted out of the mind, we should not remember it even if we were reminded. For even the thing we remember that we forgot, we had not utterly forgotten. For if we had utterly forgotten it, we should not even be able to think of looking for it.

XX

How then do I seek You, O Lord? For in seeking You, my God, it is happiness that I am seeking. I shall seek You, that my soul may live. For my body lives by my soul and my soul lives by You. What *is* the way to seek for happiness, then? Because I have no happiness till I can say, and say rightly: "Enough, it is there." How am I to seek it? Should it be by way of remembrance, as though I had forgotten it but am still aware that I have forgotten it, or is it by a kind of appetite to learn it as something unknown to me—whether as something I never have known, or something I have known and forgotten and do not even remember that I have forgotten? Is not happiness precisely what all seek, so that there is not one who does not desire it? But where did they know it, that they should desire it so? Where have they seen it, that they should love it? Obviously we have it in some way, but I do not know how. There is indeed a way by which one may have it and be blessed in having it, and there are some who have the hope of it and are blessed in that hope. These have it in a lesser way than those who are happy in its actual possession, yet they are better than those who are not happy either in the thing itself or in the hope of it. Even these last, unless they had it in some manner, could not even desire to be happy: yet it is quite certain that they do desire it. Somehow or other they have come to know it, that is they have some sort of knowledge of it. I strive to know whether or not this knowledge is in the memory, for if it is then we have at some past time been happy—whether individually, or in that man who committed the first sin, in whom we all died and of whom we are all in misery descended. Which of these two I do not ask now: my concern is whether happiness is in the memory. For I repeat we should not love it unless we had some knowledge of it. We have of course heard the name and we all admit that we want the thing, for we do not get any joy from the mere sound of the word. For when a Greek hears the word pronounced in Latin, he gets no pleasure because he does not know what has been said; but we who speak Latin get the same pleasure from it as he when he hears the word in Greek; for the thing itself is neither Greek nor Latin, but Greeks and Latins and men of all tongues are ever hot upon its pursuit. Thus happiness is known to all, for if they could be asked with one voice whether they wish for happiness, there is no doubt whatever that they would all answer yes. And this could not be unless the thing itself, signified by the word, lay somehow in their memory.

XXI

But does it lie in the memory in the way that I remember Carthage which I have seen? No. Happiness is not to be seen by the eye

because it is not a body. Is it in the memory as we remember numbers? No. For he who has knowledge of numbers does not go on
trying to gain it; but we do have knowledge of happiness, and so
we love it, and yet wish to gain it in order to be happy. Is it in our
memory then as eloquence is? No. For although when the word
eloquence is heard, people recognize the thing signified, though they
are not eloquent themselves: and again many would like to be
eloquent, so that it appears that it must be in their knowledge: the
position is different, because by their bodily senses they have observed
eloquence in others, have enjoyed it, and so have wished to possess it.
(Though obviously they would not enjoy it unless there were also
an interior notion [as well as sense perception], and would not desire
it unless they had enjoyed it.) But there is no bodily sense by which
we experience happiness in others.

Is it in the memory as we remember joy? It may be so. For even
when I am sad I remember my joy, just as when I am unhappy I
remember happiness; nor did I ever by any bodily sense see my joy
or hear it or smell it or taste it or touch it. But I experienced it in
my mind, at such times as I happened to rejoice, and the knowledge
of it remained in my memory, so that I am able to recall it—sometimes with loathing, sometimes with desire, according to the diversity
of the things I remember having enjoyed. For I have in the past
been all joyful at vile actions which I now detest and execrate when
I recall them; at other times I rejoice in good and honourable things
which I remember with longing, though I may no longer have them,
so that it is with sadness that I recall former joy.

But where and when had I any experience of happiness, that I
should remember it and love it and long for it? And not I alone, or
a handful of men besides, but surely all men whatsoever want to be
happy. And unless we knew the thing with certain knowledge, we
could not will it with so certain a will. Yet notice this: If two men
were asked whether they want to go with the army, it might happen
that one of them would say Yes, and the other No: but if they were
asked whether they wanted to be happy, each would instantly and
without hesitation say Yes—and the one would have no reason for
wanting to go with the army nor the other for not wanting to go,
save to be happy. May it be that one gets joy from this, one from
that? All agree that they desire happiness, just as they would agree,
if they were asked, that they desire joy: and indeed they think joy
and happiness are the same thing. One man may get it one way,
another another, yet all alike are striving to attain this one thing,
namely that they may be joyful. It is something that no one can say

that he has had no experience of, which is why he finds it in his memory and recognizes it when he hears the word *happiness*.

XXII

Far be it, O Lord, far be it from the heart of Thy servant who makes this confession to Thee, far be it from me to think that I am happy for any or every joy that I may have. For there is a joy which is not given to the ungodly but only to those who love Thee for Thy own sake, whose joy is Thyself. And this is happiness, to be joyful in Thee and for Thee and because of Thee, this and no other. Those who think happiness is any other, pursue a joy that is apart from Thee and is no true joy. Yet their will is not wholly without some image of joy.

XXIII

Thus it is not certain that all men do desire to be happy, since there are those who do not desire to rejoice in You, O God: and as this rejoicing is the only happiness, they do not really desire happiness. Or it may be that all men do desire true happiness but because *the flesh lusts against the spirit and the spirit against the flesh, so that they cannot do what they would,* they fall to what they can, and thus are content: because what they cannot do they do not want to do with sufficient intensity to make them able to do it. I ask all men whether they would rather have their joy in the truth or in a falsehood: they reply as unhesitatingly that they would rather have their joy in the truth as that they wish for happiness. Now joy in truth is happiness: for it is joy in You, God, who are Truth, my Light, the Salvation of my countenance and my God. This happiness all desire, this which alone is happiness all desire, for all desire to have joy in truth. I have met many who wished to deceive, but not one who wished to be deceived. But where have they come to know happiness, save where they came to know truth likewise? For they love truth, since they do not wish to be deceived; and when they love happiness, which as we have seen is simply joy in truth, they must love truth also: and they could not love it unless there were some knowledge of it in their memory. That being so, why do they not rejoice in it? Why are they not happy? Because they are much more concerned over things which are more powerful to make them unhappy than truth is to make them happy, for they remember truth so slightly. There is but a dim light in men; let them walk, let them walk, lest darkness overtake them.

Why does truth call forth hatred? Why is Your servant treated as an enemy by those to whom he preaches the truth, if happiness is loved, which is simply joy in truth? Simply because truth is loved in such a way that those who love some other thing want it to be the truth, and, precisely because they do not wish to be deceived, are unwilling to be convinced that they are deceived. Thus they hate the truth for the sake of that other thing which they love because they take it for truth. They love truth when it enlightens them, they hate truth when it accuses them. Because they do not wish to be deceived and do wish to deceive, they love truth when it reveals itself, and hate it when it reveals them. Thus it shall reward them as they deserve: those who do not wish to be revealed by truth, truth will unmask against their will, but it will not reveal itself to them. Thus, thus, even thus, does the human mind, blind and inert, vile and ill-behaved, desire to keep itself concealed, yet desire that nothing should be concealed from itself. But the contrary happens to it— it cannot lie hidden from truth, but only truth from it. Even so, for all its worthlessness, the human mind would rather find its joy in truth than falsehood. So that it shall be happy if, with no other thing to distract, it shall one day come to rejoice in that sole Truth by which all things are true.

XXIV

See now how great a space I have covered in my memory, in search of Thee, O Lord; and I have not found Thee outside it. For I find nothing concerning Thee but what I have remembered from the time I first learned of Thee. From that time, I have never forgotten Thee. For where I found truth, there I found my God, who is Truth Itself, and this I have not forgotten from the time I first learned it. Thus from the time I learned of Thee, Thou hast remained in my memory, and there do I find Thee, when I turn my mind to Thee and find delight in Thee. These are my holy delights, which in Thy mercy Thou hast given me, looking upon my poverty.

XXV

But where in my memory do You abide, Lord, where in my memory do You abide? What resting-place have You claimed as Your own, what sanctuary built for Yourself? You have paid this honour to my memory, that You deign to abide in it; but I now come to consider in what part of it You abide. In recalling You to mind I have mounted beyond those parts of memory which I have in common with the beasts, in that I did not find You among the images of corporeal things; and I came to those parts in which are kept the affections of my mind, and I could not find You there. And I came in to the innermost seat of my mind—which the mind has in my memory, since the mind remembers itself—and You were not there: because, just as You are not a corporeal image, or any affection of any living man such as we have when we are glad or sad, when we desire, fear, remember, forget and all such things: so You are not the mind itself, because You are the Lord God of the mind, and all these things suffer change, but You remain unchangeable over all: and yet You deign to dwell in my memory, ever since the time I first learned of You. And indeed why do I seek in what place of my memory You dwell as though there were places in my memory? Certain I am that You dwell in it, because I remember You since the time I first learned of You, and because I find You in it when I remember You.

XXVI

In what place then did I find You to learn of You? For You were not in my memory, before I learned of You. Where then did I find You to learn of You, save in Yourself, above myself? Place there is none, we go this way and that, and place there is none. You, who are Truth, reside everywhere to answer all who ask counsel of You, and in one act reply to all though all seek counsel upon different matters. And You answer clearly, but all do not hear clearly. All ask what they wish, but do not always hear the answer that they wish. That man is Your best servant who is not so much concerned to hear from You what he wills as to will what he hears from You.

XXVII

Late have I loved Thee, O Beauty so ancient and so new; late have I loved Thee! For behold Thou wert within me, and I outside; and I sought Thee outside and in my unloveliness fell upon those lovely things that Thou hast made. Thou wert with me and I was not with Thee. I was kept from Thee by those things, yet had they not been in Thee, they would not have been at all. Thou didst call and cry to me and break open my deafness: and Thou didst send forth Thy beams and shine upon me and chase away my blindness: Thou didst breathe fragrance upon me, and I drew in my breath and do now pant for Thee: I tasted Thee, and now hunger and thirst for Thee: Thou didst touch me, and I have burned for Thy peace.

XXVIII

When once I shall be united to Thee with all my being, there shall be no more grief and toil, and my life will be alive, filled wholly with Thee. Thou dost raise up him whom Thou dost fill; whereas being not yet filled with Thee I am a burden to myself. The pleasures of this life for which I should weep are in conflict with the sorrows of this life in which I should rejoice, and I know not on which side stands the victory. Woe is me, Lord, have pity on me! For I have likewise sorrows which are evil and these are in conflict with joys that are good, and I know not on which side stands the victory. Woe is me, Lord have mercy upon me! Woe is me! See, I do not hide my wounds: Thou art the physician, I the sick man; Thou art merciful, I need mercy. Is not the life of man on earth a trial? Who would choose trouble and difficulty? Thou dost command us to endure them, not to love them. No one loves what he endures, though he may love to endure. For though he rejoices at his endurance, yet he would rather that there were nothing to endure. In adversity I desire prosperity, in prosperity I fear adversity. Yet what middle place is there between the two, where man's life may be other than trial? There is woe and woe again in the prosperity of this world, woe from the fear of adversity, woe from the corruption of joy! There is woe in the adversity of this world, and a second woe and a third, from the longing for prosperity, and because adversity itself is hard, and for fear that endurance may break! Is not man's life upon earth trial without intermission?

XXIX

All my hope is naught save in Thy great mercy. Grant what Thou dost command, and command what Thou wilt. Thou dost command continence. And *when I knew*, as it is said, *that no one could be continent unless God gave it, even this was a point of wisdom, to know whose gift it was.* For by continence we are collected and bound up into unity within ourself, whereas we had been scattered abroad in multiplicity. Too little does any man love Thee, who loves some other thing together with Thee, loving it not on account of Thee, O Thou Love, who art ever burning and never extinguished! O Charity, my God, enkindle me! Thou dost command continence: grant what Thou dost command and command what Thou wilt.

XXX

Assuredly You command that I contain myself from *the lust of the flesh, the lust of the eyes, and the pride of life.* You commanded me also to abstain from fornication, and in the matter of marriage You advised me a better course though You allowed me a less good. And since You gave me the power, it was so done, even before I became a dispenser of Your Sacrament. Yet there still live in my memory the images of those things, of which I have already spoken much, which my long habit had fixed there. When I am awake they beset me though with no great power, but in sleep not only seeming pleasant, but even to the point of consent and the likeness of the act itself. The illusion of that image is of such avail in my soul and in my flesh, that mere visions persuade me in sleep as the realities could not persuade me when I am awake. Surely I am myself in sleep, O Lord my God? Yet there is such a difference between myself and myself, divided by that moment in which from waking I fall asleep, from sleeping I wake! Where is my reason, which when I am awake resists such suggestions, and would remain unshaken were the realities themselves presented? Is my reason closed when my eyes close? Does it fall asleep with the bodily senses? And if so how does it happen that even in dreams I often resist, mindful of my purpose, and remain most chastely fixed in it, giving no consent to such temptations? Yet there is this much difference that even when it falls out otherwise, upon waking I return to peace of conscience; and in the difference between the two states discover that I did not commit the act, though I grieve that in some way or other it was done in me.

Is not Thy hand powerful, O God almighty, to heal all the diseases of my soul, and with more abundant grace quench the lascivious motions even of my sleep? Thou, O Lord, wilt more and more increase Thy gifts in me, that my soul may follow me to Thee, utterly freed from the hold of concupiscence: so that it may not be in revolt against itself, and even in dreams may not commit, much less consent to, such baseness of corruption, by means of sense images, unto pollution of the body. For it is no great matter for the Almighty, who is able to do all things more abundantly than we can ask or understand, to prevent any such thing—or even the smallest vestige of it, so small that a mere nod would restrain it—winning the chaste mind even in sleep, even while I am in the prime of life. But now I confess to my good Lord what I still am, in this way of evil; rejoicing with trembling in what Thou hast given me and grieving that I am not yet made perfect, hoping that Thou wilt perfect Thy mercies in me unto the fullness of peace: the peace which my inward being and my outward shall have with Thee when *death shall be swallowed up in victory*.

XXXI

Another evil is of the day, and would that it were sufficient unto it. We repair the daily deteriorations of the body by eating and drinking, until the day when You will *destroy both the belly and the meats,* for You will kill our emptiness with a marvellous fullness, and You will clothe this corruptible with eternal incorruption. But for the present time the necessity is sweet to me, and I fight against that sweetness lest I be taken captive by it. I wage daily war upon it by fasting, bringing my body again and again into subjection; but the pain this gives me is driven away by the pleasure [of eating and drinking]. For hunger and thirst really are painful: they burn and kill, like fever, unless food comes as medicine for their healing. And since this medicine is ready to hand, from the comfort of Your gifts, in which earth and sea and sky serve our infirmity, this very infirmity is called delight.

This You taught me, that I should learn to take my food as a kind of medicine. But while I am passing from the pain of hunger to the satisfaction of sufficiency, in that very passage the snare of concupiscence lies in wait for me. For the passage is itself a pleasure, yet there is no other way to achieve sufficiency than that which necessity forces us to travel. And while we eat and drink for the sake of health, yet a perilous enjoyment runs at the heels of health and often enough tries to run ahead of it: so that what I say I am doing and really desire to do for my health's sake, I do in fact for the sake of the enjoyment. For there happens not to be the same measure for both: what suffices for health is too little for enjoyment; so that often it is not at all clear whether it is the necessary care of my body calling for more nourishment, or the deceiving indulgence of greed wanting to be served. Because of this uncertainty my wretched soul is glad, and uses it as a cover and an excuse, rejoicing that it does not clearly appear what is sufficient for the needs of health, so that under the cloak of health it may shelter the business of pleasure.

Day after day I fight against these temptations, and I call upon Thy right hand and to Thee refer my perplexities, for I have no clear guidance upon this matter. I hear the word of my God commanding me: *Let not your hearts be overcharged with surfeiting and drunkenness and the cares of this life.* Drunkenness is far from me, and Thou wilt have mercy that it may never come near me, but overeating has sometimes crept up on Thy servant: Thou wilt have mercy, that it may depart from me. *For no man can be continent unless Thou give it.*

Many things You give us in answer to prayer, and whatever good we received before we prayed, we received from You: even that we should come to know that we had received it from You, we received from You. Never was I a drunkard, but I have known drunkards made sober by You. Therefore I know that it is Your doing that

those are not drunkards who never were, just as it is Your doing
that those who were drunkards are drunkards no longer, and by
Your doing also that both sorts know that it is Your doing. Another
voice of Yours I also heard: *Go not after thy lusts: but turn away
from thy own will.* And this saying also I heard and very much loved:
*For neither if we eat shall we have the more: nor if we eat not, shall
we have the less:* that is to say, that the one will not make me
abundant nor the other destitute. And again I heard: *For I have
learned in whatsoever state I am, to be content therewith. I know
both how to abound and how to suffer need. I can do all things in
Him who strengthens me.* There truly speaks a soldier of a heavenly
army, not dust, as we are. But remember, Lord, that we are dust,
and that You made man of dust, that he was lost and is found. Nor
could he do this of his own power, for he was dust too—I mean this
same Paul, whom I loved as I heard him say in the breath of Your
inspiration: *I can do all things in Him who strengthens me.*

Strengthen me, that I may be able, grant what Thou dost command
and command what Thou wilt. Paul confesses that he has received
and when he glories, it is in the Lord that he glories. Another also
I heard begging: *Take from me the greediness of the belly.* From
this it is clear, O holy God, that when what You command is done,
it is You who give the power. You have taught me, Good Father, that
to the clean all things are clean, but *it is evil for that man who eats
with offense,* that *every creature of thine is good and nothing should
be rejected that is received with thanksgiving;* that *meat does not
commend us to God* and that *no man may judge us in meat or in
drink;* that *he who eats should not despise him that eats not,* and that
he who eats not should not judge him that eats. These things have I
learned, thanks and praise unto Thee, my God, my Master, who
dost knock at the door of my ears and illumine my heart: deliver me
from all temptation for it is not any uncleanness in the meat that I
fear but the uncleanness of my own gluttony. I know that permission
was given to Noe to eat of every kind of meat that was good for food:
that Elias was fed with flesh: that John the Baptist, though his ab-
stinence was marvellous, ate of animals—the locusts to wit which
were granted him for food—and was not polluted. And again I know
that Esau was defrauded owing to his greediness for the pottage of
lentils; and that David blamed himself for longing for a drink of
water: and that our King was tempted not by meat but by bread.
Therefore the Israelites in the desert deserved to be rebuked, not
because they desired meat but because in their desire for meat they
murmured against the Lord.

Placed amidst these temptations, I strive daily against greediness in eating and drinking. For this is not the kind of thing I can resolve once and for all to cut off and touch no more, as I could with fornication. For the reins of the throat are to be held somewhere between too lightly and too tightly. Who is he, Lord, that is not carried somewhat beyond the limits of the necessary? If such a man there be, he is great. Let him magnify Your name. But I am not he, for I am a sinful man. Yet I too magnify Your name, and He intercedes with You for my sins who conquered the world, who numbers me among the weak members of His body, for *Thy eyes did see my imperfect being, and in Thy book all shall be written.*

XXXII

As for the allurement of sweet scents, I am not much troubled: when they are absent I do not seek them; when they are present, I do not refuse them: yet at any time I do not mind being without them. At least so I seem to myself; perhaps I am deceived. For that darkness is lamentable in which the possibilities in me are hidden from myself: so that my mind, questioning itself upon its own powers, feels that it cannot lightly trust its own report: because what is already in it does for the most part lie hidden, unless experience brings it to light: and in this life, which is rightly called one continuing trial, no man ought to be oversure that though he is capable of becoming better instead of worse, he is not actually becoming worse instead of better. Our one hope, our one confidence, our one firm promise is Your mercy.

XXXIII

The pleasures of the ear did indeed draw me and hold me more tenaciously, but You have set me free. Yet still when I hear those airs, in which Your words breathe life, sung with sweet and measured voice, I do, I admit, find a certain satisfaction in them, yet not such as to grip me too close, for I can depart when I will. Yet in that they are received into me along with the truths which give them life, such airs seek in my heart a place of no small honour, and I find it hard to know what is their due place. At times indeed it seems to me that I am paying them greater honour than is their due—when, for example, I feel that by those holy words my mind is kindled more religiously and fervently to a flame of piety because I hear them sung than if they were not sung: and I observe that all the varying emotions of my spirit have modes proper to them in voice and song, whereby, by some secret affinity, they are made more alive. It is not good that the mind should be enervated by this bodily pleasure. But it often ensnares me, in that the bodily sense does not accompany the reason as following after it in proper order, but having been admitted to aid the reason, strives to run before and take the lead. In this matter I sin unawares, and then grow aware.

Yet there are times when through too great a fear of this temptation, I err in the direction of over-severity—even to the point sometimes of wishing that the melody of all the lovely airs with which David's Psalter is commonly sung should be banished not only from my own ears, but from the Church's as well: and that seems to me a safer course, which I remember often to have heard told of Athanasius, bishop of Alexandria, who had the reader of the psalm utter it with so little modulation of the voice that he seemed to be saying it rather than singing it. Yet when I remember the tears I shed, moved by the songs of the Church in the early days of my new faith: and again when I see that I am moved not by the singing but by the things that are sung—when they are sung with a clear voice and proper modulation—I recognize once more the usefulness of this practice. Thus I fluctuate between the peril of indulgence and the profit I have found: and on the whole I am inclined—though I am not propounding any irrevocable opinion—to approve the custom of singing in church, that by the pleasure of the ear the weaker minds may be roused to a feeling of devotion. Yet whenever it happens that I am more moved by the singing than by the thing that is sung, I admit that I have grievously sinned, and then I should wish rather not to have heard the singing. See in what a state I am! Weep with me and weep for me, all you who feel within yourselves that goodness from which good actions come. Those of you who have no such feeling will not be moved by what I am saying. But do Thou, O Lord my God, hear me and look upon me and see me and pity me and heal me, Thou in whose eyes I have become a question to myself: and that is my infirmity.

XXXIV

There remains the pleasure of the eyes of my flesh, of which I now make confession. Let the ear of Your Church, the fraternal loving ear of Your Church, hearken: that I may finish what I have to say of the temptations of bodily pleasure which still solicit me, while I *groan, desiring to be clothed with our habitation that is from heaven.* My eyes love the diverse forms of beauty, brilliant and pleasing colors. Let these things not take possession of my soul; let God possess it, who made these things and made them exceedingly good: yet

He is my good, not they. For they affect me in all the waking hours of every day, nor do I find any respite from them such as I do sometimes find in silence from all the voices of song. For light, the queen of colors, suffusing all the things I see whenever I am abroad in daylight, entices me as it flows before my sight in all its variousness, even though I am busy upon something else and not observing it. For it works its way into me with such power that if it is suddenly withdrawn, I desire it with great longing; and if it is absent too long, it saddens my mind.

O Light that Tobias beheld when though his eyes were closed in blindness he taught his son the way of life, and went before him with the feet of charity and did not err; Light that Isaac beheld when the eyes of his body were heavy and dim with age and it was granted him to bless his sons though he could not discern one from the other, yet by the act of blessing he did discern between them; Light that Jacob beheld when, though his eyes were dim in his old age, his heart was luminous and he shed light upon the tribes of the people to come, foreshown in the persons of his sons: and he laid upon his grandchildren, the sons of Joseph, hands mystically reversed [the right hand upon the younger, the left hand upon the older] not as their father seeing them from without directed, but as though he were within them and discerned from within. This is the true Light; it is one: and all who see it and love it are one. But that corporeal light of which I have spoken seasons the life of this world for its blind lovers with a dangerous enticingness. Yet those who have the knowledge to praise You for that light take up its praise in Your hymn, "O God, Creator of all," and are not carried away by it in sleep [of soul]. Of such I desire to be. I resist the enticements of the eye lest the feet with which I walk Your road should be tangled in their snare, and I raise the eyes of my soul to You that You may pluck my feet from that snare. Repeatedly You pluck them out for indeed they are ensnared. But You do not cease to pluck them out, however often I fall into the snares that are spread all about us. For *Thou shalt neither slumber nor sleep, that keepest Israel.*

How innumerable are the things made by every kind of art and workmanship in clothes, shoes, vessels and such like, in pictures also and every kind of statue—far beyond necessary and moderate use and any meaning of devotion—that men have added for the delight of their eyes, going abroad from themselves after the things they have themselves made, interiorly abandoning Him by whom they were made and destroying what He made in them. But I, O my God and my Glory, I too utter a hymn to Thee and offer my praise as sacrifice to Him who sanctifies me: for all that loveliness which passes through men's minds into their skillful hands comes from that supreme Loveliness which is above our souls, which my soul sighs for day and night. From the Supreme Beauty those who make and seek after exterior beauty derive the measure by which they judge of it, but not the measure by which it should be used. Yet this measure too is there, and they do not see it: for if they did they would not wander far from it, but would preserve their strength only for Thee and would not dissipate it upon delights that grow wearisome. But I, who speak thus and see thus, yet entangle my feet in these lower things of beauty; but Thou wilt pluck me forth, Lord, Thou wilt pluck me forth, because Thy mercy is before my eyes. For I in my wretchedness am caught and held captive, and Thou in Thy mercy wilt pluck me out—sometimes without my feeling it, because I had not wholly fallen within the trap: but sometimes I feel the pain of being drawn out, because I had fallen deep.

XXXV

At this point I mention another form of temptation, more various and dangerous. For over and above that lust of the flesh which lies in the delight of all our senses and pleasures—whose slaves are wasted unto destruction as they go far from You—there can also be in the mind itself, through those same bodily senses, a certain vain desire and curiosity, not of taking delight in the body, but of making experiments with the body's aid, and cloaked under the name of learning and knowledge. Because this is in the appetite to know, and the eyes are the chief of the senses we use for attaining knowledge, it is called in Scripture the lust of the eyes. For "to see" belongs as a property to the eyes; yet we apply the word also to the other senses, when we use them for gaining knowledge. Thus we do not say: "Hear how it flashes," or "Smell how bright it is," or "Taste how it shines," or "Touch how it glows": because all these things are said to be seen. Yet we do say not only "See how it shines," something that only the eyes can perceive; but also "See how it sounds," "See how it smells," "See how it tastes," "See how hot it is." Thus the experience of the senses as a whole, as has been said, is called the lust of the eyes. Because though the function of seeing belongs properly to the eyes, yet we apply it to the other senses by analogy when they are in pursuit of the truth about anything.

In this it is easy to distinguish between the way in which the senses serve pleasure and the way in which they serve curiosity. Pleasure goes after objects that are beautiful to see, hear, smell, taste, touch; but curiosity for the sake of experiment can go after quite contrary things, not in order to experience their unpleasantness, but through a mere itch to experience and find out. What pleasure can there be in seeing a mangled corpse, which is only horrible? Yet if there happens to be one anywhere about, people flock to it to be saddened and sickened: indeed they are in terror that they may dream about it. So that you would think that when they are awake they would not go to see it unless either they were dragged there by force, or some false report that the sight was beautiful had drawn them. It is the same with the other senses which it would be long to follow up. Because of this disease of curiosity you have the various freaks shown in the theatres. Thus men proceed to investigate the phenomena of nature—the part of nature external to us—though the knowledge is of no value to them: for they wish to know simply for the sake of knowing. We have a similar thing when for the sake of the same perverted learning inquiry is made by way of magic. And the same happens even in religion: God is tempted when signs and wonders are demanded, not for any purpose of salvation, but solely for the experience of seeing them.

In this immense forest of snares and perils, I have cut off and thrust from my heart many sins, as You have given me to do, O God of my salvation; yet when would I dare to say—with so many things of the sort buzzing about our daily life on every side—when dare I say that no such thing can draw me to look at it or through vain curiosity to desire it? Certainly the theatres no longer attract me, nor do I care to know the course of the stars, nor has my mind ever sought answers from the dead: all sacrilegious rites I detest. But, O Lord my God, to whom I owe my humble undivided service, by what subtleties of suggestion has the enemy worked upon me to desire some sign from You! I beseech You, by our King and by Jerusalem our one pure homeland, that just as any consent to such a temptation has been far from me, so it may be ever further. When I ask You for the salvation of anyone, the end of my intention is quite different: for You do as You will, and You give me the grace, and ever will give me the grace, to accept and not question.

Yet in how many tiny and inconsiderable trifles is this curiosity of ours daily tempted: and how often we slip, who shall number? When people tell idle stories, it happens only too often that we first endure them, lest we give offense to the weak, and then little by little find ourselves listening willingly. I no longer go to the Games to see a dog chasing a hare, but if in going through a field I come upon the same thing, the chase may easily draw me off from some serious thought and concentrate me upon itself, forcing me from my path not by the body of my horse but by the inclination of my heart; and indeed unless You quickly showed me my infirmity and admonished me, either by some train of thought to rise from the actual sight to You, or at least to despise and pass by the thing itself, I would simply stand gaping at it. What is to be said of me when a lizard catching flies or a spider tangling them as they fall into her net often holds my attention so close, when I am sitting at home? These are small animals, but it is precisely the same thing. I do indeed go on to praise You, the marvellous Creator and Disposer of all things, but it is not in that state that I begin to gaze so attentively. It is one thing to get up quickly, but a better thing not to fall. And of such things my life is full, and my one hope is Your immeasurable mercy. For when our heart is made the stage for such things and is overladen with the throngs of this endless vanity, our prayers are often interrupted and distracted; and though we are in Your presence, and directing the voice of our heart to Your ears, the great business of prayer is broken off through the inrush of every sort of idle thought.

XXXVI

Surely I must reckon this among things to be condemned: and is there anything to bring me back to hope save the knowledge of Your mercy, in that You have already begun to change me? And You know in what degree You have changed me, in that You have already healed me of the craving for revenge, so that You may be merciful also to my other iniquities, and heal all my diseases, redeem my life from destruction, crown me with mercy and compassion, and satisfy my desire with good things—You who have curbed my pride with Your fear and tamed my neck to Your yoke. I now bear Your yoke and it is light on me, for so You have promised, so You have done; and indeed it was always light, but I did not know it in the days when I feared to take it on me.

But tell me, Lord, You who alone reign without arrogance, because You alone are the true Lord who have no Lord: tell me whether a third kind of temptation has passed from me or can it ever pass wholly in this life—the desire to be feared and loved by men for no other reason than the joy I get from it, which is no true joy? It is a lamentable state, a base vaingloriousness. From this it comes that men neither love You utterly nor fear You with righteous fear: thus it is that You resist the proud but give grace to the humble: You thunder upon the ambition of this world and the foundations of the mountains tremble. But because certain offices in human society require the holder to be loved and feared by men, the enemy of our true beatitude presses hard upon me, spreading all about me his snares of Well done, Well done; and while I receive praises too eagerly, I lose caution and am caught by them, and so separate my joy from the truth and place it in the deceitfulness of men: I delight to be praised and feared, not for Your sake but in Your stead, and in this way the enemy has me like himself—not in any concord of charity, of course, but in the fellowship of like punishment—the devil who resolved *to establish his throne in the north,* that men darkened and frozen may serve him while he makes perverse and distorted imitation of You.

But we, O Lord, are Thy little flock: do Thou keep possession of us. Spread forth Thy wings, and let us shelter under them. Be Thou our glory; let us be loved because of Thee and let Thy word be feared in us.

A man who wishes to be praised by men when You do not praise him, will not be defended by men when You judge him, nor delivered by men when You condemn him. But it can happen, not that a sinner is praised in the desires of his soul, not that a man is blessed who does ungodlily, but that he is praised on account of some gift that You have given him: even so, if he rejoices more because he is praised than because he has the gift, then this man too is praised by men but blamed by You, and the man who praised him is better than himself who is praised: for the one took pleasure in God's gift in man, whereas the other took more pleasure in what man gave than in what God gave.

XXXVII

Daily, O Lord, are we assailed by these temptations, unceasingly are we assailed. We are daily tried in the furnace of the human tongue. And in this matter also You command us to continence: grant what You command and command what You will. You know how my heart has groaned to You about this and the tears my eyes have shed. For I cannot easily know how far I am clean from this disease, and I am in great fear of my secret sins—sins that Your eyes see, though mine do not. For in those other kinds of temptation I have some power of examining myself, but in this almost none. For I can see how far I have advanced in power to control my mind in the matter of the pleasures of the flesh and curiosity for vain knowledge: I can see it when I am without these things, either because I choose to be or because they are not to be had. For then I can ask myself how much or how little it troubles me not to have them. Similarly in the matter of riches—which are sought to the end that they may serve a man for any one of those three concupiscences, or any two of them or all three of them—if the soul cannot discern while it possesses them whether or not it despises them, it can let them go and make trial of itself that way. But how are we to be without praise in order to discover our true attitude to praise? Are we to live evilly, to live a life so monstrous and abandoned, that everyone who knows us will detest us? What greater folly could be said or thought? On the contrary if praise both is and ought to be the normal accompaniment of a good life and good works, we ought no more to abandon that accompaniment than goodness of life itself. Yet unless I am deprived of something, I cannot know whether I can bear being without it well or ill?

What then am I to confess, Lord, in this field of temptation? What, save that I rejoice at praise?—but more for the truth than for the praise. For if I were given the choice whether on the one hand I would rather be a madman, or completely wrong in everything, and yet praised by all men: or on the contrary firm and sure in the truth and abused by all men, I see clearly which I would choose. Yet I wish that the praise of another's mouth did not increase the joy I feel in any good I may have: it does increase it, I admit: worse, dispraise diminishes it. And when I am troubled at this wretchedness in myself, an excuse comes into my head, how good an excuse You know, O God, for it leaves me uncertain! You have commanded us not only continence—that is, that we should restrain our affections from certain things—but also justice—by which we must bestow love on certain things: and it is not Your will that we should love You only, but our neighbor also. Now it often seems to me that what I rejoice in is the competence or promise I see in my neighbor. I am pleased with his praise as evidence of his understanding; and similarly I am sorry for the defect in him when I hear him blame what he does not understand or what is in fact good. For I am sometimes sorry to hear my own praise, either when qualities are praised in me which I see in myself with regret, or else good qualities of no great importance are praised more than they deserve. Yet I do not know: it may be that I feel thus, simply because I do not wish the man who praises me to differ from me about myself, and this not because I am concerned about what is good for him, but simply because those good qualities which please me in myself please me all the more when they please someone else as well. For in a sense I am not being praised, when my own opinion of myself is not praised—when, that is, things are praised in me which do not please me at all, or praised more though they please me less. So it seems that I am uncertain about myself in this matter.

Behold, O Truth, in You I see that I should be moved by praise

of myself, not for my own sake but for the good of my neighbor.
But whether this is so with me, I do not know. For in this matter
I know more of You than of myself. I beseech You, O my God,
show me to myself that I may confess to my brethren what I find
defective in myself and they will pray for me. Again let me examine
myself more closely. If in rejoicing to hear myself praised I am
moved by the good of my neighbor, why am I less moved if someone else is blamed unjustly than when it happens to me? Why does
that reproach bite me deeper which is cast upon me than when
another is accused of the same sin in my presence? Am I ignorant
of this too? Or does this remain as the real truth—that I deceive
myself, and neither think nor speak the truth in Your sight? Put
such madness far from me, O Lord, lest my mouth should be *the
oil of the sinner to fatten my own head.*

XXXVIII

I am poor and needy: yet I am better when with anguish of soul
I see myself as hateful and seek your mercy, till what is damaged
in me is repaired and made perfect, to the attaining of that peace
which the eye of the proud knows not. The report of men's mouths,
and deeds known to men, bring with them a most perilous temptation from the love of praise, which goes round almost begging for
compliments and piles them up for our own personal glory. Love
of praise tempts me even when I reprove it in myself, indeed in
the very fact that I do reprove it: a man often glories the more
vainly for his very contempt of vainglory: for which reason he does not
really glory in his contempt of glory; in that he glories in it, he
does not contemn it.

XXXIX

Within us there is another evil in the same category of temptation,
by which men are made vain though they do not please others or
even displease others, and in any event have no desire to please
others: but are interiorly pleased with themselves. They please
themselves but they mightily displease You: not because they are
pleased with things not good as though they were good, but because
they are pleased with things good as though they were their own:
or even if they rejoice in them as Yours, they think they have merited
them: or even if they know that they are wholly of Your grace, yet
they do not rejoice with their fellow-men, but as grudging Your
grace to others. In all these and other similar perils and toils, You
see the trembling of my heart: and truly I feel my wounds rather

as things ever and again healed by You than as things never inflicted upon me.

XL

Where have You not walked with me, O Truth, teaching me both what to shun and what to seek, when I set before You such things as I have been able to see here below and begged Your counsel? With my bodily senses I surveyed the external world as best I could, and considered the life my body has from me and the senses themselves. From that I turned inwards to the depths of my memory, like so many vast rooms filled so wonderfully with things beyond number: and I considered and stood awe-stricken: for no one of these could I discern without You, and I found that no one of these was You. Nor was I their finder. I did indeed go through them all and I tried to distinguish and evaluate each thing according to its worth, receiving some things with the feebleness of the senses and inquiring of them, perceiving other things in which there was some admixture of myself, observing and enumerating the messengers that had brought them to me, meditating upon things preserved in the vast stores of memory, putting some of them back, drawing others out. Yet it was not myself that did these things—that is, the power by which I did them was not myself: nor was it You, because you are that unfailing Light which I consulted upon all these things, as to whether they are, and what they are, and what they are worth. But I heard You teaching and commanding. And all this I do often; for it gives me pleasure and whenever I can relax from the duties necessity lays upon me, I have recourse to this same pleasure. Nor in all these things that my mind traverses in search of You, do I find any sure place for my mind save in You, in whom all that is scattered in me is brought into one, so that nothing of me may depart from You. And sometimes You admit me to a state of mind that I am not ordinarily in, a kind of delight which could it ever be made permanent in me would be hard to distinguish from the life to come. But by the weight of my imperfections I fall back again, and I am swallowed up by things customary: I am bound, and I weep bitterly, but I am bitterly bound. So much does the burden of custom count for. I can remain in my ordinary state though unwilling, I would remain in that other state but am not able, in both states I know my misery.

XLI

Thus under the heads of that threefold concupiscence I have considered the damage wrought in me by my sins, and I have called

Thy right hand to my aid. For in my wounded heart I have seen the
shining of Thy splendor, and been beaten back, and have said:
"Who can attain thither? *I am cast away from before Thy eyes.*"
Thou art the Truth presiding over all things. But in my avarice
I was unwilling to lose Thee, yet desired to possess a lie along with
Thee: just as no man wishes to say what is false so that he himself
shall not know what is true. So I lost Thee because Thou didst
not deign to be possessed together with a lie.

XLII

Whom could I find to reconcile me to You? Was I to try to
approach the Angels? But with what prayer? What sacraments?
Many seeking to return to You and lacking the strength by themselves have, as I hear, made trial of that way, and have fallen into a
seeking for curious visions, and been found worthy to be deluded.
For they set out to find You in the conceit of their learning,
swelling their breasts instead of beating them; and they drew to
themselves through likeness in heart *the powers of this air* [fallen
angels] as ministers and companions of their pride; and by these
they were deceived with various effects of magic, seeking a mediator by whom they might be cleansed. But it was not a mediator they
found. It was the devil, transforming himself into an angel of
light. And it powerfully attracted proud flesh, that he was himself
not a fleshly body. For they were mortal and sinners; You, Lord,
to whom they wished to be reconciled, are immortal and sinless.
Now clearly a mediator between God and men should have something in common with God, something in common with men; if he
were in both points like men, he would be too far from God; if
he were in both points like God, he would be too far from men:
and in neither event could he be a mediator. But that sham mediator, by whom in Your secret judgments pride merits to be mocked,
has one thing in common with men, namely sin, and pretends to
have another thing in common with God—because he is not clothed
with the mortality of flesh, he would pass for immortal. But because
the wages of sin is death, he has this in common with men, to be condemned with them to the same death.

XLIII

But the true Mediator, whom in the secret of Your mercy You
have shown to men and sent to men, that by His example they might
learn humility—the Mediator between God and men, the man
Christ Jesus, appeared between sinful mortals and the immortal Just

One: for like men He was mortal, like God He was Just; so that, the wages of justice being life and peace, He might, through the union of His own justice with God, make void the death of those sinners whom He justified by choosing to undergo death as they do. He was shown forth to holy men of old that they might be saved by faith in His Passion to come, as we by faith in His Passion now that He has suffered it. As man, He is Mediator; but as Word, He is not something in between, for He is equal to God, God with God, and together one God.

How much Thou hast loved us, O good Father, *Who hast spared not even Thine own Son, but delivered Him up for us wicked men!* How Thou hast loved us, for whom He who *thought it not robbery to be equal with Thee became obedient even unto the death of the Cross,* He who alone *was free among the dead, having power to lay down His life and power to take it up again:* for us He was to Thee both Victor and Victim, and Victor because Victim: for us He was to Thee both Priest and Sacrifice, and Priest because Sacrifice: turning us from slaves into Thy sons, by being Thy Son and becoming a slave. Rightly is my hope strong in Him, who sits at Thy right hand and intercedes for us; otherwise I should despair. For many and great are my infirmities, many and great; but Thy medicine is of more power. We might well have thought Thy Word remote from union with man and so have despaired of ourselves, if It had not been *made flesh and dwelt among us.*

Terrified by my sins and the mass of my misery, I had pondered in my heart and thought of flight to the desert; but Thou didst forbid me and strengthen me, saying: *And Christ died for all: that they also who live, may now not live to themselves but with Him who died for them.* See, Lord, I cast my care upon Thee, that I may live: *and I will consider the wondrous things of Thy law.* Thou knowest my unskilfulness and my infirmity: teach me and heal me. He Thy only One, in whom are hidden all the treasures of wisdom and knowledge, has redeemed me with His blood. *Let not the proud speak evil of me,* for I think upon the price of my redemption, I eat it and drink it and give it to others to eat and drink; and being poor I desire to be filled with it among those that eat and are filled: *and they shall praise the Lord that seek Him.*